On Invisible Language in Modern English

Also available from Bloomsbury

Contemporary Linguistic Parameters, edited by Antonio Fabregas, Jaume Mateu, Michael Putnam
Contrastive Studies in Morphology and Syntax, edited by Michalis Georgiafentis, Giannoula Giannoulopoulou, Maria Koliopoulou, Angeliki Tsokoglou
Crossing Linguistic Boundaries, edited by Paloma Núñez-Pertejo, María José López-Couso, Belén Méndez-Naya, Javier Pérez-Guerra
The Prosody of Formulaic Sequences, by Phoebe Lin

On Invisible Language in Modern English

A Corpus-based Approach to Ellipsis

Evelyn Gandón-Chapela

BLOOMSBURY ACADEMIC
LONDON • NEW YORK • OXFORD • NEW DELHI • SYDNEY

BLOOMSBURY ACADEMIC
Bloomsbury Publishing Plc
50 Bedford Square, London, WC1B 3DP, UK
1385 Broadway, New York, NY 10018, USA
29 Earlsfort Terrace, Dublin 2, Ireland

BLOOMSBURY, BLOOMSBURY ACADEMIC and the Diana logo are trademarks of
Bloomsbury Publishing Plc

First published in Great Britain 2020
Paperback edition published 2021

Copyright © Evelyn Gandón-Chapela, 2020

Evelyn Gandón-Chapela has asserted her right under the Copyright, Designs and Patents
Act, 1988, to be identified as Author of this work.

For legal purposes the Acknowledgements on p. xiv constitute an extension
of this copyright page.

Cover design: Ben Anslow

All rights reserved. No part of this publication may be reproduced or transmitted in any
form or by any means, electronic or mechanical, including photocopying, recording or
any information storage or retrieval system, without prior permission in writing from the
publishers.

Bloomsbury Publishing Plc does not have any control over, or responsibility for, any third-
party websites referred to or in this book. All internet addresses given in this book were
correct at the time of going to press. The author and publisher regret any inconvenience
caused if addresses have changed or sites have ceased to exist, but can accept no
responsibility for any such changes.

A catalogue record for this book is available from the British Library.

A catalog record for this book is available from the Library of Congress.

ISBN: HB: 978-1-3500-6451-5
PB: 978-1-3502-7308-5
ePDF: 978-1-3500-6452-2
eBook: 978-1-3500-6453-9

Typeset by Deanta Global Publishing Services, Chennai, India

To find out more about our authors and books visit www.bloomsbury.com and sign up for
our newsletters.

On ne voit bien qu'avec le cœur. L'essentiel est invisible pour les yeux.
'One sees clearly only with the heart. What is essential is invisible to the eyes.'
Antoine de Saint-Exupéry, Le Petit Prince.

To my parents, Mª del Carmen and Daniel, and to my husband, Manel.
My three pillars.

Contents

List of Illustrations	ix
Acknowledgements	xiv
Abbreviations	xvi

1	Introduction	1
	1.1 Scope and aims of the study	7
	1.2 State of the art	9
	1.2.1 Ellipsis in comprehensive grammars of English	11
	1.2.2 Ellipsis in SFG	18
	1.2.3 Ellipsis in TGG	30
	1.2.4 The processing of ellipsis	34
	1.3 Outline of the research	48
2	Methodology	51
	2.1 Corpus-based studies on ellipsis	51
	2.2 The data	61
	2.2.1 The scope of analysis	61
	2.2.2 The corpus: The Penn Corpora of Historical English	69
	2.2.3 The query	71
	2.2.4 The database and the variables	85
3	A corpus-based analysis of Post-auxiliary Ellipsis in Modern English	113
	3.1 Core defining variables	113
	3.1.1 Grammatical variables	114
	3.1.2 Semantic, discursive variables	195
	3.2 Usage variables	223
	3.2.1 Diachronic evolution of PAE	223
	3.2.2 Genre distribution of PAE	226
	3.3 Processing variables	236
	3.3.1 Lexical distance	236
	3.3.2 Syntactic distance	246
	3.4 Concluding remarks on the characteristics of PG and VPE in Late Modern English	251
4	Conclusions and issues for further research	255

Appendix 1	267
Appendix 2	273
Notes	276
References	280
Index	288

Illustrations

Figures

1. PAE database layout 85
2. Syntactic linking 89
3. Syntactic linking and boundedness 90
4. Syntactic linking and boundedness and their relevance for type of turn 95
5. Syntactic linking 127
6. Syntactic linking and type of turn 221

Graphs

1. Representation of the relative frequencies of the licensors of PAE in Late Modern English 117
2. Distribution of PAE in Late Modern English 224
3. Graphical representation of the normalized frequencies of PG and VPE by genre 234
4. Graphical representation of the average number of words between antecedent and ellipsis site in writing and speech-related genres 238
5. Representation of the normalized average number of words between antecedent and ellipsis site per type of genre in PG and VPE 240

Tables

1. Some Previous Research on the Two Ellipsis Questions 32
2. Licensors of PAE in Late Modern English 115
3. Licensors of PAE in Late Modern English (main types) 115
4. Licensors of VPE in Present-Day English in Bos and Spenader's (2011) Study 116
5. Licensors of VPE in Writing-Related Genres in Late Modern English 116

6	Relative Frequencies of the Licensors of PAE in Late Modern English	117
7	Relative Frequencies of the Licensors of VPE in Bos and Spenader's (2011) Study	118
8	Relative Frequencies of the Licensors of VPE in Writing-Related Genres in Late Modern English	119
9	Licensors of VPE in Speech-Related Genres in Late Modern English	120
10	Relative Frequencies of the Licensors of VPE in Speech-Related Genres in Late Modern English	120
11	Licensors of PG in Writing-Related Genres in Late Modern English	121
12	Licensors of PG in Speech-Related Genres in Late Modern English	121
13	Relative Frequencies of the Licensors of PG in Writing-Related Genres in Late Modern English	122
14	Relative Frequencies of the Licensors of PG in Speech-Related Genres in Late Modern English	122
15	Auxiliary before Licensor in PG	125
16	Auxiliary(ies) before Licensor in VPE	125
17	Syntactic Linking in PG	129
18	Summary of Syntactic Linking in PG	130
19	Connectors in Coordinate Clauses in PG	130
20	Connectors in Subordinate Clauses in PG	131
21	Syntactic Linking in VPE	132
22	Summary of Syntactic Linking in VPE	134
23	Connectors in Coordinate Clauses in VPE	135
24	Connectors in Subordinate Clauses in VPE	135
25	Syntactic Linking in VPE in Writing-Related Genres	136
26	Syntactic Linking in Bos and Spenader's (2011) Study	136
27	Syntactic Domain of Ellipsis in PAE Constructions	141
28	Syntactic Linking and Syntactic Domain in PG	142
29	Syntactic Linking and Syntactic Domain in VPE	144
30	Category of the Source of Ellipsis	147
31	Category of the Target of Ellipsis Triggered by Auxiliaries *Be* and *Have* in PG	150
32	Category of the Target of Ellipsis Triggered by Auxiliaries *Be* and *Have* in VPE	150
33	Category of the Source in Bos and Spenader's (2011) Study	151
34	Category of the Source in Writing-Related Genres in Late Modern English	151

35	Split Antecedents in Late Modern English	153
36	Category of the Remnant of PG in Late Modern English	155
37	Syntactic Function of the Remnant of PG in Late Modern English	156
38	Polarity of the Source and Polarity of the Target of Ellipsis in PG	159
39	Mismatches in Polarity between the Source and the Target of Ellipsis in PG	159
40	Polarity of the Source and Polarity of the Target of Ellipsis in VPE	160
41	Mismatches in Polarity between the Source and the Target of Ellipsis in VPE	160
42	Polarity of the Source and Polarity of the Target of Ellipsis in Tag Questions	162
43	Polarity of the Source and Polarity of the Target of Ellipsis in VPE	162
44	Mismatches in Polarity between the Source and the Target of Ellipsis in VPE	163
45	Voice of the Source and the Target of Ellipsis in PG	164
46	Voice of the Source and the Target of Ellipsis in VPE	164
47	Voice Mismatches between the Source and the Target of Ellipsis in PG	169
48	Voice Mismatches between the Source and the Target of Ellipsis in VPE	172
49	Aspect of the Source and Aspect of the Target of Ellipsis in PG	173
50	Mismatches in Aspect between the Source and the Target of Ellipsis in PG	174
51	Aspect of the Source and Aspect of the Target of Ellipsis in VPE	175
52	Mismatches in Aspect between the Source and the Target of Ellipsis in VPE	176
53	Modality of the Source and Modality of the Target of Ellipsis in PG	178
54	Mismatches in Modality between the Source and the Target of Ellipsis in PG	180
55	Modality of the Source and Modality of the Target of Ellipsis in VPE	182
56	Modality of the Source and Modality of the Target of Ellipsis in VPE (continuation)	183
57	Mismatches in Modality between the Source and the Target of Ellipsis in VPE	186
58	Mismatches in Modality between the Source and the Target of Ellipsis in VPE (continuation)	187
59	Tense of the Source and Tense of the Target of Ellipsis in PG	188

60 Mismatches in Tense between the Source and the Target of Ellipsis in PG   189
61 Tense of the Source and Tense of the Target of Ellipsis in VPE   191
62 Mismatches in Tense between the Source and the Target of Ellipsis in VPE   193
63 Type of Clause of the Target of Ellipsis   196
64 Type of Clause of the Source versus Type of Clause of Target of Ellipsis in PG   199
65 Type of Clause of the Source versus Type of Clause of Target of Ellipsis in VPE   200
66 Types of Anaphora in Late Modern English   201
67 Type of Focus in PG   208
68 Focus Type in Comparative and Noncomparative PG with NP Remnants   209
69 Subjects in Noncomparative PG with NP Remnants   210
70 Subjects in Noncomparative PG with NP Remnants in Miller's (2014) and Levin's (1986) Studies   211
71 Subjects in Comparative PG with NP Remnants   212
72 Subjects in Comparative PG with NP Remnants in Miller's (2014) study   212
73 Same Subject and Different Subject PGs with NP Remnants   213
74 Same Subject and Different Subject PGs with NP Remnants in Miller's (2014) Study   213
75 Type of Focus in VPE   213
76 Sloppy Identity in PAE in Late Modern English   216
77 Turn in PAE in Late Modern English   222
78 Distribution of PAE in Late Modern English   224
79 Normalized Frequency of PAE in Late Modern English   225
80 Distribution of PAE in Late Modern English with respect to the Total Number of IPs   225
81 Genre Distribution of PG in Late Modern English   227
82 Genre Distribution of VPE in Late Modern English   227
83 Genre Distribution of PAE in Late Modern English   229
84 PAE Genre Distribution according to Culpeper and Kytö's (2010) Fine-Grained Classification of Genres   231
85 Preliminary Normalized Frequency of PAE by Genre in Late Modern English   232

86	Final Normalized Frequency of PAE by Genre in Late Modern English 233
87	Normalized Frequency of PG by Genre in Late Modern English 233
88	Normalized Frequency of VPE by Genre in Late Modern English 233
89	Absolute Frequency of PAE per Type of Genre 234
90	Absolute Frequency of PAE per Type Genre and Period 234
91	Absolute Frequency of PG per Type Genre and Period 235
92	Absolute Frequency of VPE per Type Genre and Period 235
93	Lexical Distance between the Source and the Target of Ellipsis in PAE 237
94	Average Number of Words between Antecedent and Ellipsis Site in Writing and Speech-Related Genres 238
95	Average Number of Words per IP in Writing and Speech-Related Genres 239
96	Normalized Average Number of Words between Antecedent and Ellipsis Site per Type of Genre in PG 239
97	Normalized Average Number of Words between Antecedent and Ellipsis Site per Type of Genre in VPE 239
98	Normalized Average Number of Words between Antecedent and Ellipsis Site per Type of Genre in PG and VPE 240
99	Lexical Distance and Boundedness in PG 242
100	Lexical Distance and Boundedness in VPE 244
101	Syntactic Distance between the Source and the Target of Ellipsis in PAE 246
102	Lexical and Syntactic Distance in PG 249
103	Lexical and Syntactic Distance in VPE 250

Acknowledgements

First of all, I would like to express my most sincere gratitude and appreciation to my PhD supervisor, Prof. Javier Pérez-Guerra, who has always been there to guide me and advise me throughout these years. The completion of this book would have never been possible without his tireless help and encouragement, especially during the hardest moments.

For generous financial support I gratefully acknowledge the following institutions: The Spanish Ministry of Economy and Competitiveness and the European Regional Development Fund (grant no. FFI2013-44065-P and FPI BES-2010-030869), the Autonomous Government of Galicia (grant no. GPC2014/060), the research team Language Variation and Textual Categorisation (LVTC) based at the University of Vigo and the Labex Mobility EFL Grant.

In addition, I feel especially grateful to the research team Language Variation and Textual Categorisation (LVTC) and to the English Linguistics Circle, whose team members, based at the universities of Vigo and Santiago de Compostela, have always provided me with the perfect scenario where to discuss the preliminary results of the research presented in this volume and obtain constructive, critical feedback.

I would also like to express my deepest gratitude to Dr. Lobke Aelbrecht, Prof. Liliane Haegeman, and Dr. Jeroen van Craenenbroeck for their kind help and guidance during my research stay at the University of Ghent in 2011. Their supervision and feedback at the earliest stages of the investigation presented here was crucial.

During my research stay at the University of Chicago in 2012, I had the great opportunity of being supervised by Prof. Jason Merchant. His seminal lessons on ellipsis, together with the regular meetings we used to share in order to discuss my research, contributed enormously to the correct development of my investigation. This work owes a great debt to his bright ideas and support.

Last but not least, my several research stays at the Laboratoire de Linguistique Formelle (Université Paris Diderot-Paris 7) during three consecutive years allowed me to undertake research tasks with the priceless help of both Prof. Anne Abeillé and Prof. Philip Miller. Our regular meetings and seminars served as a great source of inspiration. Their feedback has been of such incalculable value that the research presented in this book would have never been the same without their help. Most of all, I thank them both for their constant willingness to guide me and advise me, for their time and effort, and for their encouragement and interest in my work.

Abbreviations

AdP	Adverbial Phrase
AP	Adjective Phrase
BNC	British National Corpus
COCA	The Corpus of Contemporary American English
IP	Inflection Phrase
NCA	Null Complement Anaphora
NP	Noun Phrase
PAE	Post-Auxiliary Ellipsis
PG	Pseudogapping
POS	Part of Speech
PP	Prepositional Phrase
PPCMBE	Penn Parsed Corpus of Modern British English
PRONP	Pronoun Phrase
SFG	Systemic Functional Grammar
TGG	Transformational Generative Grammar
VP	Verb Phrase
VPE	Verb Phrase Ellipsis
WYHIWYG	'What you hear is what you get'
WYSIWYG	'What you see is what you get'

1

Introduction

In a communication exchange, speakers may omit information when it can be inferred from the linguistic or extralinguistic context. This implies that addressees will need to decipher not only what has been said but also what has not in order to reach a full and correct interpretation. Therefore, the recipients of the information will have the task of filling in the blanks left by their interlocutor(s), or, in other words, they will need to interpret ellipsis. This entails that actual utterances as well as omissions are equally important for the success of the communication exchange, since silence is meaningful. Ellipsis is illustrated in (1):

(1) Daniel can speak five languages, but Joseph can't ~~speak five languages~~.[1]

Example (1) is an instance of so-called VP Ellipsis[2] in which the elided verb phrase or VP (*speak five languages*) in the second conjunct can be retrieved from the first one, which serves as the antecedent.

Elliptical constructions do not occur freely. There are two main restrictions for them to be felicitous: the recoverability condition and the licensing condition.[3] On the one hand, the recoverability condition alludes to the fact that elliptical constructions need to be recoverable from the context in which they take place, be it linguistic or extralinguistic (Quirk et al. 1985: 895ff; Aelbrecht 2010; van Craenenbroeck and Merchant 2013). For instance, the example in (2) would violate the recoverability condition if uttered out of the blue, since it would not be possible to infer its meaning due to the lack of an antecedent:

(2) *I know he will.[4]

On the other hand, the licensing condition dictates what can exactly be elided depending on the syntactic context in which ellipsis takes place (Zagona 1982; Lobeck 1995; Johnson 2001; Merchant 2001; Aelbrecht 2009, 2010). Aelbrecht (2009: 15) provides an example of this:

(3) a. *Max having arrived and Morgan not having, we decided to wait.
   b. Max had arrived, but Morgan hadn't, so we decided to wait.

Although the VP could be easily retrieved from its surrounding context in the nonfinite clause, the English language only licenses the omission of the verb phrase that occurs in the finite clause ((3)b).

The mismatch between meaning (the intended message) and sound (what is actually pronounced) evinced in contexts of ellipsis poses a challenge to the traditional Saussurean concept of linguistic sign, defined as being composed of both 'signifier' (form) and 'signified' (meaning). This definition of the linguistic sign entails that every linguistic unit should have a form and a meaning for communication to be possible. However, as Merchant (2006) claims, in ellipsis there is *significatio ex nihilo* ('meaning out of nothing'), that is, 'there is meaning without form' (Merchant 2013a: 1), which implies that the interpretation of an elliptical construction is richer than what is actually pronounced (Carlson 2002; Culicover and Jackendoff 2005; Aelbrecht 2009, 2010) and therefore speakers have no problems to understand the meaning of elliptical structures.

The following would be the criteria used for the identification of elliptical structures (Bîlbîie 2011: 129): (i) the syntax is apparently incomplete, since the material that would be necessary for the correct interpretation of a structure is missing; (ii) the elements belonging to the elliptical structure must be analysable as arguments, adjuncts or predicates of the elided material; and (iii) the interpretation of an elliptical structure is obtained by means of a linguistic or an extralinguistic context, thanks to the presence of an antecedent (either explicit or implicit).[5] In addition, ellipsis also seems to defy Frege's compositionality principle (Bîlbîie 2011: 129), echoed in Chomsky's (1965: 136) words as follows: 'The semantic interpretation of a sentence depends only on its lexical items and the grammatical functions and relations represented in the underlying structures in which they appear.' This is so because elliptical sentences pose no problems for their actual interpretation even when some of their elements have been omitted.

As will be maintained in this volume, ellipsis is indeed a complex phenomenon for any theory of grammar because of its diverse characteristics, which fall between sentence and discourse grammar (Williams 1977; Gallego 2011). On the one hand, the sentence-grammar characteristics of ellipsis would be related to the different ellipsis types that have been attested and their properties (category, internal structure and morphological restrictions). The discourse-grammar characteristics present in ellipsis, on the other hand, would make reference to the context where the elliptical phenomena take place (linguistic and extralinguistic) and the thematic structure of sentences, which are formed by both given and new information (Gallego 2011). Elliptical sentences have usually been claimed to contain significant new information in discourse, avoiding unnecessary, old information.

The rationale behind the study of ellipsis, as put forward by Bîlbîie (2011: 130), is that it is present in all natural languages but not really understood in the grammar because there is the preconceived idea that ellipsis is governed by the 'principle of minimum effort' and is in free distribution with its non-elliptical counterpart. First, as a representative of the former view, Bîlbîie quotes Zribi-Hertz (1986), who claims that ellipsis remains as a choice made by the language user. Another aspect usually brought up with regard to ellipsis would be the claim that the use of ellipsis is one of the reasons why languages are so ambiguous (Hendriks and Spenader 2005: 29; Bîlbîie 2011: 130). Hendriks and Spenader (2005) and Bîlbîie (2011) confront this view by defending that ellipsis cannot be reduced to the mere instantiation of the principle of minimum effort. In ellipsis, as they contend, that said principle of minimum effort derives from the interaction of two antonymous principles which had already been captured in Grice's (1975) quantity maxim. This maxim claimed that speakers should make their contribution as informative as is required for the purpose of the communicative exchange while at the same time not making it more informative than is required. When it comes to dealing with the phenomenon of ellipsis, this amounts to saying that one can make use of ellipsis as long as our interlocutor is able to decipher our message. Therefore, only when the information can be recovered may one speaker dispense of redundant information by means of ellipsis. Hendriks and Spenader (2005: 29–30) summarize the functions of ellipsis by stating that it allows us to express things which 'are otherwise ineffable, disambiguate discourse structure, and serve as a rapport-creating device that could be relevant to automatic dialogue systems'.

Second, as will be shown below, there are numerous examples which evince differences between elliptical sentences and their non-elliptical counterparts. Indeed, there are cases where the use of ellipsis is the only means one can employ to build a grammatical sentence or obtain a certain interpretation (Bîlbîie 2011: 130). In addition, there is a great number of examples in the literature that instantiate that while certain cases of ellipsis are grammatical, their non-elliptical counterparts would be ungrammatical due to the violation of certain syntactic restrictions (like the presence of finite VPs in cases of Gapping,[6] an elliptical construction exemplified in (4)) or the violation of the so-called island constraints (as in the example of Sluicing[7] in (5), where there is a locality constraint). Ever since Ross (1969), it has been found that Sluicing appears to be insensitive to syntactic islands (Merchant 2001, 2008b: 135), that is, it allows the movement of *wh*-phrases out of islands, as in (5) and (6) (Merchant 2001, 2013a; Boeckx 2006; Bîlbîie 2011; van Craenenbroeck and Merchant 2013):

(4) a. Robin speaks French, as well as Leslie (*speaks) German.
b. Robin speaks French, and not Leslie (*speaks) German. [Bîlbîie (2011: 131); originally in Culicover and Jackendoff (2005)]

(5) They want to hire someone who speaks a Balkan language but I don't remember which (*they want to hire someone who speaks). [Merchant (2001: 5); originally in Ross (1969)]

Compare the elliptical example in (6)a with its non-elliptical counterpart:

(6) a. Ben will be mad if Abby talks to one of the teachers, but she couldn't remember which. [Merchant (2001: 88)]
b. *Ben will be mad if Abby talks to one of the teachers, but she couldn't remember which *(of the teachers) Ben will be mad if she talks to.*

Another fact that differentiates elliptical sentences from their non-elliptical counterparts from the point of view of semantics is the phenomenon known as Cross-Conjunct Binding (McCawley 1993; Hulsey 2008; Bîlbîie 2011; Johnson 2014). Cross-Conjunct Binding alludes to the fact that a quantifier in the subject of the first conjunct can bind a variable in the second conjunct, that is, there can be coreference because the quantifier of the first conjunct takes wide scope. In (7)–(9) below the pronoun belonging to the second conjunct can be coindexed with the quantified subject that appears in the first one provided that there is ellipsis:

(7) No one$_i$'s duck was moist enough or his$_i$ mussels tender enough. [McCawley (1993: 248)]
(8) Not every girl$_i$ ate a green banana and her$_i$ mother, a ripe one.
(9) No boy$_i$ joined the navy and his$_i$ mother, the army. [Johnson (2014: 29); emphasis in the original]

Compare the grammaticality of (7)–(9) above with the ungrammaticality that arises in their non-elliptical counterparts, which demonstrates that coreference is only possible in the elliptical version:

(10) *No one$_i$'s duck was most enough or his$_i$ mussels were tender enough.
(11) *Not every girl$_i$ ate a green banana and her$_i$ mother ate a ripe one.
(12) *No boy$_i$ joined the navy and his$_i$ mother can join the army.

Moreover, as reported by both Siegel (1987: 56) and Bîlbîie (2011: 131), there are cases where elliptical sentences and their non-elliptical equivalents receive different interpretations, as the meanings are in complementary distribution. This is observed in examples where the repetition of modal verbs in two conjuncts would imply a strict reading, the omission of the modal verb in the second conjunct would trigger a wide-scope reading, and the omission of the whole VP (together with the modal verb) could be interpreted as involving both types of scope:

(13) John can't eat caviar and Mary eat beans. [wide scope]
(14) John can't eat caviar and Mary can't eat beans. [narrow scope]
(15) John can't eat caviar and Mary, beans. [both] [Siegel (1987: 56)]

In (13), the modal verb *can't* negates at the same time the actions (the act of eating something) performed by two subjects, whereas in (14) the actions of both subjects are each negated independently in their respective clauses, thanks to the repetition of the modal verb *can't*. However, as noted by Siegel, (15) can receive both interpretations: *Mary eat beans* (wide scope) or *Mary can't eat beans* (narrow scope).

In addition, the lack of one-to-one semantic correspondence between elliptical and non-elliptical sentences is also evinced in those cases in which the use of ellipsis involves a restriction on the number of possible interpretations that could be given to a particular sentence. As noted earlier, ellipsis can disambiguate discourse structure (Hendriks and Spenader 2005: 29–30), a fact that was first noticed by Levin and Prince (1986). Kehler (2000: 563f, 2002: 5, 2005: 16) and Bîlbîie (2011: 132) cite and discuss some of their original examples:

(16) Sue became upset and Nan became downright angry.
(17) Al cleaned up the bathroom and Joe cleaned up the mess.
(18) One of the students was accepted at Bryn Mawr and the high school was praised on TV. [Kehler (2000: 563)]

As noted by both Kehler (2000, 2002, 2005) and Bîlbîie (2011), these sentences are ambiguous between 'symmetric' and 'asymmetric' readings. This means that each of the sentences in (16)-(18) possesses a symmetric reading, where the two actions described are understood as independent of one another (in Kehler's terms, the resemblance relation *Parallel* holds), as well as an asymmetric reading, where the first event is interpreted as being the cause of the second event (in Kehler's terms, the cause-effect relation *Result* holds). Importantly,

Levin and Prince (1986) discovered that only the symmetric reading is available in the elliptical versions of (16)-(18):

(19) Sue became upset and Nan ~~became~~ downright angry.
(20) Al cleaned up the bathroom and Joe ~~cleaned up~~ the mess.
(21) One of the students was accepted at Bryn Mawr and the high school ~~was~~ praised on TV. [Kehler (2000: 563)]

Another well-known instance where the use of ellipsis triggers a restriction in the number of interpretations of a sentence has been named 'Dahl's puzzle' after Dahl (1974). Basically, what Dahl (1974) found is that in cases where an ellipsis contains two pronouns, the first of them cannot receive a strict interpretation if the second receives a sloppy interpretation (Johnson 2009). That is, making the assumption that in (22) below the two pronouns refer to *John* in the antecedent, the expectation would be that four interpretations should be possible in principle (Hardt 1993; Fiengo and May 1994; Johnson 2009; Bîlbîie 2011), contrary to fact:

(22) John *said he saw his mother*. Bill did too.
    (a) Bill said John saw John's mother.
    (b) Bill said Bill saw Bill's mother.
    (c) Bill said Bill saw John's mother.
    (d) *Bill said John saw Bill's mother. [Hardt (1993: 115–16); emphasis in the original]

The non-elliptical version of (22), however, allows the four interpretations, where two of them would be mixed:

(23) John *said he saw his mother*. Bill said that he saw his mother too.
    (a) Bill said John saw John's mother.
    (b) Bill said Bill saw Bill's mother.
    (c) Bill said Bill saw John's mother.
    (d) Bill said John saw Bill's mother.

Although I have just shown that ellipsis may help in the disambiguation of certain discourse structures when compared to their non-elliptical versions, there are also cases in which it contributes to ambiguity. The literature has mainly dealt with two types of contexts where ambiguity seems to arise systematically: in the interpretation of pronouns and in the interpretation of unmarked nominal expressions (Bîlbîie 2011: 133). The former context involves cases such as (24), where the omission of a possessive pronoun offers the possibility of interpreting the second conjunct in a strict (24)a or in a sloppy way (24)b:

(24) Mary$_i$ kissed her$_i$ children goodbye and Anne$_j$ did too.
   (a) Anne$_j$ kissed her$_i$ children goodbye. [strict interpretation]
   (b) Anne$_j$ kissed her$_j$ children goodbye. [sloppy interpretation]

The second type of ambiguity reported in the literature can be instantiated by the following example taken from Carlson (2002: 204–5), which contains an object/subject ambiguity:

(25) Tasha called him more often than Sonya.

The remnant *Sonya* could be either the subject of the elliptical sentence (*Sonya called him more often*) or its object (*Tasha called him more often than she called Sonya*). Ambiguity lies in what type of interpretation will be chosen depending on the context where this sentence is uttered. These ambiguities have been reported for English but, according to Bîlbîie (2011: 133), they would pose fewer problems in languages which possess more morphosyntactic, lexical or prosodic marking. For example, she mentions Rumanian, a language where, on the one hand, the interpretation of the pronouns in ellipsis is alleviated (at least for the sloppy reading) thanks to the use of different pronominal forms and, on the other hand, subjects and objects receive different case markings.

As has been shown, then, the grammar of ellipsis deserves special attention and its analysis cannot be reduced to stating that it is in free distribution with its non-elliptical counterpart by any theory of grammar. In the remainder of this introductory chapter, I will deal with the scope and the aims of this volume (1.1), the state of the art on ellipsis (1.2) as well as the outline of the research (1.3).

1.1 Scope and aims of the study

In an attempt to provide an answer to the null hypothesis 'ellipsis does not undergo significant changes in the recent history of English', in this study I will undertake a corpus-based analysis of specifically Post-Auxiliary Ellipsis (PAE henceforth) in Late Modern English, using data from the Penn Parsed Corpus of Modern British English (1700–1914), and I will compare my results with those reported for Present-Day English in the relevant literature. The term PAE (Sag 1976; Warner 1993; Miller 2011; Miller and Pullum 2014) covers those cases in which a Verb Phrase (VP), Prepositional Phrase (PP), Noun Phrase (NP), Adjective Phrase (AP) or Adverbial Phrase (AdP) is omitted after one of the following licensors (those elements that permit the occurrence of ellipsis):

modal auxiliaries, auxiliaries *be*, *have* and *do* and infinitival marker *to* (the latter believed to be a defective nonfinite auxiliary verb; see Fiengo 1980; Pullum 1982; Gazdar et al. 1985; Levine 2012; Miller and Pullum 2014). This study focuses on two subtypes of PAE, namely VP Ellipsis (VPE henceforth) and Pseudogapping (PG henceforth), illustrated in (26)-(28) and (30)-(31), respectively:

(26) I have written a squib but I think that Michael *hasn't* ~~written a squib~~.
(27) A: Did he call you last night?
    B: Of course he *did* ~~call me last night~~.
(28) Jason is talkative but Sarah *is not* ~~talkative~~.
(29) A: Is your dad a plumber?
    B: Yes, he *is* ~~a plumber~~.
(30) Sheila kissed Paul, and Christina *did* ~~kiss~~ <u>Manuel</u>.
(31) If you don't tell me, you *will* ~~believe~~ <u>your mum</u>.

The examples of VPE shown in (26)-(28) illustrate the omission of VPs (*written a squib* and *call me last night*), APs (*talkative*) and NPs (*a plumber*) triggered by the licensors *have*, *do* and *be* (in italics). Notice that VPE can occur in contexts of subordination (as in (26)) and can apply across sentence boundaries (as in (29)). In turn, PG, illustrated in (30) and (31), looks like VPE but in this case a complement (usually contrastive), known as the 'remnant' (underlined), is left after the auxiliary, as illustrated by the direct objects *Manuel* or *your mum*.

In spite of the existence of a great number of studies that have studied ellipsis from a theoretical point of view (Chao 1988; Lobeck 1995; Johnson 2001; Merchant 2001, 2013a,b,c; Gengel 2007, 2013; Aelbrecht 2009, 2010; among many others), empirical analyses on the different types of ellipsis mentioned in the literature constitute a fairly recent line of investigation and have concentrated mainly on VPE and PG (see Hardt 1992a,b, 1993, 1995, 1997; Hardt and Rambow 2001; Nielsen 2003a,b, 2004a,b,c,d, 2005; Ericsson 2005; Hendriks and Spenader 2005; Hoeksema 2006; Bos and Spenader 2011; Miller 2011, 2014; Miller and Pullum 2014). These corpus-based studies have not only tried to discover new methods and algorithms for the automatic detection and retrieval of examples of ellipsis in Present-Day English, but also analysed their characteristics on the basis of empirical data. As a matter of fact, this empirical approach has proved to be a useful tool in order to test and reformulate theoretical hypotheses on ellipsis.

A methodological pillar of this study has been the implementation of an algorithm which can automatically detect and retrieve examples of PAE in a parsed corpus. This complex algorithm, which relies on the parsing conventions followed by the compilers of the Penn Parsed Corpus of Modern British English (PPCMBE) (1700–1914), has led to successful recall ratios. The novelty of this monograph lies in the fact that it not only studies PAE empirically but also proposes an algorithm for its automatic detection and retrieval in Modern English. This methodology has been a fundamental part in offering an in-depth analysis of the two subtypes of PAE mentioned earlier, namely VPE and PG, in Modern English and in comparing their characteristics with those reported in other theoretical and empirical analyses on Present-Day English data.

The variables under study have been divided into four different groups: grammatical, semantic/discursive, usage and processing variables. First, within the group of grammatical variables, I have analysed the type of licensor of PAE (modal auxiliaries, auxiliaries *be*, *have* and *do* and infinitival marker *to*); the existence of auxiliary(ies) before the licensor; the type of syntactic linking established between the antecedent and the ellipsis site (coordination, subordination, etc.); the syntactic domain where ellipsis occurs (matrix, subordinate clause, etc.); the category of the antecedent and that of the elided material (NP, VP, AP, etc.); the existence of split antecedents; the types of remnants attested in PG (classified by category and syntactic function); and, finally, auxiliary-related variables such as polarity, voice, aspect, modality and tense. Second, the semantic/discursive variables analysed include the type of clause attested in the antecedents and in the ellipsis sites (declarative, interrogative and imperative); the type of anaphora (anaphoric, cataphoric and exophoric); the type of focus (subject choice, auxiliary choice, object choice, etc.); the existence of sloppy identity, and the type of turn (i.e. whether there is a change of speaker or not). Third, I have paid attention to usage variables such as the distribution of PAE constructions by period (eighteenth and roughly nineteenth centuries) and genre (speech-related vs. writing-related genres). Finally, I have also analysed processing variables such as the lexical distance (in number of words) and the syntactic distance (in number of clauses) existing between the antecedent and the ellipsis site in PAE constructions.

1.2 State of the art

The term 'ellipsis' (from Greek ἔλλειψις, *élleipsis*, 'omission'), as it is conceived in current linguistic research, refers to structures in which expected syntactic elements are missing in certain constructions, creating a mismatch between meaning (the intended message) and sound (what is in fact uttered).

Put differently, ellipsis is an instance of indirect mapping between meaning and form.

Ellipsis is nowadays studied with respect to the syntactic structures, the contexts and the discourse conditions in which it is attested. Thus, modern linguistics is mainly concerned with the description and establishment of all the different criteria for the use of ellipsis, providing the rules that license its occurrence. As Sundby et al. (1991: 241) point out, 'in modern linguistics, ellipsis hinges on the rules specifying the conditions for its use, and the term is most frequently used in describing complex sentence structures, particularly coordination.' Over the past fifty years, the 'mechanism' of ellipsis has become a central issue of debate for researchers working on semantics, syntax, pragmatics, psycholinguistics and corpus linguistics, as will be shown. The notion of ellipsis is discussed in great detail not only in the comprehensive grammars of English such as Quirk et al. (1985), Biber et al. (1999) and Huddleston and Pullum (2002) (see Section 1.2.1 below), but also in books and articles dealing with its diverse types and subtypes from very diverse angles and frameworks. Ellipsis has helped anaphora theorists, ellipsis theorists, syntacticians, semanticists and psycholinguists to make progress on the aims of their own investigations.

Nevertheless, even though many attempts have been made in order to provide an exact and detailed taxonomy of all of the different types and subtypes of ellipsis, so far one could state that 'so little is known about ellipsis that even its taxonomy is up for grabs' (Johnson 2008: 2).

In addition, as more languages started to be studied with respect to the phenomenon of ellipsis, new findings have emerged, either challenging or supporting the existing theories on ellipsis. In the past few years, there has also been an increase in the use of corpora in order to test and reformulate theoretical hypotheses on ellipsis by examining new empirical evidence (see Section 2.1).

The focus of this volume is not to extend or discuss ellipsis from a specific theoretical framework, but to provide an empirical (more descriptive) account of this syntactic phenomenon in Modern English. In an attempt to determine the research questions and the variables at work in the description of ellipsis, a number of the most relevant theoretical accounts of this linguistic strategy will be thoroughly discussed: the characteristics of ellipsis as mentioned in the three most influential comprehensive grammars of English (Quirk et al. 1985; Biber et al. 1999; Huddleston and Pullum 2002); formal (mostly, generative) approaches, which provide an extensive and up-to-date analysis and discussion of the main theoretical issues as regards licensing, structure and identity (Sag 1976; Williams 1977; Dalrymple et al. 1991; Hardt 1993;

Fiengo and May 1994; Ginzburg and Sag 2000; Merchant 2001, 2004, 2013a,b; Culicover and Jackendoff 2005; Aelbrecht 2009, 2010; van Craenenbroeck 2010a,b; Thoms 2010, 2013; Chung et al. 1995; Chung 2006, 2013; to name but a few); and also non-syntactocentric approaches to ellipsis such as Systemic Functional Grammar, in which ellipsis has been studied basically as a cohesive agency which 'contributes to the semantic structure of the discourse' (Halliday 1994: 316; Thompson 2003: 149; Halliday and Matthiessen 2004: 562) and as a special instance of thematic structure in a clause, where some parts are presupposed from previously mentioned pieces of discourse. The theoretical accounts of ellipsis mentioned so far are then complemented with a discussion of the findings provided by empirical studies from the field of psycholinguistics. As will be shown, the realm of psycholinguistics has proved its importance as a resource where to look for answers to theoretical proposals. This will pave the way for Chapter 2, where I present the main findings from the field of corpus linguistics, whose approach has served as a tool in order to test and reformulate theoretical hypotheses on ellipsis (see Hardt 1992b, 1993, 1995, 1997; Hardt and Rambow 2001; Nielsen 2003a,b, 2004a,b,c,d, 2005; Ericsson 2005; Hendriks and Spenader 2005; Hoeksema 2006; Bos and Spenader 2011; Miller 2011, 2014; Miller and Pullum 2014) and the results of the analysis of the different variables taken into account (see Chapter 3). Since the approach adopted in this study is not merely descriptive, the statistical findings have been justified by alluding to the different theoretical frameworks previously surveyed.

First, I will offer a general overview of the treatment that the concept of ellipsis has received in three seminal comprehensive grammars of English, such as Quirk et al. (1985), Biber et al. (1999) and Huddleston and Pullum (2002) (Section 1.2.1). Then, Section 1.2.2 will be devoted to the description of ellipsis as conceived within the framework of Systemic Functional Grammar (SFG), mainly represented by M. A. K. Halliday. Section 1.2.3 will tackle this syntactic phenomenon from the point of view of Transformational Generative Grammar (TGG). Section 1.2.4 provides an overview of the main empirical findings on ellipsis in the field of psycholinguistics.

1.2.1 Ellipsis in comprehensive grammars of English

In an attempt to draw some generalizations about the treatment of the syntactic phenomenon of ellipsis, this section explores three influential comprehensive grammars of English: Quirk et al. (1985), Biber et al. (1999) and Huddleston and Pullum (2002).

To start with, both Quirk et al. (1985) and Huddleston and Pullum (2002) provide a thorough description of the concept of ellipsis and propose a taxonomy of the diverse types and subtypes of the strategy with a meticulous explanation of the conditions under which ellipsis takes place,[8] that is, the recoverability and the licensing conditions mentioned earlier in the introduction to this monograph. On the one hand, Quirk et al. (1985) devote a whole chapter to describe the syntactic phenomenon of ellipsis (omission) in contrast with pro-forms *do so, do it, do that, do this*, and so on (i.e. substitution) and consider both mechanisms a means for grammatical reduction, namely, the abbreviation of grammatical structures in order to avoid redundancy of expression and contribute to clarity. On the other hand, Huddleston and Pullum (2002) deal with the concept of ellipsis with respect to anaphor and deixis and regard ellipsis as a kind of anaphor used to obtain reduction as well. Both grammars discuss ellipsis and substitution and include in their discussions not only a comparison of the differences among the pro-forms *do so, do that, do it, do this* and *so* but also a description of their most common contexts of use in contrast with ellipsis.[9] In turn, Biber et al. (1999) discuss ellipsis as a phenomenon that takes place in clause grammar and complement clauses, basing their description on some examples taken directly from corpora with genre, register and dialect variation.

In general, ellipsis is described as grammatical omission, that is, as a means to achieve reduction by leaving out material which can be recovered from the context. In addition, ellipsis is also considered a tool that contributes to the cohesion of discourse (see also Section 1.2.2 for the cohesive characteristics of ellipsis from the perspective of SFG). The rationale behind the use of ellipsis, as defended in these grammars, is mainly to avoid redundancy of expression, since there is a general preference for economy in the language. For instance, according to Quirk et al. (1985: 860; italics in the original), example (32) would be preferable to (33) because it is slightly more economical:

(32) She might sing tonight, but I don't think she will (sing tonight).[10]
(33) She might sing tonight, but I don't think she will *do so*.

The syntactic phenomenon of ellipsis has been shown to be quite frequent in coordination contexts, where there is usually a parallelism between two or more units with regard to structure, meaning and/or function, thus allowing reduction to come into the picture to avoid a possible redundant overlap. For instance, the clauses *Pushkin was Russia's greatest poet* and *Tolstoy was Russia's greatest novelist* (Quirk et al. 1985: 858) could be coordinated into the following structure:

(34) Pushkin was Russia's greatest poet, and Tolstoy her greatest novelist.
[Quirk et al. (1985: 858)]

The intensive verb *to be* has been omitted in the second conjunct under identity with the verb of the first conjunct. In addition, the possessive phrase *Russia's* in the first conjunct has been replaced with the possessive pronoun *her* in the second conjunct. Thus, coordination is believed to be so strongly tied in with ellipsis that Quirk et al. (1985: 859) claim that 'so close is the association between coordination and ellipsis that we cannot very well understand the one phenomenon without understanding the other'.

However, it has also been highlighted that ellipsis tends to be avoided in contexts where the omission of the given information would lead to ambiguity, as in (35) below, where the omission of the verb *kills* (a case of Gapping) causes problems for the actual understanding of this sentence, which is further obscured by the use of Greek names:

(35) In the course of the play, Atreus kills his wife Aerope, Aegisthus his uncle Atreus, and Pelopia herself. [Quirk et al. (1985: 860)]

Reduction is considered to be a syntactic phenomenon because it is the particular syntax of a language that will allow the reduction of linguistic elements (see Section 1.2.3 on the licensing condition on ellipsis as put forward by TGG). They provide the following example, showing that the reduction of the string *was Russia's greatest* in order to avoid repetition renders the sentence ungrammatical:

(36) *Pushkin was Russia's greatest poet, and Tolstoy novelist. [Quirk et al. (1985: 859)]

In their view, there exists a necessity to find an explanation as to why some examples of reduction are grammatical whereas others are not, and as to what the allowed degrees of reduction are.

In addition, these grammars also broach the recoverability condition in cases of ellipsis. As Quirk et al. (1985: 861) explain, ellipsis acts as a cohesive device in the sense that 'the full form of what has been reduced is generally RECOVERABLE FROM CONTEXT' (emphasis in the original). Quirk et al. (1985) defend that there exist three types of recoverability: textual recoverability (the elided material is recoverable from the immediate linguistic context),[11] situational recoverability (the extralinguistic context provides the key to the understanding of the omitted elements, that is, it would be a case of exophoric reference) and structural recoverability (the knowledge of grammatical structure will be crucial to retrieve the absent material). Here are some examples illustrating the different types of recoverability:

Textual recoverability:

(37) I'll buy the red *wine* if you'll buy the white Δ.¹²
(38) If you want me to Δ, I'll lend you my pen.

Situational recoverability:

(39) *How could you* Δ? [Quirk et al. (1985: 895); italics in the original]

Structural recoverability:

(40) It is strange (*that*) nobody heard the noise. [Quirk et al. (1985: 862); italics in the original]

Of all these, only textual recoverability is said to contribute to cohesion in discourse. Besides, textual recoverability can be of two kinds: anaphoric (37) or cataphoric (38). It is anaphoric when the antecedent to the elided material appears first, and cataphoric when the reverse situation takes place. Note, however, that the term 'antecedent', although it literally means 'going before', is applied to both anaphoric and cataphoric reference.

Biber et al. (1999: 156) also distinguish between textual and situational ellipsis when mentioning that elements need to be recoverable from a context, but do not recognize the category of structural ellipsis. Textual ellipsis is said to take place in 'coordinated clauses [...], comparative clauses [...], question-answer sequences [...], and other contexts where adjacent clauses are related in form and meaning' (Biber et al. 1999: 156). As far as situational ellipsis goes, it is said to depend upon the context of the situation in which an utterance occurs and to be more frequent in conversation, including under this label those cases where there is omission of function words. Here are some of the examples provided:[13]

(41) You've become part of me, and I <*have become part*>, of you.
(42) She looks older than my mother <*does*>.
(43) A: Have you got an exam on Monday?
     B: <*I've got*> two exams <*on Monday*>.
(44) What was the mileage when we got there? <*Was it*> A hundred and eleven?
(45) <*I*> Saw Susan and her boyfriend in Alder weeks ago.
(46) What <*are*> you going to do? <*Are*> You going to do her a postcard?
     [Biber et al. (1999: 156-8)]

On the one hand, examples (41)-(44) illustrate textual ellipsis: (41) in a coordinated clause, (42) in a comparative clause, (43) in question–answer sequences and (44) in a full interrogative question followed by a more specific question which is elliptic in form. On the other hand, (45) and (46) instantiate situational ellipsis, where (45) shows the omission of a function word, in this case, ellipsis of the subject and (46) ellipsis of the auxiliaries.

On their part, Huddleston and Pullum (2002: 1456) distinguish between retrospective and anticipatory ellipsis:[14]

(47) a. If you want me to <u>invite Kim as well</u>, I will __. [retrospective ellipsis]

b. If you want me to__ , I will <u>invite Kim as well</u>. [anticipatory ellipsis]

Material is said to be reduced or 'ellipsed' in this grammar. Even though they do not distinguish between textual, situational and structural ellipsis, they allude to the possibility of what they term 'ellipted antecedents', that is, the omission of the antecedent of a structural gap, as in:

(48) Now __ hug each other.
(49) __ Keeping a wary eye on each other, they woo Concordia.
[Huddleston and Pullum (2002: 1504)]

In the imperative clause in (48) the understood antecedent *you* is omitted, whereas 'the covert subject of the subordinate clause is itself anaphorically linked to the following *they* in the matrix clause' in (49) (Huddleston and Pullum 2002: 1504).

As for the classification of ellipsis, Quirk et al.'s (1985: 888) grammar provides the criteria required for ellipsis, whereas the other two grammars focus their attention on mentioning the different existing ellipsis types and the syntactic restrictions that each of them needs to comply with. Quirk et al. (1985: 888) contend that ellipsis in a strict sense would need to comply with the following five criteria:

(a) The ellipted words are precisely recoverable.
(b) The elliptical construction is grammatically 'defective'.
(c) The insertion of the missing words results in a grammatical sentence (with the same meaning as the original sentence).
(d) The missing word(s) are textually recoverable.
(e) The missing expression is an exact copy of the antecedent.

Criterion (a) implies that there should be no doubt as to what words are missing in contexts. This is the example provided (Quirk et al. 1985: 884; italics in the original), where one can easily deduce that the missing information is the verb *sing*.

(50) She can't *sing* tonight, so she won't Δ.

Criterion (b) alludes to the fact that ellipsis needs to be postulated to give an account of those examples that lack usual obligatory elements in the sentence. While in (50) grammatical defectiveness is obvious, it may not be so in the following example (Quirk et al. 1985: 885):

(51) Visit me tomorrow, if you wish (to visit me tomorrow).

It is difficult to decide whether the lack of the infinitive clause, which may be optional, represents a case of grammatical defectiveness. As suggested by Quirk et al. (1985: 885), this will depend on our acceptance of intransitive *wish*.

Criterion (c) entails that the insertion of the absent elements yields a grammatical sentence while keeping the same meaning as the reduced counterpart. Here are the examples offered (Quirk et al. 1985: 886; italics in the original):

(52) He always wakes up earlier than *I*. [formal]
(53) He always wakes up earlier than *me*. [informal]

Observe that while one could add the omitted words *wake up* to (54), doing so in (55) yields an ungrammatical sentence:

(54) He always wakes up earlier *than I wake up*.
(55) *He always wakes up earlier *than me wake up*.

Quirk et al. (1985: 886) argue that (54) is 'a more definite example of ellipsis' than (55) because the insertion of the omitted words renders the sentence grammatical, and add that that may have been the rationale behind favouring (54) over (55) in prescriptive teaching. The bracketed part of criterion (c) – 'with the same meaning as the original sentence' – is necessary because ellipsis is assumed to take some elements as 'understood'. Synonymy between the elliptical and the non-elliptical counterpart is, then, crucial. The importance of this part of criterion (c) is shown in (56) below (Quirk et al. 1985: 886):

(56) The poor (people) need more help.

Whereas the NP *the poor* is assumed to presuppose a general noun like *people*, when this noun is inserted, the elliptical and the non-elliptical counterparts do not convey the same meaning: the elliptical sentence *the poor* has a generic meaning, while *the poor people* would have a specific one. As put forward by Quirk et al. (1985: 886), 'generic meaning requires that we delete the article: *Poor people need more help*'.

Criterion (d), that is, the missing elements are textually recoverable, is postulated in order to know exactly what has been omitted in the light of the antecedent of the ellipsis site, making it possible to agree on what the missing elements are. But Quirk et al. (1985: 887) add criterion (e), that is, the missing words are present in the text in exactly the same form, to further distinguish two types of textual recoverability:

(57) She might *sing tonight*, but I don't think she will (sing tonight).
(58) She rarely *sings*, so I don't think she will (sing) tonight. [Quirk et al. (1985: 887); italics in the original]

In (57) the omitted part is an exact copy of the antecedent (*sing-sing*), but this is not the case in (58), where there is a morphological variation in the verb (*sings-sing*). In this case, criterion (c) might have applied as well, since (59) would be ungrammatical:

(59) *She rarely *sings*, so I don't think she will *sings* tonight.

Therefore, although Quirk et al. (1985: 885) invoke the principle of verbatim recovery so as to differentiate ellipsis from other types of omission in language (aphaeresis, clipping), they acknowledge that 'verbatim recovery does not necessarily mean that the items replaced are morphologically identical to the items constituting the antecedent' (Quirk et al. 1985: 885), as shown in (58) above. But there are cases, especially in coordinated structures, in which the application of criterion (e) would be significant, as in (60) and (61) below:

(60) The club always has *paid its way*, and always will (pay its way).
(61) ?The club always has (paid its way) and always will *pay its way*. [Quirk et al. (1985: 887); italics in the original]

In these sentences, there is a mismatch between the antecedent and the ellipsis site since both conjuncts require the presence of two different forms of the verb *pay*: *pay* and *paid*. However, Quirk et al. (1985: 887) state that (60) seems to be quite acceptable, while (61) is widely considered as incorrect.

In conclusion, Quirk et al. (1985: 887–8; italics in the original) declare that 'the technicalities of ellipsis are not *mere* technicalities, but have importance in enabling us to make different generalizations about what kinds of reduction are possible in English grammar'. Ellipsis, then, seems to follow some specific rules depending on the type of elliptical construction dealt with.

Moreover, ellipsis has also been classified by formal type, that is, according to the location of the ellipsis site. Three kinds of ellipsis have been proposed: initial (also known as 'ellipsis on the left'; Quirk et al. 1985: 893), medial and final ellipsis ('ellipsis on the right'; Quirk et al. 1985: 893), illustrated in (62)-(64):

(62) He squeezed her hand but <he> met with no response.
(63) He and his mate both jumped out, he <jumped out> to go to the women, his mate <jumped out> to stop other traffic on the bridge.
(64) Perhaps, as the review gathers steam, this can now change. It needs to <change>. [Biber et al. (1999: 156)]

Whereas Biber et al. (1999: 156) limit their discussion to mentioning the three classes and providing an example of each type, Quirk et al. (1985: 893) engage in an interesting debate on the consideration that medial ellipsis does not really exist since it 'is a structural illusion which results from looking at too large a constituent in the sentence' which can be subsumed under the category of special cases of either initial or final ellipsis.

Lastly, according to Quirk et al. (1985: 894), final ellipsis is much more frequent than initial and medial ellipsis. This does not accord with Biber et al.'s (1999: 1108) corpus data, which show that initial ellipsis tends to be more frequent than final ellipsis, the latter being also more common than medial ellipsis. The data also display dialect variation with regard to the choice of initial, medial or final ellipsis, and show that 'this tendency is more marked in BrE than in AmE' (Biber et al. 1999: 1108). As a consequence, as has been shown, there is no consensus as for the frequency of each of these types.

Following, in Section 1.2.2 I will address the concept of ellipsis as conceived of within the framework of SFG.

1.2.2 Ellipsis in SFG

The SFG framework focuses on understanding the meaning and function of language in context. SFG sets out to describe the different – meaningful – choices speakers make among the systems available to them. Therefore, language is conceived of as a means for communicative interaction among human beings, serving their particular needs depending on the context in which the act of communication takes place. In consequence, the text as a suprasentential unit of meaning is of paramount importance for this theory: every sentence contained in a text is considered to contribute to the meaning of the whole unit. This is why concepts such as cohesion, coherence and the thematic structure of sentences within discourse are relevant for SFG. Within this framework, mainly represented by M. A. K. Halliday, ellipsis has been principally studied as a cohesive agency which 'contributes to the semantic structure of the discourse' (Halliday 1994: 316; Thompson 2003: 149; Halliday and Matthiessen 2004: 562) and as a special instance of thematic structure in a clause, where some parts are presupposed from previously mentioned pieces of discourse.

SFG widely tackles the issue of ellipsis as well as of the usual contexts where ellipsis tends to occur. While Halliday (1994) and Halliday and Matthiessen (2004) broach the concept of ellipsis both from the point of view of its possible thematic structures and its role with respect to cohesion in discourse, ellipsis as a cohesive agency receives an extensive treatment in Halliday and Hasan's (1976) book, devoted to the description of cohesion in English in general. In this book, ellipsis is studied in relation to other cohesive agencies like reference, substitution, conjunction and lexical cohesion. As was the case with the comprehensive grammars of English reviewed, ellipsis and substitution (pro-forms *do so*, *do it*, *do that*, etc.) are both regarded as cohesive agencies within this framework. In other words, ellipsis and substitution are considered flipsides of the same coin: whereas in cases of ellipsis there is substitution by zero, in cases of substitution there is a place-holding device that is left occupying the space of the omitted material. Since discourse is composed of both given and new information, ellipsis is regarded as a mechanism which allows one to omit old/given information that can be easily recovered from the context in which it appears. Hence, ellipsis is studied as a phenomenon that manifests itself as the text develops, establishing a cohesive relation with respect to what has been mentioned before in the discourse and avoiding unnecessary repetition. In addition, the different discourse variables that play an important role in ellipsis as a cohesive mechanism are described in detail in Halliday and Hasan (1976), as will be shown below. I will start by mentioning the special status of the thematic structure of elliptical clauses and then move on to describe the role of ellipsis as a cohesive agency.

According to SFG, elliptical clauses have a special status in relation to thematic structure, that is, with respect to Themes and Rhemes. As is well known, the Theme of a clause is defined in SFG as 'the element which serves as the point of departure of the message; it is that which locates and orients the clause within its context' (Halliday and Matthiessen 2004: 64). The Rheme, in turn, refers to 'the remainder of the message, the part in which the Theme is developed' (Halliday and Matthiessen 2004: 64). SFG tries to decipher the conditions under which certain elements may be presupposed from previous sentences and what the intended meaning of that presupposition would be in a particular context by studying the thematic structure of sentences in texts. As Thompson (2003: 149) claims, 'Either Theme or Rheme may be missing [...] in elliptical clauses, where part of a message may be "carried over" from an earlier message (e.g. in the answer to a question), or may be understood from the general context.'

Halliday (1994) and Halliday and Matthiessen (2004) draw a distinction between independent clauses, which are 'major and explicit' in the sense that they possess both Theme and Rheme (Halliday and Matthiessen 2004: 99) and special instances of thematic structure such as bound (dependent bound and embedded bound clauses), minor (normally used as greetings, calls, exclamations, alarms; Halliday and Matthiessen 2004: 99) and elliptical clauses. Elliptical clauses are, in turn, divided into two subtypes: anaphoric ellipsis and exophoric ellipsis. Anaphoric ellipsis refers to those instances where 'some part of the clause is presupposed from what has gone before, for example in response to a question' (Halliday and Matthiessen 2004: 100). The resulting forms after ellipsis has taken place are very diverse, some of them being 'indistinguishable from minor clauses, for example *Yes. No. All right. Of course.*; these have no thematic structure, because they presuppose the whole of the preceding clause' (Halliday and Matthiessen 2004: 100). However, there are other instances of anaphoric ellipsis which presuppose only part of the previous clause. Those instances possess a thematic structure, albeit the form of these thematic structures will largely depend on the size of the presupposition. The second subtype of ellipsis, exophoric ellipsis, does not make reference to any previously mentioned material. In this case, the speaker exploits 'the rhetorical structure of the situation, specifically the roles of speaker and listener. [...] Hence the Subject, and often also the finite verb, is "understood" from the context; for example *Thirsty?* ("are you thirsty?"), *No idea.* ("I've no idea")' (Halliday 1994: 63; Halliday and Matthiessen 2004: 100). This kind of elliptical clauses also have a thematic structure, but only consisting of Rheme in this case. Therefore, the Theme of the clause is part of what goes unsaid. Here are some instances of the thematic structure of both anaphoric and exophoric ellipsis clauses:

(a)

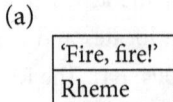

cried the town crier; 'There's a fire!'

(b)

'Where?, Where?'
Rheme

said Goody Blair; 'Where is it?'

(c)

'Down the town'
Rheme

said Goody Brown; 'It's down the town'

(d)

'I	'll go see it'
Theme	Rheme

said Goody Fleet; (not elliptical)

(e)

'So	Will	I'
Conjunctive	Finite	Topical
Theme		

said Good Fry; 'So will I go see it' (Halliday and Matthiessen (2004: 101))

As shown above, the first three examples (a)-(c) represent the thematic structure of exophoric ellipsis clauses, where only the Rheme part survives after ellipsis by relying on the context of the situation (*Fire, fire!*, *Where?, Where?, Down the town*). The last two clauses ((d) and (e)) in turn, represent an instance of anaphoric ellipsis. Notice that the first one is non-elliptical but serves as the appropriate antecedent for the second clause, in which the Rheme part of the clause is presupposed: *go see it*.

In addition, since ellipsis creates cohesion by means of presupposing material, SFG has studied those circumstances under which some items can be presupposed within verbal groups by examining the conditions and restrictions imposed by the syntax and the systemic choices available. With respect to the limits imposed by the syntax, it is claimed that cohesion in the verbal group in certain cases cannot be achieved by means of ellipsis: if the verbal group that is being presupposed is within an embedded clause ('rankshifted' as they term it), presupposition by means of ellipsis is impossible (Halliday and Hasan 1976: 196):

(65) a. A: The policeman paid no attention to the girl who was driving the car. B: Was she?

b. A: The policeman paid no attention to Mrs Jones, who was driving her car. B: Was she?

Example (65)a represents the impossibility of presupposing the VP which is embedded in an NP: *the girl who was driving the car*.[15] This is not the case of (65)b, where the non-restrictive relative clause is not embedded, thereby allowing presupposition by ellipsis.

As for the systemic choices available in order to create cohesion by means of ellipsis, polarity, finiteness, modality, voice and tense have been studied in SFG in order to check how they affect the meaning of elliptical sentences.

i. Polarity

Polarity is expressed in the Mood part of the clause, that is, in the verbal operator. There are some sequences in which everything may be presupposed except for polarity, while the elided material would be taken for granted. This is observed in examples of lexical ellipsis[16] and yes/no ellipsis:

(66) a. Were you laughing? – No, I wasn't.
b. Cats like cheese. – They don't, do they? – Yes, they do. – Well, some do and some don't. [Halliday and Hasan (1976: 177)]

Halliday and Hasan (1976: 177) explain that polarity always needs to be made explicit, because the other material can already be presupposed. But what happens in cases of operator ellipsis (i.e. ellipsis 'from the left', where the operator is missing and the only remnant is the lexical verb), since in this type of ellipsis the element that expresses the polarity is omitted? Is polarity presupposed in this elliptical construction? Halliday and Hasan (1976: 178) claim that polarity is not presupposed. This type of construction usually takes place when the only element that is left as a remnant is the lexical verb and has 'the specific function of supplying, confirming or repudiating a lexical verb'. It typically appears in contexts where there is an answer to a *wh*-question like *What are you doing?* or to a yes/no question. However, in answering a yes/no question polarity cannot be presupposed (Halliday and Hasan 1976: 178):

(67) A: What are you doing? (positive)
B: Thinking. (positive; 'I'm ...')
(68) A: Not day dreaming? (negative; 'aren't you ...?')
B: No, thinking (positive; 'I'm ...')

Among the choices available to speakers, one implies the repetition of the lexical verb in order to either confirm or deny what has been previously stated. As a matter of fact, operator ellipsis in these cases is possible only if it is explicitly introduced by a polarity item: *yes* or *no*, as illustrated below:

(69) Weren't you complaining? – (No), Not complaining.
(70) Were you complaining? – Yes, complaining. [Halliday and Hasan (1976: 178)]

In sum, even though in operator ellipsis its structure does not require the expression of polarity, for semantic reasons this is largely limited to those contexts in which the answer is positive, given that in cases of yes/no questions polarity cannot be taken for granted, that is, it must be explicitly stated.

The cases of marked polarity, that is, 'the assignment of special prominence to the selection of positive or negative in order to draw attention to it' (Halliday and Hasan 1976: 179), are also of importance here. Marked polarity is achieved thanks to the use of non-contracted forms of the finite operator or the negative, for example, '*is*, *had [...]* etc. instead of the reduced forms '*s*, '*d [...]* etc., *not* instead of *n't*' (Halliday and Hasan 1976: 179). Whereas it is impossible to have marked polarity in examples of operator ellipsis (even in cases where the presupposed material has it), as in (71), in lexical ellipsis it 'must have the polarity marked;[17] so the finite operator cannot be reduced' (Halliday and Hasan 1976: 180), as in (72):

(71) What is he DOING all this time? – Reading, probably.
(72) a. Who'll put down five pounds? – I will. (not I'll)
    b. John's arrived, has he? – Not yet; but Mary has. (not Mary's)

Marked polarity in (71) is simply not available in the response. In the case of (72), marked polarity is present in all positive forms, but it is optional in the negative ones: one could have replied *I won't* to (72)a or *Mary hasn't* to (72)b. This obviously has to do with the fact that 'the negative is itself a kind of marked polarity' (Halliday and Hasan 1976: 180). The reason behind this preference for marked polarity in this type of verbal ellipsis, according to Halliday and Hasan (1976: 180), seems to be that in this kind of sequences the main aim is to express polarity.

ii. Finiteness and modality

Like in Halliday and Hasan (1976: 180ff), the systems of finiteness and modality will be treated together because both of them have an impact on the first position of the verbal group. Verbal groups can be either finite or nonfinite. If finite, finiteness will be expressed in the first word of the verbal group by means of a tense operator ((a)–(e)) or a modal operator ((f)–(h)):

(a) am, is, are; was, were [*ie* finite forms of *be*]
(b) have, has; had [*ie* finite forms of *have*]

(c) do, does; did
(d) shall, will
(e) used (to)
(f) shall, will, should, would, can, could, may, might, must, ought (to)
(g) am to, is to, are to; was to, were to [*ie* finite forms of *be*, plus *to*]
(h) need, dare (in one use) [Halliday and Hasan (1976: 180)]

If a verbal group does not contain a finite form, then it is nonfinite (infinitives, participles and gerunds). Given that they are expressed in the first position of the verbal group, both finiteness and modality can normally be presupposed by operator ellipsis and not presupposed in lexical ellipsis. The latter type of ellipsis, then, cannot carry over the selections made by the verbal group it presupposes. Halliday and Hasan (1976: 181) add that 'there is no restriction of the presupposition of a finite verbal group by a nonfinite or vice versa':

[finite presupposed by finite]
(73) The picture wasn't finished. If it had been, I would have brought it.

[finite presupposed by nonfinite]
(74) He's always being teased about it. I don't think he likes being.

[nonfinite presupposed by finite]
(75) What was the point of having invited all those people? – I didn't; they just came.

[nonfinite followed by nonfinite]
(76) It was hard work parcelling all those books. – I'm sure it was; and I'd much prefer you not to have.

In the case of operator ellipsis, as mentioned earlier, the situation is the opposite: the first part of the verbal group is what is actually omitted and, therefore, this systemic choice between finite and nonfinite cannot be expressed. What happens in these cases is that finiteness is carried over from the presupposed clause:

[finite: 'they are finishing']
(77) What are they doing now? – Finishing their essays.

[nonfinite: 'to be finishing']
(78) What would you like them to be doing while you're away? – Finishing their essays. [Halliday and Hasan (1976: 181)]

The same arguments apply to modality (i.e. the systemic choice between modal and non-modal). Modality is said to be 'a subcategory of "finite" and is expressed by the presence or absence of a modal operator' (Halliday and Hasan 1976: 182). Therefore, once more, in lexical ellipsis there are no restrictions with regard to what can be presupposed by what:

[modal presupposed by non-modal]
(79) I could help them. – Why don't you?

[non-modal presupposed by modal]
(80) Are you going to tell her? – I ought to.

[modal presupposed by same modal]
(81) He must have destroyed them. – Someone must have, certainly.

[modal presupposed by different modal]
(82) He must have destroyed them. – He may have, I suppose. [Halliday and Hasan (1976: 182)]

It goes without saying that operator ellipsis, as was the case with finiteness, carries over the modality expressed in the presupposed clause (that is, it is never explicit):

[non-modal: 'they are finishing']
(83) What are they doing now? – Finishing their essays.

[modal: 'they will be finishing']
(84) What will they be doing now, do you think? – finishing their essays, probably. [Halliday and Hasan (1976: 182)]

iii. Voice
The system of voice gives one the option of choosing between active or passive voice. Its position in the verbal group is 'expressed towards the end [...] by the presence (passive) or absence (active) of some form of *be* or *get* just before a lexical verb, with the lexical verb in the passive participle form' (Halliday and Hasan 1976: 182). SFG claims that in lexical ellipsis voice is presupposed from the previous clause, that is, there should be no mismatches in voice between the presupposed (antecedent) and the presupposing (elliptical) clause. According to Halliday and Hasan (1976: 182–3), the following examples are ungrammatical even though they 'make perfectly good sense' just because the elliptical clause repudiates the voice selection in the presupposing clause:

[active followed by passive: 'if it had been finished']
(85) They haven't finished the picture. If it had been, I would have brought it.

[passive followed by active: 'if she does beat him']
(86) Johnny hates being beaten at any game by his sister. If she does, he sulks.

[active followed by passive: 'she has never been loved']
(87) Mary could love very deeply. Unfortunately she never has been.

[passive followed by active: 'she has forgiven them']
(88) She is forgiven, apparently. But I don't think she has them.

The explanation offered for the ungrammaticality of these examples is that when one reaches the elliptical clause, 'there is a change in the alignment of structural positions' (Halliday and Hasan 1976: 183). For example, in (85) and (86) the subject changes, whereas the actor/goal relationship is the same in the presupposing and presupposed clause. In (87) and (88) the situation is reversed: the actor/goal relationship changes, while the subjects remain the same. As a matter of fact, in these cases one gets the feeling that the proposition should be completely rephrased again. However, as will be shown in Section 1.2.4 Merchant (2008a: 169) points out that there are some instances of VPE that allow for mismatches in voice:

(89) This problem was to have been looked into, but obviously nobody did ~~look into this problem~~. [Merchant (2008a: 169)]

In (89), the presupposed clause is passive (*was to have been looked into*), whereas the elliptical one is active (*look into this problem*). Therefore, this is counter-evidence to the affirmation made by Halliday and Hasan (1976: 183) that states that 'the voice selection [...] cannot be repudiated by an elliptical structure'.

As far as voice in operator ellipsis is concerned, Halliday and Hasan (1976: 183) contend that since the subject is always elided in this type of ellipsis, it must be presupposed from the previous clause. For example:

(90) Were Australia leading England at the time, then? – No, England were winning.

The answer *No, England winning* would be ungrammatical in this case, and this means that voice must be presupposed too if the presupposing part is elliptical. However, Halliday and Hasan (1976: 183) mention one exception to this rule:

those cases where the subject is the same but the actor/goal changes, as in the following instances:

(91) Will you be interviewing today? – No; being interviewed.
(92) John has loved Mary for a long time. – Or at least been loved by her.

As observed in (91) and (92), these examples of operator ellipsis are perfectly grammatical even though the voice in the presupposed clause has been repudiated by the presupposing clause.

iv. Tense

According to Halliday and Hasan (1976: 186ff), there may be many different types of presupposition of tense selections in verbal ellipsis, as illustrated in the following examples:

(93) a. I protest. – Do you?
b. He usually talks all the time. He didn't, yesterday.
c. It doesn't turn. It will if you press it in first.
d. She won't agree. – She did last time.
e. Is he arguing? – Yes, he always does.
f. Was he going to apologize? – He won't now.
g. Has she heard about it yet? – No, but she soon will.
h. You have been forgetting every morning. Today you did again.
[Halliday and Hasan (1976: 188)]

The choice of tenses in the elliptical groups of the examples just mentioned would be as follows (Halliday and Hasan 1976: 188):

Presupposed group	Elliptical group
(a) present	present
(b) present	past
(c) present	future
(d) future	past
(e) present in present	present
(f) future in past	future
(g) past in present	future
(h) present in past in present	past

The elliptical verbal group chooses a simple tense choice, explicitly expressing it in the operator (*did, does, will*). Therefore, the only part that is presupposed is the lexical verb (in its base form), and the tense selection is not carried over from the presupposed clause. Things are different when the elliptical group makes a compound tense selection, since there are some differences in acceptability depending on the construction. Here are some acceptable examples in Halliday and Hasan (1976: 189):

(94) a. At least Stan has tried. I don't think Bob has.
　　b. I'm going home this weekend. I shall be every weekend now.
　　c. Are you dieting? – I have been for some time.
　　d. He was going to build it himself. He isn't any longer.
　　e. She really has been working hard. – And she is going to be again before long.

And here are the corresponding tense selections (Halliday and Hasan 1976: 189):

Presupposed group	Elliptical group
(a) past in present	past in present
(b) present in present	present in future
(c) present in present	present in past in present
(d) future in past	future in present
(e) present in past in present	present in future in present

As mentioned earlier, there are some examples that become less acceptable when they make a choice of compound tense, according to Halliday and Hasan (1976: 189):

(95) a. Have you discussed it yet? – No, we are now.
　　b. You've been forgetting every morning. Today you have again.
　　c. He was going to tell us. But he still hadn't, yesterday.

Below are the tense selections chosen for these examples (Halliday and Hasan 1976: 189):

Presupposed group	Elliptical group
(a) past in present	present in present
(b) present in past in present	past in present
(c) future in past	past in past

Halliday and Hasan claim (1976) that, in order for examples in (95) to become acceptable, they should use the lexical verb that has been omitted or a verbal substitute. Therefore, in (95)a, the verbal group should be rephrased containing *discussing it/doing*; (95)b should use the past participle of the lexical verb *forgotten* or the substitute *done*; and in (95)c *told us* or *done* should be present for it to become grammatical.

The reason behind the behaviour of compound tense selections in elliptical groups seems to be that

> in compound tenses, the tense selection is not made clear by the finite verbal operator alone; other elements are needed, and the form of the lexical verb itself may change. If the tense in the elliptical verbal group is a compound one, then it must be such that the lexical verb carried over IN THE SAME FORM. [Halliday and Hasan (1976: 189); capitals in the original]

This explains the contrast between examples in (94) and (95). Whereas in (94) all the examples could insert the lexical verb present in the presupposed clause ((a) *tried*, (b) *going*, (c) *dieting*, (d) *(going to) build*, (e) *working*), this cannot be done with the examples shown in (95); in Halliday and Hasan's (1976: 189; capitals in the original) words, the 'last-order tense, the one that is EXPRESSED last in the verbal group (though it appears first in the NAME of the tense), is carried over from the presupposed group'. If the last-order tense changes, the form of the lexical verb has been modified and in that case it must be either repeated or substituted.

It is also claimed that the principles that have been mentioned regarding tense in finite verbal groups could be applied to nonfinite verbal groups, even in those cases where there is a mismatch in finiteness between the presupposed and the presupposing clause. Here are two examples of this fact (Halliday and Hasan 1976: 190):

(96) a. He shows no sign of having been studying. – He hadn't/hasn't/wasn't.
b. She intends to come. – She won't.

These are the tense selections that have been made (Halliday and Hasan 1976: 190):

Presupposed group	Elliptical group
(a) nonfinite: present in past (corresponding to all three:)	finite: present in past in past
	finite: present in past in present
	finite: present in past
(b) nonfinite: tenseless	finite: future

Tense selections in operator ellipsis, as may have been guessed by now, are presupposed, that is, the tense choice in the presupposed clause will be the same in the presupposing clause too. Since this construction normally appears in the context of question–answer sequences, the focus is normally on the lexical verb, leaving the tense selection unchanged, as in (Halliday and Hasan 1976: 191):

(97) a. What is he going to do with all that paraphernalia? – Catch fish.
[=He is going to catch fish]
b. Have you been digging? – No, weeding. [=I've been weeding]

Of course, the elliptical verbal group could also repudiate the tense from the presupposed clause, but this has to be done explicitly (Halliday and Hasan 1976: 192):

(98) He must have mended it. – Or been going to mend it, rather.

As will become clearer in Chapter 2 and Chapter 3 (see Sections 2.2.4 and 3.1), the observations on polarity, finiteness, modality, voice and tense are of paramount importance for this study, since all of these auxiliary-related variables will be subject to an in-depth analysis in cases of PAE.

In the coming section, I will offer a brief review of ellipsis from the point of view of TGG.

1.2.3 Ellipsis in TGG

Whereas ellipsis has traditionally been approached in the domains of rhetoric, diction or discourse, its formal characteristics were studied in a rigorous systematic way with the success of TGG in the 1960s. Since the dawn of TGG, ellipsis has centred the attention of many linguists aiming at explaining the mismatch between meaning (the intended message) and sound (what is actually uttered) in natural language communication. The literature on ellipsis within this framework has mainly focused on describing the characteristics of the existing elliptical phenomena across languages – and English is still by far the most studied language – as well as on trying to decipher what kind of relationship is established between an ellipsis site and its antecedent, usually believed to be governed by some kind of parallelism. As highlighted by Merchant (2013a: 1), 'It is no exaggeration to say that debates over the nature of this parallelism have formed the core of most of the Generative work on ellipsis over the last forty years.' The importance of these debates, as he argues, has to do with the fact that they are used in order to prove the preference for a particular kind of linguistic representation over another:

> Most of the debate is located in the arena of semantics and abstract syntactic structures – it is clear that surface syntactic or phonological parallelism is not at stake – and as such, elliptical structures often play an important role in fundamental ontological debates in linguistics. The logic is clear: if the

parallelism or identity conditions found in ellipsis resolution require reference to certain kinds of objects, then our theories of linguistic competence must countenance objects of that kind. [Merchant (2013a: 1)]

Transformational Generative grammarians have been mainly concerned with trying to answer the following three questions (see Aelbrecht 2009, 2010; Bîlbîie 2011; Gallego 2011; Merchant 2013a): the structure question, the identity question and the licensing question.[18] In what follows, I will briefly describe the implications of the answers given to each of these questions. To begin with, the structure question can be summarized as follows:

(99) In elliptical constructions, is there syntactic structure that is unpronounced? (Is there syntax internal to the ellipsis site?) [Merchant (2013a: 4)]

The two possible answers to this question have crucial consequences for the theory of grammar. If the answer is affirmative, the theories of grammars must allow the existence of 'unpronounced phrases and heads' (Merchant 2013a: 4). If, by contrast, the answer is negative, one would be postulating that syntax would be 'wysiwyg' ('what you see is what you get') (Aelbrecht 2010: 3) or 'wyhiwyg' ('what you hear is what you get') (Merchant 2013a: 4), that is, there is no need to postulate the existence of more syntax than what is present.

Second, the identity question tries to decipher the following:

(100) What is the relationship between the understood material and its antecedent? [Merchant (2013a: 4)]

The identity question has centred most of the debates since the dawn of TGG given that identity issues are at stake in one of the restrictions on the occurrence of ellipsis: the recoverability condition, as pointed out earlier, posits that elided elements need to be recoverable from the (either linguistic or extralinguistic) context in order for them to be omitted (Aelbrecht 2009, 2010; van Craenenbroeck and Merchant 2013). Several identity relationships have been put forward in the literature, since the ellipsis site must be identical to some antecedent phrase. However, this identity has been argued to be semantic (Dalrymple et al. 1991; Hardt 1993; Ginzburg and Sag 2000; Merchant 2001; Merchant 2004; Culicover and Jackendoff 2005; van Craenenbroeck 2010a; Aelbrecht 2009, 2010; Thoms 2010, 2013), syntactic (Sag 1976; Williams 1977; Fiengo and May 1994; Chung et al. 1995) or both (Chung 2006, 2013; van Craenenbroeck 2010a; Merchant 2013b). Merchant (2013a: 5) offers a summary of the different positions that linguists have defended when trying to answer the first two questions mentioned so far (see Table 1).

Third, the purpose of the so-called licensing question is to answer the following questions:

(101) What heads or positions or structures allow for ellipsis, and what are the locality conditions on the relation between these structures and ellipsis? [Merchant (2013a: 5)]

The licensing question has been addressed by Zagona (1982); Lobeck (1995); Johnson (2001); Merchant (2001); Aelbrecht (2009, 2010); van Craenenbroeck (2010a); Thoms (2011a) and Johnson (2013), among others. The key issue in this question is to try to discover what makes an elliptical construction felicitous in a given syntactic context and what elements, also known as 'licensors' of ellipsis, allow or 'license' it in a certain construction. This notion will be of particular importance for this study; in fact, in Section 3.1.1. I will focus on the frequency of the different licensors of PAE in Modern English in an attempt to determine whether variation is at work or not. Van Craenenbroeck and Merchant (2013: 702) exemplify this requirement with the following example:

(102) *John read the long book and I read the short [NP *e*].[19]

Example (102) constitutes a case of ungrammatical NP Ellipsis since this type of ellipsis is not licensed in this context even though it would be perfectly recoverable from its antecedent (that is, it is given information in the context). An interesting fact about ellipsis sentences is that not all types of elliptical phenomena take place in all languages (Aelbrecht 2010), which poses a major

Table 1 Some Previous Research on the Two Ellipsis Questions

Is identity syntactic or semantic?	*Is there syntax in the ellipsis site?*	
	Yes	No
Syntactic	Sag (1976); Williams (1977); Fiengo and May (1994); Chung et al. (1995); Kehler (2002); etc.	N/A (incoherent)
Semantic	Sag and Hankamer (1984); Merchant (2001); van Craenenbroeck (2010a); Aelbrecht (2010); etc.	Keenan (1971); Dalrymple et al. (1991); Hardt (1993); Ginzburg and Sag (2000); Culicover and Jackendoff (2005); etc.

challenge for the type of crosslinguistic generalizations and hypotheses required by frameworks such as TGG. To give an example, Sluicing is said to be more frequent crosslinguistically than VPE, and, as pointed out by Aelbrecht (2010: 14), the example of VPE in (103) is allowed (licensed) in English but not in languages such as Dutch, French or Italian (or Spanish, of which I have added its counterpart in (103)):

(103)
    a. Monika has paid already, but Alice hasn't.
    b. *Jelle heft al betaald, maar Johan heft nog niet.   [Dutch]
    Jelle has already paid but Johan has still not
    c. *Aurélie a déjà payé, mais Jonathan n'a
    Aurélie has already paid but Jonathan NE.has
    pas encore.   [French]
    not yet
    d. *Antonio ha già pagato, ma Stefano non ha ancora.   [Italian]
    Antonio has already paid but Stefano not has yet.
    e. *Manuel ya ha pagado, pero Ana aún no ha.   [Spanish]
    Manuel already has paid, but Ana yet not has.

In addition, it should be noted that not all languages follow the same licensing criteria for the different elliptical phenomena, as they vary greatly from language to language – as an illustration of this, Merchant (2001: 3) contends that 'VP-ellipsis as attested in English seems to be quite rare among the world's languages'.

In sum, TGG has mainly concentrated on trying to answer questions on structure (whether there is syntax internal to the ellipsis site), identity (what kind of relationship is established between the ellipsis site and its antecedent) and licensing (what heads, positions or structures permit the occurrence of ellipsis and what the locality conditions established between these structures and ellipsis are). As has been pointed out, ellipsis has played an important role in ontological debates regarding the theory of grammar, given that if one needs to claim the existence of certain elements to justify the occurrence of ellipsis, then linguistic theories need to allow those kinds of elements to be part of their theories.

In the following section, I will concentrate on describing the main findings that have been reported from the perspective of psycholinguistics.

1.2.4 The processing of ellipsis

In recent years the realm of psycholinguistics has become a resource of paramount importance in order to achieve empirical support or refute evidence of theoretical proposals about ellipsis. As will be shown, VPE is by far the type of ellipsis which has received most of the attention, followed by Sluicing.[20] It should also be noted that most of the experiments obtained their results by means of acceptability judgements or self-paced readings. Not only were linguistic theories about ellipsis put to the test (such as Kehler's 2000, 2002 theory of ellipsis and discourse coherence and the binding theory; or Merchant's 2008a theory voice mismatches in VPE and PG), but also developed in the light of the psycholinguistic data obtained (such as the 'recycling hypothesis', the 'main assertion hypothesis' or the 'parallelism hypothesis'). Therefore, investigating the processing of elided elements has contributed to shed some light on how the language processor works and on the interaction between syntax and discourse in an attempt to elucidate the role of language processing with respect to judgements of acceptability. This section summarizes the main empirical findings on ellipsis reported in the field of psycholinguistics and processing.

As mentioned above, psycholinguistics has aimed at providing empirical evidence for theoretical proposals. Frazier and Clifton (2006), for example, evaluated Kehler's (2000, 2002) proposal regarding the link between a particular discourse coherence relation type and its corresponding (in)sensitivity to syntax in examples of VPE via comprehension experiments. The elegance of Kehler's (2000, 2002) theory resides in the fact that he makes 'a connection between the operations needed to establish the appropriate discourse coherence relation and the applicability/non-applicability of syntactic conditions' (Frazier and Clifton 2006: 3). Kehler (2000, 2002) distinguished between three different discourse coherence relation types: cause-effect, resemblance – which were the focus of Frazier and Clifton's (2006) study – and contiguity relations – which describe situations where there is a sequence of events. In sentences where the cause-effect relation holds proposition P plausibly implies Q. Those sentences where the resemblance coherence type is involved highlight similarity or contrast between entities or events. On the one hand, Kehler (2000, 2002) proposed that the cause-effect type is insensitive to syntax and therefore does not predict a syntactic antecedent for an elided VP, that is, there is no syntactic reconstruction in the ellipsis site. On the other hand, the resemblance type works the opposite way and hence VPE is sensitive to syntax. It requires a syntactic antecedent because there is syntactic reconstruction in the ellipsis site. The following examples illustrate this contrast (Kehler 2002: 5):

(104) This problem was to have been looked into, but obviously nobody did ~~look into the problem~~.
(105) #This problem was looked into by John, and Bob did ~~look into the problem~~ too.

In Kehler's (2000, 2002) theory, example (104) illustrates the cause-effect relation, since it can be interpreted as an implicational relation, while in (105) the resemblance relation is instantiated (the same actions are described of two different entities). Whereas the cause-effect example is grammatical, the opposite is true in the resemblance example.

Kehler's (2000, 2002) theory also predicts grammatical violations of the binding theory in cases where the cause-effect coherence relation holds (as in (106)), but not in those examples where the resemblance coherence type holds (as in (107)):

(106) John's$_i$ lawyer defended him$_i$ because he$_i$ wouldn't.
(107) #John's$_i$ lawyer defended him$_i$, and he$_i$ did too. [Kehler (2000: 550ff)]

In (106) condition B of the binding theory is violated (a (non-anaphoric) pronominal (expression) must be free within its local domain), since it allows the coreference between the noun *John* and the pronoun *him*. However, coreference between these two items is not allowed in (107). Bearing these data in mind, Frazier and Clifton (2006) analysed the predictions of Kehler's (2000, 2002) coherence theory empirically. They noticed that Kehler's examples were extracted from corpora and did not constitute true minimal pairs. For this reason, they undertook five comprehension experiments using standard minimal pair materials. Two of their experiments (an auditory and a written acceptability judgement) tested the hypothesis that the discourse coherence relation involved is the relevant factor for classifying ellipsis into syntactically sensitive versus syntactically insensitive types. In the auditory acceptability judgement experiment, subjects had to listen to sixteen experimental sentences like (108), which were constructed with four different versions (Frazier and Clifton 2006: 4–5):

(108) a. The problem was looked into by Kim because Lee did. (Because, no adverb)
b. The problem was looked into by Kim last time because Lee did. (Because, adverb)

c. The problem was looked into by Kim just like Lee did.
(Resemblance, no adverb)
d. The problem was looked into by Kim last time just like Lee did.
(Resemblance, adverb)

As can be observed, the first clause is always passive and the second one containing VPE is always active. Subjects were asked to indicate whether they had understood the sentences they would be presented with. In the written acceptability judgement experiment, these sentences were slightly modified by substituting the connective *because* by *even though*. Subjects were told to rate their acceptability. The results for both experiments showed that 'syntactic matching is preferred for resemblance relations AND for cause-effect relations' (Frazier and Clifton 2006: 7; capitals in the original).

The remaining three experiments tested the processing of pronominals and reflexives in sentences containing VPE. In another written acceptability questionnaire, they tested whether Principle A of the Binding theory (a reflexive must be bound in its local domain) must be obeyed in cases of ellipsis involving resemblance relations but not in those involving cause-effect relations. Subjects were presented with sentences like (109) and had to choose between two possible interpretations, that is, either 'everyone else blamed Doug' (strict reading) or 'everyone else blamed himself' (sloppy reading):

(109) a. Doug blamed himself for the band's collapse because everyone else did.
b. Doug blamed himself for the band's collapse just like everyone else did. [Frazier and Clifton (2006: 8)]

Importantly, Shapiro et al. (2003) in a previous work on on-line processing of VPE had found some evidence showing that the subjects of the first clause in examples like (110) and (111) below are reactivated at the elided position of the second clause. This means that the strict reading is computed, at least temporarily, even if its meaning is unpreferred (as in (110)), or impossible because of the nature of the verb (as in (111)):

(110) The policeman defended himself and the fireman did too, according to someone who was there.
(111) The policeman perjured himself and the fireman did too. [Shapiro et al. (2003: 3)]

In the remaining two experiments (two written questionnaires and one self-paced reading test) Frazier and Clifton (2006) tested the effect imposed by syntactic parallelism between the antecedent clause and the one containing the ellipsis site on the preference for either a strict or a sloppy interpretation of pronominals or reflexives. To that end, they used examples where the discourse coherence relation did not vary. Here are some of the sample sentences used (Frazier and Clifton 2006: 9):

(112) a. John saw a snake near him and Bill did too.
b. John saw a snake near his backpack and Bill did too.

The results of these three experiments showed that strict readings were as likely to take place in cause-effect sentences as in resemblance sentences. Also, they proved that if the coherence relation was held constant and parallelism was increased by means of the *and ... did too* construction, the number of sloppy interpretations for pronouns, possessive pronouns and reflexives increased. These findings, according to Frazier and Clifton (2006), are in line with Carlson's (2002) work, which studied the effects of parallelism with respect to the processing of ellipsis. Carlson (2002) proposed that once structural similarities have been acknowledged, analyses that strengthen further similarities are favoured, something that was evinced in Frazier and Clifton's (2006) data. In conclusion, this study has shown that Kehler's (2000, 2002) theory does not have an empirical basis. The lack of a syntactically appropriate antecedent affects the grade of acceptability of all sentences containing VPE, not just those involving resemblance relations. Moreover, it has been shown that parallelism is favoured both in cause-effect and resemblance relations.

In a similar vein, Arregui et al. (2006) offered some evidence for Frazier and Clifton's (2006) concluding insights and proposed that a processing theory coupled with a syntactic account would better explain and describe examples of VPE. This is known as the 'VP recycling hypothesis', and contends that 'when a syntactically-matching antecedent is not available, the listener/reader creates one using the materials at hand' (Arregui et al. 2006: 1). The central idea behind this hypothesis is that the resolution of elided VPs requires a syntactically parallel antecedent. If this type of antecedent is absent, then the processor has the option of *recycling* the surrounding material in order to create an adequate structure:

> The VP recycling hypothesis predicts that missing antecedent examples should be acceptable to various degrees depending on what material is present to provide

an antecedent, what operations need to be performed on the antecedent, and what evidence is available to aid the processor in performing those operations. [Arregui et al. (2006: 4)]

In order to test this hypothesis, Arregui et al. (2006) undertook five acceptability judgement experiments (on-line processing studies and written questionnaires). In the first two of them, they analysed antecedents containing verb phrases versus antecedents containing adjective phrases, as well as antecedents appearing in predicate position versus others appearing as a constituent of the sentence's subject NP, that is, sentences ranged from perfect to impossible. In the second experiment non-elliptical versions of the second clause were also added. Following, some of the sample sentences are cited (Arregui et al. 2006: 4):

(113) a. None of the astronomers saw the comet, /but John did. (Available verb phrase)
b. Seeing the comet was nearly impossible, /but John did. (Embedded verb phrase)
c. The comet was nearly impossible to see, /but John did. (Verb phrase with trace)
d. The comet was nearly unseeable, /but John did. (Negative adjective)

The results of both experiments confirmed the recycling hypothesis, as the acceptability judgements corresponding to examples (113)a through (113)d evinced a significant decrease in their acceptability levels. The inclusion of the non-elliptical versions of the second clause also showed that it is not easy to understand the ellipsis when an adequate antecedent is not present.

Two other experiments have led to the comparison between verbal and nominal gerund antecedents, their prediction being that verbal gerunds would be judged more acceptable than nominal gerunds. These are some of the sample sentences (Arregui et al. 2006: 9):

(114) a. Singing the arias tomorrow night will be difficult/but Maria will. (Verbal, -mod)
b. Singing the arias slowly tomorrow night will be difficult/ but Maria will. (Verbal, mod)
c. Tomorrow night's singing of the arias will be difficult/but Maria will. (Nominal, -mod)
d. Tomorrow night's slow singing of the arias will be difficult/but Maria will. (Nominal, +mod)

The hypothesis was borne out: participants judged antecedents containing verbal gerunds more acceptable than those with nominal gerunds.

In another experiment Arregui et al. (2006) tested whether speakers are prone to ignore the grammar and produce elided constituents without perfect matching antecedents in cases where the required antecedent is less marked than the antecedent actually produced. To that end, they compared active (unmarked) and passive antecedents (Arregui et al. 2006: 12):

(115) a. The dessert was praised by the customer after the critic did already.
b. The dessert was praised by the customer and the critic did.
c. The customer praised the dessert after the appetizer was already.
d. The customer praised the dessert and the appetizer was.

The results showed that the level of acceptability was higher for mismatching examples which possessed a passive antecedent and an active elided VP than for those with an active antecedent and a passive elided VP.

In conclusion, Arregui et al.'s (2006) work provided important evidence in favour of the VP recycling hypothesis: that examples of VPE with mismatching antecedents in a standard verb phrase position may be judged acceptable largely depends on their particular characteristics.

Contrary to this view, Kim et al. (2011) argue that a strict syntactic identity criterion can be defended in a modern deletion analysis of VPE, and thus propose a processing model of relative acceptability levels in VPE. They contend that listeners/readers do not repair mismatched structures but prioritize the search for syntactic structure. Mismatches are believed to be essentially grammatical, but the more searching work the parser does, the less acceptable an example will be judged. When parsing a sentence, one follows some 'hints' that help its comprehension. These hints are known as parsing heuristics in Kim et al.'s (2011) work. They propose the existence of two heuristics (Kim et al. 2011: 16):

- MaxElide: VP Ellipsis preferentially targets configurationally higher rather than lower nodes.
- Canonical Realization: Surface subjects preferentially are underlying subjects as well.

In order to test why examples like (116) below are grammatical, Kim et al. (2011: 2) conducted three acceptability judgement studies using the magnitude estimation paradigm.

(116) a. This information could have been released by Gorbachev, but he chose not to ~~release this information~~. [Hardt (1993)]
b. In March, four fireworks manufacturers asked that the decision be reversed, and on Monday the ICC did ~~reverse the decision~~. [Dalrymple et al. (1991)]

In this type of experiment, participants had to judge the acceptability of a set of sentences. The first experiment tested the acceptability of voice and category mismatches using sample sentences like these:

(117) Voice match
a. Active-Active: Jill betrayed Abby, and Matt did ~~betray Abby~~, too.
b. Passive-Passive: Abby was betrayed by Jill, and Matt was ~~betrayed by Jill~~, too.

(118) Voice mismatch
a. Active-Passive: Jill betrayed Abby, and Matt was ~~betrayed by Jill~~, too.
b. Passive-Active: Abby was betrayed by Jill, and Matt did ~~betray Abby~~, too.

(119) Category mismatch
a. Noun-VP: The criticism of Roy was harsh, but Kate didn't ~~criticize Roy~~.
b. Adjective-VP: The report was critical of Roy, but Kate didn't ~~criticize Roy~~. [Kim et al. (2011: 17–18)]

The results concluded that there was a main effect of mismatch, such that sentences that contained structural mismatches between conjuncts were judged less acceptable than those that matched structurally. In addition, ellipsis had a main effect on the results: examples with ellipsis were judged less acceptable than their non-elliptical counterparts. However, there was a significantly greater negative impact on acceptability judgements when there was ellipsis in the second conjunct, which means that 'the condition on matching conjuncts is specific to cases of ellipsis' (Kim et al. 2011: 23).

In order to check the role of Canonical Realization in the acceptability of examples of VPE, Kim et al. (2011) carried out two experiments in which they crossed factors such as ellipsis, match and canonicality. In both experiments there were category mismatches with adjectival and nominal antecedents in the first conjunct and the antecedents varied with regard to canonicality: half of the sentences represented canonical order (i.e. agent-verb-theme) (see (120)a) and half non-canonical order ((120)b) (Kim et al. 2011: 27):

(120) Mismatching adjectival antecedents
a. of Theme: The parents were critical of the uniforms, but the cheerleaders didn't ~~criticize the uniforms~~.
b. -able: The boy's exhaustion was understandable, and the coach did ~~understand the boy's exhaustion~~.

When the results of the three experiments were compared, it was found that both canonicality and mismatch influence acceptability in a general way regardless of the presence of ellipsis. However, while canonicality only affects acceptability because it is a general processing pressure, syntactic mismatches have a stronger effect on acceptability judgements due to the presence of ellipsis.

Similarly, Miller and Hemforth (2014) studied cases of VPE with nominal antecedents and proposed, as Kim et al. (2011), that these kinds of antecedents are always grammatical. However, Miller and Hemforth (2014) argued that these nominal antecedents need to comply with certain discourse conditions on VPE, as VPE always requires a salient alternative in the discourse model. According to them, the discourse model is 'a mental representation which coherently combines information from the text (linguistic or nonlinguistic utterance acts) and from the nonlinguistic context' (Miller and Hemforth 2014: 2). Therefore, if nominal antecedents of VPE comply with the requirement of expressing such an alternative, then they are fully grammatical. Thanks to three on-line acceptability judgement experiments, Miller and Hemforth (2014) found that VPE was rated as more acceptable than *do it* in cases where a salient polar alternative was present in the context regardless of whether this polar alternative was expressed by a verb or a noun. In addition, it was determined that in these cases nominal antecedents were judged slightly less acceptable than verbal antecedents. The reason behind this difference, as they claimed, would reside in the fact that, independently of the ellipsis, nouns are judged less acceptable than verbs when they are required to express a polar alternative. In conclusion, they propose that VPE needs to access an antecedent that complies with discourse constraints within the discourse model but that the heuristic strategies of the parser make use of all available evidence (including syntactic structure in short memory) in order to find a suitable antecedent. Therefore, syntactically identical antecedents will be easier to find and thus more acceptable.

Martin and McElree (2008), on their part, analysed the on-line processing of VPE taking into account factors such as distance between an ellipsis and its antecedent, and the length and complexity of the antecedent. In order to do so, they carried out an eye-tracking experiment and four speed-accuracy trade-off experiments (whereby participants are asked to read sentences presented phrase by phrase and respond whether what they have read is sensible or not). In two of the experiments they analysed the effect of distance between an ellipsis and its antecedent with regard to speed and comprehension accuracy. The results of these experiments revealed that the longer the distance, the lower accuracy was. They explained that by claiming that intervening material between an ellipsis and its antecedent had an impact on the quality of the retrieved information about the antecedent. Interestingly, however, they found that distance did not affect the speed of the interpretation of ellipsis, which argues contra a search process in order to access antecedents for VPE and favours an analysis where they are accessed directly. The remaining experiments investigated whether antecedents are copied into the ellipsis site by manipulating the length and complexity of the antecedent. The results showed that complexity, especially due to the number of discourse entities in the antecedent, reduced the level of accuracy. However, the speed of interpretation was not affected by either complexity or length, which, according to Martin and McElree (2008), suggests that ellipsis interpretation does not involve a copy operation, but a pointer to existing structures in memory.

Another factor that was studied in relation to the acceptability of VPE examples was the influence of antecedents appearing in either main or subordinate clauses (Garnham and Cain 1998; Clifton and Frazier 2010). On the one hand, Garnham and Cain (1998) tried to test the assumption that verbal ellipses are interpreted indirectly by means of a representation of superficial form of nearby text. To that end, they tried to find some evidence of the different availability of superficial representations of two clauses in main-subordinate pairs. They carried out two self-paced reading studies in which they tested the influence of the order of appearance of main and subordinate clauses (either main-subordinate or subordinate-main) on the processing of ellipsis. Subjects had to read sentences on a computer screen and then judge whether their continuation was sensible or not. Here are some of the examples tested (Garnham and Cain 1998: 24):

MAIN-SUBORDINATE, ellipsis takes meaning from MAIN

(121) The art thieves might have taken both the Van Gogh's from the gallery, if they hadn't set the alarm off, but fortunately they didn't.

SUBORDINATE-MAIN, ellipsis takes meaning from MAIN

(122) If the art thieves hadn't set the alarm off, they might have taken both the Van Gogh's from the gallery, but fortunately they didn't.

MAIN-SUBORDINATE, ellipsis takes meaning from SUBORDINATE

(123) The art thieves might have taken both the Van Gogh's from the gallery, if they hadn't set the alarm off, but fortunately they did.

SUBORDINATE-MAIN, ellipsis takes meaning from SUBORDINATE

(124) If the art thieves hadn't set the alarm off, they might have taken both the Van Gogh's from the gallery, but fortunately they did.

As can be observed, in these conditional sentences the order of the type of clause varies (main-subordinate/subordinate-main) as well as the sentence from where the elliptical clause obtains its meaning. As Clifton and Frazier (2010: 6) point out, the fact that the ellipsis site can find its antecedent in either the *if*-clause or the consequent clause of the conditional has to do with the counterfactual nature of these sentences. The results showed that acceptability was reduced in cases where the ellipsis took its meaning from a main clause and this main clause was followed by a subordinate one, as only 42 per cent of the examples tested were judged acceptable. However, the other three combinations scored around 80 per cent of acceptability. In addition, they found that there were two factors that influenced faster positive acceptability judgements: (1) the presence of the antecedent in a subordinate clause rather than in a main clause (which according to Garnham and Cain (1998: 19) suggests that the superficial form of a subordinate clause is more important) and (2) the immediate precedence of the antecedent of the ellipsis (instead of being two clauses back).

Similarly, Clifton and Frazier (2010) examined VPE examples whose antecedents were in a conditional clause by carrying out two experiments: a written questionnaire study and an acceptability judgement study. In a previous work, Frazier and Clifton (2005), by studying the discourse-syntax interface and how it affects processing, had found that speakers seem to follow the 'main assertion hypothesis'. This hypothesis contends that 'other things being equal, comprehenders prefer to relate material in a new sentence to the main assertion of the preceding sentence' (Frazier and Clifton 2005: 14). That is, readers and listeners normally prefer that the antecedent of the ellipsis be a main clause, rather than a subordinate one. Evidence for this hypothesis was found in the light of the following examples (Frazier and Clifton 2005: 14–15):

(125) a. John said Fred went to Europe and Mary did too.
b. John said Fred went to Europe. Mary did too.

Frazier and Clifton (2005) discovered that whereas readers were more likely to take the immediately preceding phrase *went to Europe* as the antecedent of the VPE within a single sentence (as in (125)a), in the presence of a sentence boundary (as in (125)b), they were more likely to take the matrix VP of the preceding clause as the antecedent of the ellipsis site. The explanation given for this fact was that ellipsis is subject to both syntactic and discourse conditions. While syntactic representations dominate in one single sentence, discourse representations do so across sentence boundaries. As Clifton and Frazier (2010: 3) put it, 'after a sentence has been parsed and interpreted, the syntactic representation becomes less salient, and the discourse representation becomes relatively more salient.' Clifton and Frazier (2010) tested whether the main assertion tendency was linked to ellipsis in a self-paced reading study. By analysing the following sentences, they discovered that it is a very general tendency which is not restricted to sentences containing anaphoric or elided elements (Clifton and Frazier 2010: 4):

(126) a. Stacy will publish a novel. Her sister won't.
b. Jim announced that Stacy will publish a novel. Her sister won't.
c. Stacy will publish a novel. Her sister won't publish anything.
d. Jim announced that Stacy will publish a novel. Her sister won't publish anything.

The results of their study showed that in sentences like (126)a, where the antecedent of the elliptical clause is the main assertion of the preceding sentence, the second elliptical sentence was read faster than in sentences like (126)b, where the antecedent appeared in the subordinate clause of the preceding sentence. However, as mentioned above, this tendency also seemed to hold in the remaining non-elliptical examples, since the second sentence of (126)c was read faster than the second one of (126)d. This led them to propose that 'the same discourse integration preferences may hold for overt material in a sentence and for the unpronounced material we claim exists inside an ellipsis site' (Clifton and Frazier 2010: 4)

Discourse constraints in examples of ellipsis had been claimed to be part of its grammar (Kehler 2002; Hardt and Romero 2004). However, the other experiments in Clifton and Frazier (2010) provided new insights supporting the idea that there is at least one discourse constraint which is part of the processing mechanism, not the grammar: the main assertion of an utterance. Examples of VPE with antecedents in conditional sentences were tested in both a written questionnaire and a self-paced study. The first study made use of sentences containing examples of VPE and Bare Argument Ellipsis[21] like the following (Clifton and Frazier 2010: 5):

(127) a. If John went to the store, he bought Twinkies. George did too.
b. If John went to the store, he bought Twinkies. George too.
c. Mary is sure that John went to the store. If John went to the store, he bought Twinkies. George did too.
d. Mary is sure that John went to the store. If John went to the store, he bought Twinkies. George too.

Subjects had to choose between two alternative interpretations of the sentences. In one of interpretations, the antecedent of the ellipsis would be only the consequent clause *It's also true of George that he bought Twinkies*. In the other one, the antecedent of the ellipsis would be the whole conditional sentence *It's also true of George that if he went to the store he bought Twinkies*. The results revealed that, due to the main assertion tendency, processors take into account full conditionals and not only verb phrases as antecedents (examples (127)a and (127)b). Nevertheless, in cases like (127)c and (127)d, where the antecedent of the conditional clause contains old and redundant information, fewer full conditional antecedents are taken to be the antecedents of VPE, as though 'the consequent clause has become the assertion of the conditional sentence with the *if*-clause essentially cancelling out' (Clifton and Frazier 2010: 1).

In the second experiment, a modal was added to the *if*-clause, thus yielding the conditional counterfactual:

(128) a. If John went to the store he bought Twinkies. George did too. [simple past, hypothetical, simple past ellipsis]
b. If John went to the store he bought Twinkies. George would have too. [simple past, hypothetical, modal ellipsis]
c. If John had gone to the store he would have bought Twinkies. George would have too. [simple past, non-actuality, modal ellipsis]

In this experiment, they wanted to check whether the results of the previous experiment might be due only to the fact that the consequent implied the antecedent rather than to the size of the linguistic antecedent chosen as the correct interpretation. In that case, examples in which the antecedent was implied should be judged more acceptable than those in which it was not implied, as 'the main assertion requirement could be satisfied by entailment while still choosing a VP antecedent' (Clifton and Frazier 2010: 287). The results demonstrated that the non-actuality entailment or implicature increases the acceptability ratings of examples like (128)c with respect to the hypothetical sentences in (128)a and (128)b.

Moving now to other studies which have dealt with different ellipsis types other than VPE, Kim and Runner's (2013) work deserves some mention here, as they put to the test Merchant's (2008a) theoretical proposal about the observation that VPE can tolerate voice mismatches between the antecedent and the ellipsis site, whereas PG cannot, as illustrated below:

(129) VPE
    a. This problem was to have been looked into, but obviously nobody did <look into this problem>.
    b. The system can be used by anyone who wants to <use it>.

(130) Pseudogapping
    a. *Roses were brought by some, and others did <bring> lilies.
    b. *Klimt is admired by Abby more than anyone does <admire> Klee. [Merchant (2008a: 169-70)]

Merchant (2008a) claims that this asymmetry in the tolerance of voice mismatches is due to a difference in the height of the ellipsis: while the elided constituent in PG contains the voice feature on v,[22] this is not the case in VPE (see Merchant 2008a for more specific details on the analysis). The consequence of this analysis is that voice is subject to syntactic identity in PG, a restriction which does not apply in VPE. As Kim and Runner (2013) put it, 'the claim is that all ellipsis types require syntactic identity, but whether voice parallelism matters depends on whether the voice features are inside the ellipsis site.' However, Kertz (2008: 284) proposed another source for the differences in acceptability of examples of VPE:

> The crucial difference [...] between the cases of acceptable and unacceptable [VP] ellipses examined so far is not syntactic structure, and not discourse structure, but information structure: cases of unacceptable mismatch tend to focus the subject argument of the target clause, while cases of acceptable mismatch instead focus the auxiliary verb.

Some examples of VPE which support her view are presented below (Kertz 2008: 285):

(131) *The material was skipped by the instructors and [the TA's]$_{top/foc}$ did too.
(132) *The problem was looked into by the committee, just like [the chair]$_{top/foc}$ did.
(133) A lot of this material can be skipped, and often I [do]$_{foc}$.
(134) This problem was to have been looked into, but obviously nobody [did]$_{foc}$.

As (131) and (132) show, subject focus causes a strong mismatch effect. By contrast, in (133) and (134), which are examples of auxiliary focus, this mismatch effect is reduced. However, auxiliary focus is not typically possible in PG examples, as it normally focuses subjects and objects, not auxiliaries (Kim and Runner 2013):

(135) a. Some brought roses and others did lilies.
b. *Some brought roses and others [did]$_{foc}$ lilies.

As a result, Kim and Runner (2013) contend that Merchant's VPE examples enjoy orthogonal advantage, as the grammatical examples of VPE mentioned involve auxiliary focus, which is known to improve the acceptability of voice mismatches. The ungrammatical examples of PG used by Merchant, however, involve subject/object focus, which inevitably leads to lower acceptability. If those examples of PG were turned into examples of VPE, this would be the result (Kim and Runner 2013):

(136) a. *Roses were brought by some, and others did ~~bring roses~~, too.
b. *Some brought roses, and lilies were ~~brought by some~~, too.

In their view, then, there is a need to 'compare apples to apples'. With that purpose in mind, they tested examples of VPE and PG (examples with no ellipsis were included as well), keeping them as similar as possible by means of a magnitude estimation acceptability study. Here are some of the materials used:

(137) VP Ellipsis
Match: Jane blamed Alex for the disastrous performance, and Neil did, too.
Mismatch: Jane was blamed by Alex for the disastrous performance, and Neil did, too.

(138) Pseudogapping
Match: Jane blamed Alex for the disastrous performance, and Neil did Emma.
Mismatch: Jane was blamed by Alex for the disastrous performance, and Neil did Emma.

The results of this study showed that ellipsis was judged less acceptable than absence of ellipsis. In addition, mismatch was judged less acceptable than match. However, mismatch received lower acceptability judgements only in the cases of ellipsis. It was also shown that the mismatch penalty was greater for VPE than for PG. These results led Kim and Runner (2013) to claim that Merchant's 'height of ellipsis' account about the differences between VPE and PG is not supported, given that once the confounds from Merchant's examples were excluded, the mismatch effect on ellipsis was actually stronger for VPE than for PG. Moreover, Kim and Runner (2013) highlight that 'it is not clear what independent evidence would point towards VPE being "big" (lower) VP Ellipsis and Pseudogapping being "little" (higher) VP Ellipsis'.

This section on psycholinguistics leads us to the following chapter of this volume, where the field of corpus linguistics has also served as a valuable tool to check the theoretical (im)plausibility of these hypotheses via empirical data.

1.3 Outline of the research

As this study presents the results of a corpus-based analysis of PAE in Modern English, in Chapter 2 I first offer an overview of the contributions of the different corpus studies on ellipsis (Section 2.1). Then, I define the main aims of the present monograph and the scope of the data under analysis: those cases of PAE attested in the Penn Parsed Corpora of Modern British English (1700–1914) (Section 2.2.1). In Section 2.2.2 I offer a general description of the Penn Corpora of Historical English, whose texts have been the data source of this investigation. In Section 2.2.3, I describe the programme CorpusSearch 2 and deal with the characteristics of the retrieval algorithm used to detect and retrieve cases of PAE automatically (precision, recall and F1 ratios). In Section 2.2.4, I present the database of PAE in Late Modern English and the variables that have been object of study.

Chapter 3 is devoted to an in-depth analysis of the data, divided into three different blocks: core defining variables (Section 3.1), usage variables (3.2) and processing variables (Section 3.3). Section 3.4 offers some concluding remarks on the characteristics of PG and VPE in Late Modern English.

Finally, Chapter 4 provides the summary and concluding remarks of this study, together with some suggestions for further research.

2

Methodology

Since this study constitutes a corpus-based analysis of Post-Auxiliary Ellipsis (PAE) in Modern English, in this chapter I will first provide an overview of the contributions of the different corpus studies on ellipsis to then focus on the description of the types of PAE analysed in the present volume. Following that, I will mention the characteristics of the corpora that have served as a basis for the empirical analysis of PAE, that is, the Penn Corpora of Historical English. Then, I will make reference to the software (CorpusSearch 2) and the retrieval algorithm used in order to obtain the data, mentioning its main characteristics. Finally, I will thoroughly explain the methodology and the variables studied.

2.1 Corpus-based studies on ellipsis

Despite the existence of a significant number of studies that have analysed the properties of VPE and PG from a theoretical point of view (Lobeck 1995; Johnson 2001; Gengel 2007; Aelbrecht 2010; Gengel 2013; Merchant 2013b, among others), it has been only recently that these ellipsis types have been studied empirically by means of corpora (see Hardt 1992b, 1993, 1995, 1997; Hardt and Rambow 2001; Nielsen 2003a,b, 2004a,b,c,d, 2005; Ericsson 2005; Hendriks and Spenader 2005; Hoeksema 2006; Bos and Spenader 2011; Miller 2011, 2014; Miller and Pullum 2014). These corpus studies have tried to discover new methods and algorithms for the automatic detection and retrieval of examples of different ellipsis types in Present-Day English.[1] Therefore, this empirical approach has served as a tool in order to test and reformulate theoretical hypotheses on ellipsis. I agree with Bos and Spenader (2011: 464–5) in that the following are the reasons why corpus studies on VPE are so scarce:

> In contrast to the numerous theoretical studies, corpus studies on VPE are rare, as are implementations of theoretical VPE resolution algorithms in practical

NLP [Natural Language Processing] applications. We believe that there are at least two reasons for this. First, from a purely practical perspective, automatically locating ellipsis and their antecedents is a hard task, not subsumed by ordinary natural language processing components. Recent empirical work (Hardt 1997; Nielsen 2005) indeed confirms that VPE identification is difficult. Second, most theoretical work begins at the point at which the ellipsis example and the rough location of its antecedent are already identified, focussing on the resolution task. Moreover, the complex ellipsis phenomena described by theoretical work on ellipsis are not terribly frequent in ordinary texts such as newswire.

Hardt's (1992b) was the first work to propose an algorithm to determine antecedents for VPE automatically. Using a group of 304 cases of VPE extracted from the Brown corpus, Hardt's algorithm on a first stage eliminated impossible antecedents to then assign preference levels to other plausible antecedents. The input to the algorithm was an elliptical VP and what he called a 'VPlist' (Hardt 1992b: 9), that is, a list that contained the VPs present in the same sentence as the VPE, as well as those taking place in the two immediately preceding sentences. Hardt (1992b) reports an accuracy of 94 per cent of his algorithm for antecedent detection.[2] In his (1993) dissertation, Hardt also implemented two computer programmes, testing them on hundreds of examples of VPE automatically retrieved from corpora. One of them would resolve VPE by copying the antecedent into the ellipsis site, while the other would identify the antecedent of VPE. Furthermore, in his (1995) study, Hardt developed another system that would both identify[3] and resolve cases of VPE from the Penn Treebank by matching tree patterns thanks to the utility called 'tgrep'. According to Hardt (1995: 53), an immediate application of this system would be to annotate the Penn Treebank for VPE resolution. In this work, new preference factors for the selection of possible antecedents of VPE such as recency, syntactic position, priming and similar parallel elements were added with respect to Hardt (1992b).[4] The system was able to detect the correct antecedent in 83.5 per cent of VPE examples from the Penn Treebank. This study paved the way for Hardt (1997), which 'was the first systematic corpus-based study of VPE resolution' (Hardt 1997: 525). In this work, the system was able to resolve VPE cases automatically in the 644 examples retrieved from the parsed Penn Treebank. As in the previous works, the system first determined the possible antecedents for each case of VPE based on structural constraints and discourse preference factors like recency, clausal relations and parallelism. The success of the system presented in this work was evaluated by comparing its output with that of human coders. Hardt (1997) reported a success rate of 94.8 per cent for his algorithm. Finally,

Hardt and Rambow (2001) was the first study to present work on VPE generation by focusing its attention on those factors that bear an influence on VPE. These factors include a variety of surface-oriented, morphological, syntactic, semantic and discourse features (Hardt and Rambow 2001: 2f):

- Surface-oriented features: sentential distance (number of clauses between antecedent and ellipsis site), word distance (number of words between antecedent and ellipsis site) and antecedent VP length (size of the antecedent in number of words).
- Morphological features: presence of auxiliaries in antecedent and ellipsis site (including infinitival marker *to*).
- Syntactic features: voice (of the antecedent and the ellipsis site), syntactic structure (the syntactic relation holding between the head verbs of the two VPs: conjunction, subordination, comparative constructions, and *as*-appositives) and subcategorization frame (for each verb: transitive or intransitive).
- Semantic and discourse features: adjuncts (adjuncts being identical in meaning in both antecedent and ellipsis site, similar in meaning, only the antecedent or candidate VP having an adjunct, the adjuncts being different or there being no adjuncts at all), in-quotes (whether the antecedent and/ or ellipsis site are within a quoted passage), discourse structure (whether the discourse segments containing the antecedent and candidate are directly related in the discourse structure) and polarity (whether the antecedent or ellipsis site contains the negative marker *not* or one of its contractions).

Hardt and Rambow (2001) analysed the data in order to find out which of the factors described above affect VPE and the results were as follows: the distance between antecedent and ellipsis site, the syntactic relation between antecedent and ellipsis site, and the presence or absence of adjuncts. Bearing in mind these results, they trained an algorithm for VPE generation with the help of machine learning techniques that would decide whether or not to perform VPE.

Ericsson (2005) carried out another corpus study that would generate elliptical utterances in a dialogue system. First, she investigated elliptical utterances in human–human dialogue (focusing on question–answer dialogues) and then generated appropriate elliptical utterances in a dialogue system.

In Nielsen (2005) and in earlier works (2003a,b, 2004a,b,c,d) where he presented the intermediate stages of his research leading to his (2005) dissertation, he put to the test both the syntactic and semantic accounts of ellipsis by carrying out a corpus-based empirical approach to ellipsis. To that end, he made use of machine learning techniques in order to resolve ellipsis. Nielsen's work was highly influenced by that of Hardt (1992b, 1993, 1995, 1997) and Hardt and Rambow (2001), as will become clear below. These were the steps he followed: first, ellipsis occurrences were detected by spotting elided verbs. Then, antecedents were identified, trying to find the suitable VP which served as the antecedent of VPE. Finally, ellipses were resolved. In this final step, as he mentions, 'for most cases of ellipsis, copying of the antecedent clause to the VPE site, with or without some simple transformations, is enough for resolution' (Nielsen 2005: 28). For the first two stages of ellipsis resolution, Nielsen (2005) made use of machine learning techniques. For the last one, however, he generated rules by hand. As Nielsen (2005: 28–9) states, previous existing methods had focused their attention on the resolution of ambiguous or difficult cases but had taken for granted the identification of both elliptical sentences and their corresponding antecedents. The main claim of Nielsen's (2005: 29) work is that 'it is possible to produce the components of a VPE resolution system, using a corpus-based, knowledge-poor approach'. He concentrated mainly on the detection of instances of VPE and PG (due to the similarity of the latter to the former) and the identification of their antecedents. This was done by means of experiments carried out with the help of different machine learning techniques that allowed him to assess the performance of the algorithms used in order to retrieve the data.[5] The corpora used were the British National Corpus (BNC) and the Penn Treebank. The sections from the BNC under study were samples of written text with extracts from novels, autobiographies, scientific journals and plays. On the other hand, the data from the Penn Treebank was composed of 1989 *Wall Street Journal* material and parts of the Brown Corpus.

    Nielsen (2005) succeeded in providing a robust system for VPE detection that automatically tags and parses data, extracting syntactic features. Then, machine learning was employed to classify the examples obtained. According to Nielsen (2005: 131), his study 'offers clear improvement over previous work, and is the first to handle un-annotated free text, where VPE can still be done with good recall[6] and precision'.[7] As far as the identification of the antecedent of VPE is concerned, Nielsen (2005) also improved previous works on this task, as his algorithm was able to identify antecedents successfully even with automatically parsed data. Finally, with respect to ellipsis resolution, Nielsen (2005) offered a classification of the data gathered with respect to the degree of the complexity of resolution required. The measure used in order to determine this degree of complexity was readability, namely whether the sentence made sense after reconstruction. According to Nielsen (2005: 174), 'in a number of cases, straightforward copying of the antecedent VP to the VPE site will result in an intelligible sentence. For a variety of constructions this is not enough, and further processing needs to be done.' Nielsen's classification of ellipsis resolution is illustrated below:

- Trivial cases:

This label was used for those cases in which resolving the ellipsis was trivial because it could be done by simply copying the antecedent or by using simple rules that depended on the syntactic context (approximately 83 per cent of the data). Here are some of the examples he provides (adapted from Nielsen 2005: 175–6):

(1) Jewelry makers rarely pay commissions and aren't expected to ~~pay commissions~~ anytime soon.

(2) In 1893 while recovering from a bout of influenza he wrote: You will see from this heading that I am not dead yet, nor likely to be ~~dead yet~~.

(3) a. You said something – about getting caught up in the action –
b. PLAYER: (Gaily freeing himself) I did ~~say something about getting caught up in the action~~, I did ~~say something about getting caught up in the action~~, – You're quicker than your friend.

As can be observed, in (1) simply copying the antecedent is enough for ellipsis resolution. In (2), however, the negative marker from the antecedent (*not*) needs to be removed before copying the antecedent in the ellipsis site. Finally, in (3) one can observe a case where the tense in the antecedent requires modification so as to adjust to that of the VPE site.

- Intermediate cases:

This category was used for those cases 'where it is possible to generate rules for resolution, but in a less straightforward way than for the trivial cases' (Nielsen 2005: 177). These cases comprise around 8 per cent of the corpus. Here are some examples (Nielsen 2005: 177–8):

(4) a. The party divisions between leading reformers such as Lloyd George, Mosley and Macmillan also hindered co-operation, as did personal hostility within political parties (on all occasions between Mosley and Ernest Bevin in the Labour movement and intermittently between Lloyd George and Keynes in the Liberals).

b. The party divisions between leading reformers such as Lloyd George, Mosley and Macmillan also hindered co-operation, as personal hostility within political parties (on all occasions between Mosley and Ernest Bevin in the Labour movement and intermittently between Lloyd George and Keynes in the Liberals) *hindered co-operation*.

c. The party divisions between leading reformers such as Lloyd George, Mosley and Macmillan also hindered co-operation, *and* personal hostility within political parties (on all occasions between Mosley and Ernest Bevin in the Labour movement and intermittently between Lloyd George and Keynes in the Liberals) hindered co-operation *too*.

In these cases of *as*-appositives, where VPE takes place right after an *as*, the antecedent would need to be located after the clause following the VPE (as in (4) b), although, as Nielsen (2005) points out, personal preference may lead one to modify the structure slightly and produce something like in (4)c.

- Difficult cases:

This category was for those examples which create considerable problems for automatic methods of ellipsis resolution, but not for humans (around 8 per cent of the data; Nielsen 2005: 181ff):

(5) a. Take care of yourself$_i$ then.
 b. I$_i$ will ~~take care of myself$_i$~~.
(6) a. Fancy a trip to the theatre?
 b. The question was close to being a statement.
 c. 'I'd – I'd love to ~~go to the theatre~~,' I said.
(7) a. Cigarette?
 b. No, I didn't think you would ~~smoke/want a cigarette~~.
 c. You don't mind if I do ~~smoke a cigarette~~?
(8) And besides, you do not look, you do not choose, do you ~~look and/or choose~~?

In (5) one can observe a case of pronominal ambiguity, also known as 'sloppy identity', where in order to resolve the ellipsis the syntactic form needs to be changed so that it can reflect a change in speaker. Example (6) would be a case requiring inference, as there is not a syntactic source for the ellipsis site. Example (7), in turn, would illustrate cases where the antecedent is unspoken (also known as 'exophoric VPE' in Miller and Pullum's 2014 work). Finally, (8) instantiates a case of split antecedents 'where syntactic data from separate phrases, even sentences have to be assembled' (Nielsen 2005: 183).

Bos and Spenader (2011), in turn, annotated twenty-five sections of the *Wall Street Journal* distributed with the Penn Treebank semi-automatically. They used theory-neutral annotation in order to code the auxiliary verb causing VPE, the beginning and end of the antecedent, the syntactic type of the antecedent (VP, TV,[8] NP, PP or AP) and the type of syntactic pattern between antecedents and ellipsis sites. More than 500 instances of VPE and related phenomena (including PG and the *do so* anaphora) were marked up. As Bos and Spenader (2011: 467) state, 'the resulting annotation is publicly available in stand-off format. With respect to precision, recall, coverage, usability, and detail of annotation, this corpus is a considerable improvement on previous annotation efforts.' This improvement is especially evident when compared to 118 cases of VPE of Nielsen (2005) and 260 of Hardt (1997) in the *Wall Street Journal* part of their annotated corpora. Three annotators (including the two co-authors) marked up cases of VPE and their corresponding antecedents in a number of sections of the *Wall Street Journal* individually. Then, they used section nineteen in order to check for inter-annotator agreement. As Bos and Spenader (2011: 480) mentioned, this section contained twenty-one cases of VPE and, whereas two of the annotators found all these twenty-one cases, one of them found only eighteen. Their corpus study revealed, as will be mentioned in Section 3.1.1, the great value of corpus studies on VPE, given that the VPE source–target patterns found deviated enormously from those standard examples normally quoted in the theoretical linguistics literature on VPE.

Miller (2011) carried out a corpus investigation of the different conditions underlying the choice among several anaphors in English: PAE with auxiliary *do* (that is, what is traditionally known as VPE with auxiliary *do*) versus *do so* and *do it/this/that* constructions. His study of the Corpus of Contemporary American English (COCA)[9] revealed that several factors influenced this choice:

> (i) Register (Spoken, Fiction, Newspaper or Academic): Post-Auxiliary Ellipsis appears to be more frequent in Fiction and Spoken registers.
> (ii) The presence or absence of an accessible polar alternative: cases where there exist contrasts in polarity or contexts that allow the

possible choice between two branches of a polar alternative strongly favour the occurrence of Post-Auxiliary Ellipsis.

(iii) Whether the sentence that contains the anaphor makes reference to the same state of affairs as that containing the antecedent: in *do so* constructions normally the subject of the antecedent and of the *do so* construction are the same, otherwise the state of affairs would be different.

(iv) The presence of a non-contrastive adjunct: it is typical of *do so* constructions (83 per cent of the cases) and specifies 'some additional property of the state of affairs' (Miller 2011: 10), because otherwise the *do so* construction would be redundant. This is a constraint that, according to Miller, does not apply to *do it* (60 per cent) or PAE (1.6 per cent).

(v) The identity of the subject of the anaphor and its antecedent (this applies to *do so* constructions).

(vi) The saliency of the antecedent: The main difference between *do it*, *do this* and *do that* on the one hand, and PAE and *do so* on the other, lies in the fact that the former forms 'do not require the same degree of saliency of their antecedent. The data suggest that an activated referent (in the sense of Gundel et al. 1993) is sufficient for the use of *do it*, *do this* and *do that*' (Miller 2011: 8).

Miller and Pullum (2014), based on a large corpus analysis of the COCA, demonstrated the existence of examples of exophoric PAE (which do not have a linguistic antecedent and therefore need to be inferred from the context) and thoroughly explained the reasons for their – apparent – rarity. Hankamer and Sag (1976) had shown the following contrast, where exophoric PAE was not possible:

(9) [Context: Sag raises a cleaver and prepares to hack off his left hand.]
 a. Hankamer: #Don't worry, he never actually does___. [PAE][10]
 b. Hankamer: Don't worry, he never actually does it. [do it]

Schachter (1977) responded to Hankamer and Sag's (1976) paper by producing several counterexamples to this claim, arguing that PAE could be freely exophoric. Hankamer (1978), in turn, responded to this paper by claiming that the range of exceptional examples of exophoric PAE were limited and semantically conventionalized, that is, they would be the result of idiomatization (as in, for example, the question *Shall we?*). Besides, the fact that there are cases where PAE is not acceptable but *do it/do this/do that* are demonstrated that the antecedent is recoverable from the context. Miller and Pullum (2014: 11) entered this debate and, on the basis of the data found, argued, 'Our claim is that Hankamer was wrong about exophoric PAE in that it can indeed be freely deployed in exophoric uses in all the situations where it satisfies the general discourse conditions on its use that apply in anaphoric contexts, too.' In their view, it is not true that exophoric PAE is rare, as it 'seems to occur as often as the demands of the nonlinguistic context happen to motivate it – it is free to occur exophorically within the range of the circumstances that allow it to occur at all' (Miller and Pullum 2014: 11). Here are some of the examples of exophoric PAE found in the COCA (Miller and Pullum 2014: 19–20):

(10) Once in my room, I took the pills out. 'Should I?' I asked myself. [COCA]

(11) [Entering a construction site, A hands a helmet to B]. B: Do I have to?

Exophoric PAE, therefore, needs to meet certain restrictive discourse conditions to licence its occurrence. Miller and Pullum (2014) conclude that while meeting these discourse conditions for nonlinguistic contexts is not easy, it is by no means impossible.

So far I have concentrated on those corpus studies that have mainly analysed examples of VPE. Two other corpus works have dealt with PG. First, Hoeksema (2006) studied PG thanks to a survey of speaker judgements and a small corpus study that allowed him to propose the existence of a gradient acceptability for cases of PG, which would be dependent on two factors: the type of context and the type of elided element. He argued that violations of preferences are cumulative, leading to ever-worse judgements. His proposal was that the acceptability of examples of PG would be the result of different threshold levels for binary responses in terms of acceptability or non-acceptability, and not of different underlying grammars. The data gathered from his corpus revealed that the most frequent contexts where PG takes place was the comparative (87 per cent), followed by coordination (4 per cent). In his survey of speakers' judgements, Hoeksema confirmed these results: comparative contexts are favoured over coordinative ones. In addition, he also found that PG with direct object remnants (12) was preferred over PG with predicate remnants (13) (Hoeksema 2006: 14; capitals in the original):

(12) Mary made as many WOMEN happy as she did MEN.

(13) Let's do as many people HAPPY as we do UNHAPPY.

What is more, he also found that examples of PG which contain complex predicates, like the one illustrated in (14), are somewhat better than examples such as (15), despite the fact that in the former the omitted material is composed by a discontinuous string and the latter is not (Hoeksema 2006: 12–13; capitals in the original):

(14) She found her CO-WORKER more attractive than she did her HUSBAND.
(15) ?She found her co-worker more ATTRACTIVE than she did INTERESTING.

Second, Miller (2014) carried out a large-scale corpus study of PG using the COCA. His work focused on the use of the NP remnant of this type of elliptical construction (see Section 3.1 for more details). He divided cases of PG into non-comparative PG (16) and comparative PG (17):

(16) Your weight affects your voice. It does mine, anyway. [(Miller 2014: 78)]
(17) It hurt me as much as it did her. [Miller (2014: 79)]

Miller (2014) presented the different discourse conditions that these two types of PG follow and their distribution per genres. His in-depth analysis of PG based on the COCA corpus allowed him to contradict the mainstream generative analysis of PG, which claims that PG is the result of remnant raising. In other words, PG would be considered a subcase of VPE where 'the remnant has been moved out of the VP before ellipsis' (Miller 2014: 81). Miller (2014) argues convincingly against such an analysis on the basis of the examples found in COCA, which show that they do not respect typical island constraints (nothing can be moved out of an island):

(18) According to current ideas, the frothiness of space retards the arrival of a burst's highest-energy photons more than it does *the lowest-energy photons*. [Complex NP Constraint, *What does it retard the arrival of?; *The photon was retarded the arrival of.] [Miller (2014: 82)]

He gathered sixty cases of island violations like this one (4.2 per cent of the occurrences). In his opinion, 'this seems far too great a rate to make it plausible to consider them as speech errors. All the more so that they clearly do not have the flavor of island variations. My feeling is that they range between perfectly acceptable and slightly sloppy, rather than ill-formed' (Miller 2014: 83). These data led him to suggest an alternative interpretive analysis of PG in the sense of Kubota and Levine (2014), where 'the flexibility of constituency in the system allows analyses where both the syntax and semantics of the ellipted material are explicitly represented as a constituent in the derivation of the antecedent clause' (Miller 2014: 86). Miller, however, is aware of the fact that this approach leads to overgeneration and that it would be necessary to constrain the flexibility just mentioned in order to avoid claiming that just anything can undergo ellipsis.

In this volume, I extend these studies by presenting a complex algorithm for the automatic detection and retrieval of cases of PAE in Late Modern English, using data from the PPCMBE (1700–1914), and by carrying out an in-depth analysis of examples of VPE and PG. This analysis will pave the path for a comparison between the characteristics of these PAE constructions in Late Modern English and those reported in theoretical and empirical works on PAE in Present-Day English.

In the following sections, I will focus on the description of the types of PAE that will be analysed in this study, namely, VPE and PG. Following that, I will also mention the characteristics of the corpora and the programme that has been used in order to obtain the data that have been the object of this piece of research.

2.2 The data

2.2.1 The scope of analysis

This volume will focus on the study of instances of PAE. The term Post-Auxiliary Ellipsis (Sag 1976; Warner 1993; Miller 2011; Miller and Pullum 2014) covers those cases in which a VP, NP, AP, PP or AdP is elided after one of the following licensors (that is, those elements that license the occurrence of ellipsis): modal auxiliaries, non-modal auxiliaries *be*, *have* and *do* and infinitival marker *to*.[11] It was Sag (1976: 53) who suggested that the term 'Post-Auxiliary Ellipsis' should be used instead of the misnomer VP Ellipsis, since neither does this type of ellipsis necessarily require the omission of a VP nor is it enough for it to occur. As Miller and Pullum (2014: 6) put it, 'the defining characteristic [of PAE] is not that a VP is omitted but that a constituent or constituent sequence immediately following an auxiliary is missing'. Miller and Pullum (2014: 6) make use of the following examples to illustrate this:

(19) We don't want to cancel the parade, but we could [c̶a̶n̶c̶e̶l̶ ̶t̶h̶e̶ ̶p̶a̶r̶a̶d̶e̶]$_{VP}$. [PAE]

(20) You think I'm dumb, but I'm not [d̶u̶m̶b̶]$_{AP}$, you know. [PAE]

(21) He said there would be results quite soon, and indeed there were [~~results~~]$_{NP}$ [~~quite soon~~]$_{AdP}$. [PAE]
(22) I couldn't reach him, though I tried [~~to reach him~~]$_{VP}$ several times. [NCA]

As can be observed, in (19) a VP has indeed been elided. However, this is not true of examples (20) and (21), where what has undergone ellipsis is an AP in the former and an NP together with an AdP in the latter. Note that, as Miller and Pullum (2014: 6) point out, (21) 'does not even form a constituent according to classical constituency tests; for example, it cannot be clefted'. Finally, (22) constitutes a case of Null Complement Anaphora (NCA), which illustrates a construction where a VP has indeed been omitted, but not after an auxiliary, as in the other cases (see Hankamer and Sag 1976; Depiante 2000; van Craenenbroeck and Merchant 2013 for more details). Therefore, NCA would not be considered a case of PAE.[12] The present study focuses on two subtypes of PAE: VPE and PG, illustrated in (23) and (24), respectively:

(23) I have written a squib but he hasn't ~~written a squib~~.
(24) John kissed Sarah, and Mary did ~~kiss~~ Paul.

Below I will provide the general characteristics of these two subtypes of PAE. Notice, however, that the definition of PAE given in the present study could be argued to include also cases of British English *do*. This type of construction is found only in British dialects of English. As Thoms (2011a: 3) points out, in British English *do* 'a superfluous *do* appears at the edge of what appears to be a VP ellipsis site after a modal or auxiliary', as shown in (25):

(25) a. Rab should leave, and Morag should *do*, too.
b. Rab has left, and Morag has *done*, too.

Thoms (2011a: 3) claims that the *do* found in the previous examples has no lexical semantic content, similar to what happens with standard *do*-support. In addition, the occurrence of this construction is optional in the sense that it is in free distribution with respect to cases of VPE without *do*.

British English *do* has been claimed to be both a verbal pro-form (Halliday and Hasan 1976; Quirk et al. 1985; Huddleston and Pullum 2002; Baltin 2006; Haddican 2007) and the result of ellipsis (Miller 2002; Aelbrecht 2009, 2010; Thoms 2011a,b; Baltin 2012), and so far no consensus has been reached. Underlying the debate would be the classification of *do* in British English *do* constructions either as a main verb or as an auxiliary verb. To give an example of features which are relevant to the discussion, main verb *do* (like in the construction *do so*) has been claimed not to be possible with stative antecedents, which British English *do* allows, and this would favour the analysis of British *do* as an auxiliary. Here are some examples that illustrate this fact (Thoms 2011b: 4):

> (26) a. John might seem to enjoy that, and Fred might, too.
> b. John might seem to enjoy that, and Fred might do, too.
> c. ??John might seem to enjoy that, and Fred might do so, too.

Nevertheless, large corpus-based studies like Houser (2010) and Miller (2013) have shown that there are cases of *do so* which can indeed have stative antecedents (in italics), as in these examples taken from Houser (2010: 50):

> (27) The six genes that *have the largest t-statistics* do so by virtue of having denominators close to zero, implying near constant expression levels.
> (28) Even in the aftermath of the Tiananmen Square massacre, the power of corporate interest has always *prevailed over other concerns*. Clinton can be quietly confident that it will do so again.

This weakens the relevance of the previous argument in favour of *do* as an auxiliary verb in British English *do* constructions. If, as a consequence of Houser's and Miller's findings, British English *do* cannot be taken as an auxiliary, then its analysis would lie beyond the scope of this piece of research, in which I focus on strictly ellipsis after an auxiliary (PAE).

Furthermore, the adscription of *do*, not necessarily British English *do*, to the class of main verb or auxiliary verb is controversial. In this respect, I have already reported that Huddleston and Pullum (2002: 1524) distinguish between what they term 'primary forms of *do*' (present in all dialects of English) and secondary forms of *do* (attested only in British English, that is, cases of British English *do*). Whereas examples (29) to (32) would illustrate the primary uses of *do*, (33) to (36) would exemplify secondary uses of *do*:

> (29) I liked it, but Kim *didn't* ___. [primary verb negation]
> (30) I liked it; *did* YOU___? [subject-auxiliary inversion]
> (31) He says she doesn't like him, but she DOES ___. [emphatic polarity]
> (32) I liked it, and Kim did too. [Huddleston and Pullum (2002: 1523–4); emphasis in the original]
> (33) %I didn't tell you at the time; I wish now that I had done. [past participle][13]
> (34) %I wasn't enjoying the course then, but I am doing now. [gerund participle]

(35) %I haven't written the letter yet, but I will do soon.
(36) %I like it now, but I didn't do then. [Huddleston and Pullum (2002: 1524); emphasis in the original]

This uneven distribution of *do* in the dialects of English raises the question as to whether *do* is a supportive auxiliary or a lexical pro-form. Huddleston and Pullum (2002: 1524) claim that in the dialects of English which permit only primary forms of *do*, this *do* 'is best regarded as a special case of supportive auxiliary *do*'. Auxiliary *do* must be present in order to license the reduction of the VP in the auxiliary stranding construction, just as it happens with primary verb negation, subject-auxiliary inversion and emphatic polarity. However, in British English, a dialect which allows both primary and secondary forms of *do*, this auxiliary is regarded as a pro-form 'substituting for a verb alone [...] or a verb together with internal dependents [. ...] Pro-form *do* is a lexical verb, and combines with supportive auxiliary *do* in constructions like the negative' (Huddleston and Pullum 2002: 1524). Moreover, Quirk et al. (1985: 874), when referring to examples of British English *do*, state that in British English 'many allow the possibility of adding after the operator an optional *do* as an intransitive substitute verb'. Halliday and Hasan (1976) also refer to this construction as an example of substitution within the verbal group. Therefore, all three grammars claim that this *do* which only appears in British English is an instance of substitution and not ellipsis, and this reinforces the view that British English *do* should not be accounted for in terms of ellipsis.

The exclusion of the analysis of British English *do* in the present study is also justified on methodological grounds since my database comprises only two examples of this construction, quoted below, which, for obvious reasons, cannot undergo any kind of statistical treatment:

(37) We must even let it go on, as it has *done*, and will *do*.[14]
CARLYLE-1835,2,256.43
(38) Yet I know very well what is meant by that, and that our Affairs don't go so well as they should *do*, because of Bribery and Corruption.
FIELDING-1749,2,10.162

In what follows, I will provide the general characteristics of the two constructions of ellipsis under study, namely VPE and PG.

2.2.1.1 VP Ellipsis

The term VP Ellipsis, the most widely discussed type of ellipsis in the literature by far, is used here in order to refer to cases where a VP, NP, AP, PP or AdP has undergone ellipsis after modal auxiliaries, non-modal auxiliaries *be*, *have* and *do* and infinitival marker *to*. Therefore, the name VPE is merely used for classification purposes so as to keep the distinction between this subtype of PAE and PG. Here are some further examples that illustrate cases of VPE (the licensors of ellipsis, that is, those auxiliaries that license the occurrence of ellipsis, appear in italics):

(39) A: Can you pass me the salt?
B: Yes, of course I *can* [pass you the salt]~VP~.

(40) Look, Dr. Briant, I've been with you on this from the word go, you know I *have* [been with you on this from the word go]~VP~. [Adapted from the BNC]

(41) A: I have a book written by my granny.
B: *Have* you [a book written by your granny?]~NP~

(42) Will likes playing the piano and I think Karen *does* [like playing the piano]~VP~ too.

(43) A: Did you phone Alice?
B: No I *didn't* [phone]~VP~. Sorry, I forgot.

(44) She hadn't seen him in seven years and didn't really want *to* [see him]~VP~. [Adapted from the BNC]

(45) You say John is doing a great job, but Anne *is* [doing a great job]~VP~ too!

(46) John is a doctor and Anne *is* [a doctor]~NP~ too.

(47) Paul is handsome but one cannot ignore that Peter *is* [handsome]~AP~ too.

(48) Bill's son is on the beach, although he shouldn't *be* [on the beach]~PP~ because he's allergic to the sun.

(49) She told me she was there, but she *wasn't* [there]~AdP~.

As can be observed, VPE is possible in contexts of subordination (as in (40), (42) and (47)) and can apply across sentence boundaries, as observed in examples (39), (41) and (43). Notice that auxiliary *have* licenses the omission of either a VP (see (40)) or an NP (41). Auxiliary *be*, in turn, licenses the omission of VPs (see (45)), NPs (46), APs (47), PPs (48) and AdPs (49). Van Craenenbroeck and Merchant (2013: 703) use the term 'Predicate Phrase Ellipsis' in order to refer to those cases in which auxiliary *be* licenses the ellipsis of non-verbal material such as NPs, APs, PPs or some other constituent.

As Gengel (2013: 8) points out, 'VP Ellipsis can be constructed backwards, with the Ellipsis site in the first part of the sentence […] . VP Ellipsis is often assumed to involve special polarity marking, which is encoded with the emphatic marker *too*, or negation' (see (42) and (45), for example). Gengel (2013: 8–9) quotes examples extracted from Lobeck's (1995) work to illustrate the capacity of VPE to be cataphoric in some, but not all contexts:

(50) Because Pavarotti *couldn't* [~~sing the part~~]$_{VP}$, they asked Domingo to sing the part. [Lobeck (1995: 20); adapted from Gengel (2013: 8)]

(51) a. *Sue *didn't* [~~eat meat~~]$_{VP}$ but John ate meat.
b. Because Sue *didn't* [~~eat meat~~]$_{VP}$, John ate meat. [Lobeck (1995: 22); adapted from (Gengel 2013: 9)]

2.2.1.2 Pseudogapping

As mentioned earlier, the second subtype of PAE considered in this study is PG, a category of ellipsis that is very similar to VPE, in which a complement, known as the 'remnant', is left after the auxiliary, as illustrated by the direct objects *me* and *the weatherman* in (52) and (53) (licensors appear in italics and remnants are underlined):

(52) Does that make you mad? It *would* ~~make~~ <u>me</u> ~~mad~~! [Adapted from Levin (1986: vii)]

(53) If you don't believe me, you *will* ~~believe~~ <u>the weatherman</u>. [Carlson (2002: 11)]

(54) And because we can communicate so much visually – for instance, by the expressions on people's faces – you don't need quite so many words as you *do* ~~need words~~ <u>in a novel</u>. [Sue Birtwistle and Susie Conklin, *The Marking of Pride and Prejudice*, Penguin/ BBC Books, London, 1995, p.13; adapted from Gengel (2013: 11)]

Remnants in PG are most often NPs (as in examples (52) and (53) (*me* and *the weatherman*)) or PPs (as in example (54) *in a novel*) (see Gengel 2013: 9). Remnants are also contrastively paired with a complement of the antecedent: *me* contrasts with *you* in (52), and *me* with *the weatherman* in (53). Levin (1986: 3) defines PG as 'a "hole" created by a deleted main verb, one which is flanked on the left by either a modal auxiliary, aspectual (perfective *have* or progressive *be*), or supportive *do*, and on the right by a contrastive object'. As Lasnik (1995) highlights, this type of ellipsis displays some characteristics of Gapping (there is a right side remnant) together with some properties of VPE (there is a finite auxiliary) (see also Gengel 2013). PG can take place in both noncomparative (55) and comparative structures (56) (Levin 1986;

Miller 2014). Here are some examples extracted from the COCA corpus provided by Miller (2014: 73):

(55) 'It doesn't bother me,' I said untruthfully. 'Well, it *does* ~~bother~~ me,' he growled, and I let it rest.
(56) We'll let you know if it deals with the heat and humidity as well as it *did* ~~deal with~~ the frigid slop.

However, unlike VPE, PG is more constrained since it shows a preference for coreferential subjects and comparative contexts (Levin 1986; Aelbrecht 2010). This preference is illustrated in (57), where PG takes place in a comparative sentence whose subject corefers with the one present in the antecedent clause (*he*).

(57) He realized that he could make more money in some other position than he *could* ~~make money~~ farming. (Adapted from Levin 1978: 229)

With respect to the acceptability of instances of PG, Levin (1986: 3) mentions that 'deleting a repeated main verb when its object is contrastive is perfectly natural for some speakers'. In this sense, Lasnik (1995) even quotes linguists like Jackendoff (1971) and Lapin (1992), who offer examples which they considered ungrammatical and that in current studies fall under the category of PG:

(58) a. Bill ate the peaches and Harry *did* ~~eat~~ the grapes.
     b. Bill ate the peaches and Harry *will* ~~eat~~ the grapes. [Jackendoff (1971)]
(59) John reviewed the play and Mary *did* ~~review~~ the book. [Lappin (1992)]

Examples like (58) and (59), Lasnik (1995) contends, are not infrequent in written and spoken English. He goes on to add that 'a number of researchers have labelled them marginal, or even fully grammatical' (see Levin 1986; Gengel 2013; Miller 2014 for more details). In this sense, Gengel (2013: 9) mentions the fact that 'sometimes a Pseudogapping configuration is ungrammatical in coordinate structures [...] but perfectly grammatical in comparative structures', as seen in (60) and (61):

(60) *You probably just feel relieved, but I *do* ~~feel~~ jubilant.
(61) I probably feel more jubilant than you *do* ~~feel~~ relieved. [Levin (1978: 232); adapted from Gengel (2013: 11)]

In Miller's (2014) corpus-based study of PG noncomparative PG proved to be less acceptable than comparative PG and typical of the spoken register.

2.2.1.3 Differences between VPE and PG

There are a number of differences between VPE and PG that have been reported in the literature (Levin 1986; Hoeksema 2006; Gengel 2013; Miller 2014). Levin (1986: 53–4) mentions six differences between these two subtypes of ellipsis, which are reported below (all of the examples have been extracted from Levin 1986: 53–4):

> a. VPE is possible in contexts of subordination, while embedded PGs 'rapidly become awkward' (Levin 1986: 53):

(62) Since tornadoes petrify Harold, I can't for the life of me figure out *why he's so surprised about the fact that* * they do ø me too/ hurricanes do ø too.

> b. As a consequence of (a), cataphoric examples are possible in VPE, but not in PG (Levin 1986: 53):

(63) *Although it *doesn't ø me*, it takes Karen a long time to clean the hamster's cage.
(64) Although it *doesn't always ø*, it sometimes takes a long time to clean the hamster's cage.

> c. VPE is possible in infinitival clauses whereas PG is not (Levin 1986: 54):

(65) It [an enema] leaves some water in you. At least, it seems *to* *ø me / ø.
(66) Speaker A: Van Gogh's work is beginning to impress me.
Speaker B: *It's starting *to* ø me, too / Well! It's finally starting *to* ø.

> d. The elliptical V in VPE can 'belong to any [semantic] class whatever; the elliptical V in PG must belong to a certain class(es)' (Levin 1986: 54).

(67) The one they choose might *be* Gail, but it *won't ø me/ might not ø.
(68) Speaker A: Tim's preface *has* me in it!
(69) Speaker B: *It does ø me ø, too / I'm not surprised it does ø.

> e. In VPE the subject in the elided clause is not required to be coreferential with the subject in the antecedent clause. However, as mentioned by Levin (1986: 54), the subject of the pseudogapped clause must be coreferential with the subject of the antecedent clause for most speakers.

(69) Speaker A: That thunderstorm bothered Millicent last night.
Speaker B: ??Well, *your stereo* did ø me/ I'm afraid *my stereo* did ø, too.

f. Whereas a great variety of auxiliary combinations is permitted in VPE (as in example (70), attested in the British National Corpus) in PG a single auxiliary is involved. More than one auxiliary in PG would be rather marginal (as in (71)), although Levin reports one case (shown in (72)) (Levin 1986: 54):

(70) I saw it and obviously so did Arnold, but nobody else *could have*.
(71) Speaker A: Cream rinse makes my hair get dirty faster.
Speaker B: ??It *may have* ø mine ø once, too.
(72) I processed everybody's check last week, but I *must not've* ø yours.

Therefore, as can be deduced from above, the only similarity that VPE and PG share is the type of licensor, that is, the auxiliary(ies) that allow(s) the ellipsis of verbal material in both constructions.[15]

2.2.2 The corpus: The Penn Corpora of Historical English

The databases used in order to carry out this investigation are commonly known as the Penn Corpora of Historical English, formed by a collection of running texts and text samples of British English prose from different historical periods which range from the Middle English period up to the First World War.[16] The collection is divided into three different corpora: Penn-Helsinki Parsed Corpus of Middle English, 2nd ed. (PPCME2), Penn-Helsinki Parsed Corpus of Early Modern English (PPCEME) and Penn Parsed Corpus of Modern British English (PPCMBE). The PPCMBE corpus, which provides the empirical basis for this investigation, contains 948,895 words and is made up of eighteen different genres. I have classified these genres into two groups: speech related and writing related. Speech-related genres include Diary, Drama comedy, Fiction, Non-private letters, Private letters, Trial proceedings and Sermon. Writing-related genres comprise Bible, Biography autobiography, Biography other, Educational treatise, Handbook other, History, Law, Science medicine, Science other, Philosophy and Travelogue.

Importantly, the texts are available in three different formats with their corresponding filename extensions: raw text (.txt), part-of-speech tagged text (.pos) and syntactically annotated text (.psd). The original layout of the text is not preserved; instead, it is divided into tokens. These tokens usually include main clauses along with any subordinate clauses that they may contain and are 'associated with a token ID, enclosed in parentheses, which contains the name of the file, a page reference to the printed text (possibly including a volume reference)' (Kroch, Santorini and Diertani 2010),[17] as in (73):

(73) I am sure I may on this occasion call Kitty Foote, as Hastings did H. Egerton, my 'very valuable Friend.' AUSTEN-180X,179.421.

The ID *AUSTEN-180X,179.421* has been named after its author, in this case the writer Jane Austen (1775–1817), followed by its year of composition. In this case, since the text spans several years within a decade, it contains an 'x' rather than the last digit (180x).

The syntactic annotation or parsing of these corpora has been crucial for the present study, as it provides the possibility of looking for words or word sequences, in addition to syntactic structure. Therefore, syntactic constructions which follow a general pattern can be easily retrieved automatically. However, a word of caution should be noted with respect to the philosophy behind the annotation of these corpora. The main goal of the Penn Treebank-style annotation is to facilitate automated search to the detriment of offering a linguistically accurate annotation. This is the reason why this annotation is rather 'flat' if compared with current linguistic theories like minimalism, and does not use binary-branching. As a consequence, therefore, the labels employed in the annotation have served primarily as atheoretical tools that would allow the automatic classification of sentences taking into account several properties and patterns. Hence, labels should not be interpreted as descriptive claims about the language.

To give an example of the Penn Treebank annotation conventions, the simple sentence 'This spider was of an ash colour' would be encoded as follows:

(74) This spider was of an ash colour.

((IP-MAT (IP-MAT-1 (NP-SBJ (D This) (N Spider))
       (BED was)
       (PP (P of)
           (NP (D an) (N ash) (N colour))))
(ID ALBIN-1736,1.15)

In (74), a pair of parentheses ( ) describes each level (node in a tree), where each of them is made up of two components: a label on the left (a phrase label (e.g. NP), a part-of-speech (POS) label (e.g. D), etc.) and content on the right (phrase(s) such as 'This spider', or word(s) like 'of', etc.).

The list of the basic POS labels used in the Penn Treebank, necessary for the understanding of both the algorithm proposed in this monograph and the output data, can be found in Appendix 1.[18]

The automatic retrieval of examples of PAE has been made possible thanks to the use of a programme called CorpusSearch 2, whose characteristics are described below. CorpusSearch 2 query language is thoroughly explained in Appendix 2.

2.2.3 The query

2.2.3.1 *CorpusSearch 2*

CorpusSearch 2 is a Java programme that helps carry out research in corpus linguistics. It offers the possibility of searching corpora as well as building an annotated corpus. It can be used under any Java-supported operating system, such as Linux, Macintosh, Unix or Windows. CorpusSearch allows implementing the following activities automatically:

- find and count lexical and syntactic configurations of any complexity;
- correct systematic errors;
- code the linguistic features of corpus sentences for later statistical analysis. [CorpusSearch Home (2005)]

CorpusSearch 2 requires two elements: a corpus of parsed labelled sentences where to search for linguistic information (i.e. the source file(s)) and a command file which contains a query that specifies what structures should be searched for in any particular node(s) (i.e. a search domain, for example, IPs and NPs) in the corpus under study. The command file (also known as 'query file', with the file extension .*q*) returns an output text file (with the extension .*out*) with all the results which comply with the query. This output file includes the actual examples together with some information regarding the position where those structures were found. In addition, 'statistics are kept detailing the number of "hits", that is, distinct constituents containing the structure, the number of matrix sentences ("tokens") containing hits, and the total number of tokens in the file' (CorpusSearch Home 2005). The basics of CorpusSearch 2 query language, necessary for the understanding of the specific query used in this study, are described in Appendix 1.

2.2.3.2 *The retrieval algorithm: Precision and recall*

In order to develop a specific algorithm and check the parsing conventions used by the compilers in the analysis of examples with ellipsis, I manually analysed

12 raw texts out of 102 files (112,347 words analysed out of almost one million words), all belonging to different genres and periods of time of the PPCMBE. The syntactic patterns followed by the examples of PAE were examined to draw some generalizations that would allow the creation of an algorithm for their automatic retrieval. Importantly, this manual analysis revealed that PAE is not annotated uniformly in the PPCMBE. For example, the general patterns of PAE found manually showed that while auxiliaries *do* and *have* were licensors of PAE which had already been tagged in the parsed texts in the vast majority of cases, this was not the case with instances of PAE whose licensor was auxiliary *be*, as they were not coded. Here are two examples of PAE after auxiliaries *do* and *have*:

(75) — On the Monday morning he came again? A. He *did*.
WATSON-1817,1,84.97

((IP-MAT (META (CODE <font>)
       (NP (N A.))
       (CODE <$$font>))
    (NP-SBJ (PRO He))
    (DOD did)
    (VB *)
    (. .))
(ID WATSON-1817,1,84.97))

(76) But we have proved that one is the very same thing as good. 'We *have*.'
BOETHJA-1897,114.249

((IP-MAT-SPE (' '
    (NP-SBJ (PRO We))
    (HVP have)
    (VBN *)
    (. .)
    (' '))
(ID BOETHJA-1897,114.249))

As can be seen in (75), the tag *VB* followed by an asterisk * indicates that the verb has been elided after auxiliary *do*. Simply searching for the tag *VB* indicating that it immediately dominates (iDoms) the * symbol (thus escaping the wild card use) returns a fair amount of PAE instances. The same applies to auxiliary *have*, as shown in (76). As regards *have*, first, those instances of ellipsis of ordinary verbs after auxiliary *have* were coded as such in the vast majority of cases, as illustrated in (76). Nevertheless, as will be shown later, there were a few exceptions to this (see (90) below). Second, when auxiliary *have* licenses the ellipsis of the perfect participle of *have*, this is annotated as *HVN ** in the corpus. However, only two examples of this kind were found in the corpus, instantiated in (77).

(77) Council. Have you had any Promise of a Pardon? M'Cormack. I *have not*. TOWNLEY-1746,37.343

((IP-MAT (META (CODE <font>)
      (NP (NPR M'Cormack))
      (, ,)
      (CODE <$$font>))
    (NP-SBJ (PRO I))
    (HVP have)
    (NEG not)
    (HVN *)
    (. ,))
(ID TOWNLEY-1746,37.343))

Third, there were also five cases where the omission of the perfect participle of auxiliary *be* after the licensor *have* was annotated with the tag *BEN **, as in (78):

(78) Q. Have you been examined as a witness before the Grand Jury at Hicks's Hall? A. I *have*. WATSON-1817,1,168.2270

((IP-MAT (META (CODE <font>)
      (NP (N A.))
      (CODE <$$font>))
    (NP-SBJ (PRO I))
    (HVP have)
    (BEN *)
    (. .))
(ID WATSON-1817,1,168.2270))

Fourth, there was a third pattern regarding cases of auxiliary *have* as the licensor of PAE, namely those instances where non-verbal material was omitted were not coded in the corpus:

(79) you had a Command from his Royal Highness to go to the Church where the Officers were Prisoners, and to take their Names? Capt. Nevet. Yes, I had, Sir. TOWNLEY-1746,48.613

```
((IP-MAT (META (NP (NPR Capt.) (CODE <font>) (NPR Nevet))
    (, .)
    (CODE <$$font>))
    (INTJ Yes)
    (, ,)
    (NP-SBJ (PRO I))
    (HVD had)
    (, ,)
    (NP-VOC (N Sir))
    (. .))
(ID TOWNLEY-1746,48.613))
```

Due to the lack of annotation in the corpus for these last cases, the rest of the examples of this type had to be found using another strategy. The solution adopted here was to look for contexts where auxiliary *have* (with either positive or negative polarity) would be immediately followed by any kind of punctuation mark, which is a typical context for PAE to occur. Actually, the five examples of PAE where the omission of the perfect participle of *be* (*BEN* *) after licensor *have* was annotated were found without having to resort to a new condition in the algorithm such as BEN iDoms * thanks to this condition.

However, there are cases of PAE with auxiliary *be* as the licensor which are not tagged, as in (80):

(80) and therefore it cannot be learn'd by Conversation, as the Modern Languages *are*; ANON-1711,12.125

```
    (PP (P as)
    (CP-ADV (WADVP-2 0)
        (C 0)
        (IP-SUB (ADVP *T*-2)
        (NP-SBJ (D the) (ADJ Modern) (NS Languages))
        (BEP are))))))))))
(, ;)
(ID ANON-1711,12.125))
```

In the annotation of (80) there is no clue that PAE is taking place. Therefore, as will be shown later, the same decision was made as with those cases of PAE whose licensor was auxiliary *have* and non-verbal material was omitted: some conditions were included in the algorithm to try to retrieve instances of PAE after auxiliary *be* which were followed by any kind of punctuation mark, just like in (80), where *be* is followed by a semicolon.

Modal auxiliaries, on the other hand, also followed a pattern: the script was designed in such a way that it would return examples of modal auxiliaries that were not followed by any kind of verb, with the exception of auxiliaries *have* and *be*, which could be present in some examples of PAE, like the following:

(81) Cha. Sir George is ready to depart. But I *could not have* departed without returning to say farewell! COLLIER-1835,26.952

(82) their experiences and travels are not appreciated as they *should be* appreciated by their friends of the chapel. BRADLEY-1905,204.104

Consequently, an algorithm was created that would retrieve both those syntactic contexts of ellipsis that had already been tagged, as well as those that had not been but were prone to contain examples of ellipsis. The following was the initial script used as a query file to obtain the examples of PAE in Late Modern English:

(83)

```
node: *
query: (VB* iDoms \*)
OR (HV* iDoms \*)
OR (MD* hasSister !VB*|BE*|DO*|HV*)
OR ((MD* iPrecedes HV*)
AND (HV* iPrecedes [.,]))
OR ((MD* iPrecedes NEG)
AND (NEG iPrecedes HV*)
AND (HV* iPrecedes [.,]))
OR ((MD* iPrecedes HV*)
AND (HV* iPrecedes BE*)
AND (BE* iPrecedes [.,]))
OR ((MD* iPrecedes NEG)
AND (NEG iPrecedes HV*)
AND (HV* iPrecedes BE*)
AND (BE* iPrecedes [.,]))
OR (BE* iPrecedes [.,])
OR ((BE* iPrecedes NEG)
AND (NEG iPrecedes [.,]))
OR (HV* iPrecedes [.,])
OR ((HV* iPrecedes NEG)
AND (NEG iPrecedes [.,]))
OR ((HV* iPrecedes NP-SBJ)
AND (NP-SBJ iPrecedes [?]))
```

OR ((DO* iPrecedes NEG)
AND (NEG iPrecedes NP-SBJ)
AND (NP-SBJ iPrecedes [.,?]))
OR (DOI iPrecedes [.,])
OR (CP* hasLabel CP-QUE-TAG*)

Due to its methodological importance, this algorithm will be described step by step in what follows. First, the search domain, that is, the node, had to be defined. In this case, the programme should look for examples of PAE in every possible node by making use of the asterisk *, which is a wild card that can stand for any string. The first condition of the algorithm, 'VB* iDoms *', looks for any kind of verb (represented by the tag *VB**) that immediately dominates a *, which is the symbol used in the PPCMBE to annotate that ellipsis has occurred (in its escape use). This condition alone retrieves the vast majority of cases of PAE found by the algorithm. The second condition, 'HV* iDoms *', does the same as the previous condition, but in this case with auxiliary *have*: it searches for examples where the auxiliary *have* immediately dominates an asterisk (i.e. an elided element). This type of annotation was used in the corpus to code the ellipsis of auxiliary *have* in its perfect participle form. This is illustrated in (84), where the tag *HVN* followed by an asterisk indicates that there has been an ellipsis of the perfect participle of auxiliary *have*:

(84) Q. Had you no preventer Braces?
A. I believe we had at the lower Yards, but don't know whether we had at Topsail-Yards or not, but I believe not, because if *we had* we should certainly have made use of them. HOLMES-TRIAL-1749,67.1248

```
(PP (P+N because)
  (CP-ADV-SPE (C 0)
    (IP-SUB-SPE (PP (P if)
      (CP-ADV-SPE (C 0)
        (IP-SUB-SPE (NP-SBJ (PRO we))
          (HVD had)
          (HVN *))))
      (NP-SBJ (PRO we))
      (MD should)
      (ADVP (ADV certainly))
      (HV have)
      (VBN made)
      (NP-OB1 (N use))
```

```
                    (PP (P of)
                         (NP (PRO them))))))
        (. .))
(ID HOLMES-TRIAL-1749,67.1248))
```

The third condition of the algorithm, '(MD* hasSister !VB*|BE*|DO*|HV*),' aims at searching for instances of PAE that are licensed by a modal auxiliary, with no verbal material or auxiliaries *be*, *have* and *do* as its sister. This would be one output example:

> (85) But still you would reckon the injuring person more unhappy than he who had suffered the wrong? – I certainly *would*.
> BOETHRI-1785,160.349

```
((IP-MAT-SPE (, -)
        (NP-SBJ (PRO I))
        (ADVP (ADV certainly))
        (MD would)
        (. .))
(ID BOETHRI-1785,160.349))
```

However, the two conditions '((MD* iPrecedes HV*) AND (HV* iPrecedes [.,]))' and '((MD* iPrecedes HV*) AND (HV* iPrecedes BE*) AND (BE* iPrecedes [.,]))' – together with their negative counterparts '((MD* iPrecedes NEG) AND (NEG iPrecedes HV*) AND (HV* iPrecedes [.,]))' and '((MD* iPrecedes NEG) AND (NEG iPrecedes HV*) AND (HV* iPrecedes BE*) AND (BE* iPrecedes [.,]))' – would search for the other two possible combinations with modal auxiliaries that may license the occurrence of PAE. The combination '((MD* iPrecedes HV*) AND (HV* iPrecedes [.,]))' will retrieve examples of PAE where a modal auxiliary immediately precedes auxiliary *have* and this auxiliary also immediately precedes any kind of punctuation mark. An illustration of this condition can be observed in (86):

> (86) but in a little time I hope to do all you *would have*.
> JOHNSON-1775,2,9.177

```
                    (IP-SUB (NP-OB1 *T*-1)
                         (NP-SBJ (PRO you))
                         (MD would)
                         (HV have)))))
(. .))
(ID JOHNSON-1775,2,9.177))
```

The negative counterpart of this condition '((MD* iPrecedes NEG) AND (NEG iPrecedes HV*) AND (HV* iPrecedes [.,]))' did not yield any examples of PAE. The second possible combination with modal auxiliaries that may license PAE, '((MD* iPrecedes HV*) AND (HV* iPrecedes BE*) AND (BE* iPrecedes [.,]))', would look for examples where a modal auxiliary immediately precedes auxiliary *have* and this auxiliary also immediately precedes auxiliary *be* and *be* immediately precedes any kind of punctuation mark, as exemplified in (87):

(87) That the wicked, who suffer the chastisement which they merit, are happier than they *would have been*, BOETHRI-1785,154.295

>> (IP-SUB-SPE (ADJP *T*-3)
>> (NP-SBJ (PRO they))
>> **(MD would)**
>> **(HV have)**
>> **(BEN been)**
>> (, ,)
>> (ID BOETHRI-1785,154.295))

Once again, the negative counterpart of this second combination with modal auxiliaries '((MD* iPrecedes NEG) AND (NEG iPrecedes HV*) AND (HV* iPrecedes BE*) AND (BE* iPrecedes [.,]))' did not yield any examples of PAE either.

The following condition of the algorithm, '(BE* iPrecedes [.,]) OR ((BE* iPrecedes NEG) AND (NEG iPrecedes [.,]))', would look for instances of PAE licensed by auxiliary *be* where this auxiliary (in either positive or negative form) immediately precedes any punctuation mark, a syntactic context which would be prone for PAE to occur. As mentioned earlier, this condition was necessary because none of the instances of PAE after auxiliary *be* was coded in the corpus. Here are two of the output examples retrieved (instantiating *be* with both positive and negative polarity):

(88) that it cannot be so quickly learn'd as the Modern Tongues *are*. ANON-1711,12.126

>> (PP-2 (P as)
>> (CP-CMP (WADVP-3 0)
>> (C 0)
>> (IP-SUB (ADVP *T*-3)
>> (NP-SBJ (D the) (ADJ Modern) (NS Tongues))
>> **(BEP are))))))**
> (. .))
> (ID ANON-1711,12.126))

(89) Does not every Affection necessarily imply, that the Object of it be itself loved? If it *be not*, 'tis not the Object of the Affection. BUTLER-1726,271.326

```
((IP-MAT (PP (P If)
         (CP-ADV (C 0)
            (IP-SUB (NP-SBJ (PRO it))
                    (BEP be)
                    (NEG not))))
         (, ,)
 (ID BUTLER-1726,271.326))
```

The next condition of the algorithm, '(HV* iPrecedes [.,]) OR ((HV* iPrecedes NEG) AND (NEG iPrecedes [.,]))', was included to retrieve examples of PAE where auxiliary *have* (with either positive or negative polarity) immediately preceding any punctuation mark licenses the occurrence of ellipsis. This is another syntactic context where instances of PAE tend to occur that was not always coded in the corpus. As mentioned earlier, it should be highlighted that most occurrences of PAE licensed by auxiliary *have* where what has undergone ellipsis is verbal material were coded, though see (90) below for illustration of one of the exceptions. However, those examples where auxiliary *have* licenses the ellipsis of non-verbal material, as in (91), were never annotated in the corpus.

(90) but in a little time I hope to do all you would *have*. JOHNSON 1775,2,9.177

```
                              (IP-SUB (NP-OB1 *T*-1)
                                      (NP-SBJ (PRO you))
                                      (MD would)
                                      (HV have)))))
         (. .))
 (ID JOHNSON-1775,2,9.177))
```

(91) Bare. Indeed, Mrs. Liddy, I have a very great Opinion of you; and to let you see I *have*, will entrust you with a Secret, DAVYS-1716,32.269

```
((IP-MAT (CONJ and)
         (IP-INF-PRP (TO to)
            (VB let)
            (IP-INF (NP-SBJ (PRO you))
                    (VB see)
                    (CP-THT (C 0)
```

           (IP-SUB (NP-SBJ (PRO I))
                   (HVP have)))))
      (, ,)
(ID DAVYS-1716,32.269))

The final condition concerning auxiliary *have* '((HV* iPrecedes NP-SBJ) AND (NP-SBJ iPrecedes [?]))' constituted an ad-hoc solution to retrieve examples like (92), which had been found in the manual analysis of the corpus but could not be found automatically. This condition makes the software look for examples where auxiliary *have* immediately precedes a subject which is an NP and this NP, in turn, immediately precedes a question mark.

   (92) I had much rather you would go. Sir Simon. *Had you?*
        (COLMAN-1805,46.884)

   (IP-SUB (HVD Had)
           (NP-SBJ (PRO you)))
      (. ?))
(ID COLMAN-1805,46.884))

The manual analysis of the texts also revealed that there were cases where auxiliary *do* in imperative clauses was not coded in the corpus as a licensor of PAE. Therefore, the next two conditions of the algorithm constitute again two ad-hoc solutions. First, '((DO* iPrecedes NEG) AND (NEG iPrecedes NP-SBJ) AND (NP-SBJ iPrecedes [.,?]))' looks for examples where auxiliary *do* immediately precedes a negator. This negator, in turn, immediately precedes a subject which is an NP and is immediately followed by any punctuation mark, as exemplified in (93). Second, the condition '(DOI iPrecedes [.,])' retrieves examples where auxiliary *do* is imperative and immediately follows any punctuation mark, as in (94).

   (93) Bur. Don't take on so – *don't you*, now! COLMAN-1805,33.483

      (IP-IMP-PRN **(DOI $do)**
              (NEG $n't)
              (CODE {TEXT:don't})
              (NP-SBJ (PRO you)))
      (, ,)
      (ADVP-TMP (ADV now))
      (. !))
(ID COLMAN-1805,33.483))

(94) Make haste after me, *do*, now! COLMAN-1805,36.601

((IP-IMP **(DOI do)**
    (, ,)
    (ADVP-TMP (ADV now))
    (. !))
(ID COLMAN-1805,36.601))

Finally, the query '(CP* hasLabel CP-QUE-TAG*)' was used to look for cases of CPs whose label was 'CP-QUE-TAG', that is, cases of tag questions where PAE necessarily occurs, thus getting rid of redundant material. Here is an example of a tag question found by the algorithm:

(95) We have nothing to consult about, *have we, William?*
    BROUGHAM-1861,10.345

(CP-QUE-TAG (IP-SUB (HVP have)
                 (NP-SBJ (PRO we))))
(, ,)
(NP-VOC (NPR William))
(. ?))
(ID BROUGHAM-1861,10.345))

The examples which had been found manually were later compared with an automatic search of the parsed files by means of CorpusSearch 2 which relied on the algorithm just explained. The evaluation of the efficiency of the algorithm was calculated taking into account its recall, precision and the F1-measure, defined as follows:

$$\text{Recall} = \frac{\text{No}(\text{correct ellipses found})}{\text{No}(\text{all ellipses in test} = \text{all ellipses found manually})}$$

$$\text{Precision} = \frac{\text{No}(\text{correct ellipses found})}{\text{No}(\text{of answers given by the algorithm})}$$

$$\text{F1} = \frac{2 \times \text{Precision} \times \text{Recall}}{\text{Precision} + \text{Recall}}$$

As is well known, recall is calculated by dividing the number of relevant examples retrieved automatically by the gold standard (the number of examples found manually). That is, it provides us with the measure of how much coverage the algorithm has, namely, the number of correct examples of PAE obtained automatically with respect to the ones found manually. Precision, in turn, is calculated by dividing the number of relevant examples of PAE found by the number of attempts, providing a measure of the accuracy of the algorithm. Finally, the F1-measure allows one to combine recall and precision at a 1/1 ratio, giving 'the harmonic mean of these two' (Nielsen 2005: 60). The recall of this initial algorithm was 0.89 (140/156=0.89), whereas its precision was 0.55 (140/251=0.55) and the F1=0.67. However, since some examples of ellipsis like 'Since the Law was given by Moses, Grace and Truth was ~~given~~ by Jesus Christ' could not be retrieved by this algorithm, a new condition was included to retrieve cases of *be* (with either positive or negative polarity) followed by PPs and AdPs:

>OR (BE* iPrecedes PP|ADVP)
>OR ((BE* iPrecedes NEG)
>AND (NEG iPrecedes PP|ADVP))

Here is one of the examples retrieved by this new condition:

>(96) for their propensity to vice is really as much a disease of the mind, as any of the ordinary human distempers *is ~~a disease~~ of the body.*
>BOETHRI-1785,161.361

```
    (PP-1 (P as)
(CP-CMP-SPE (WNP-2 0)
        (C 0)
        (IP-SUB-SPE (NP-MSR *T*-2)
            (NP-SBJ (Q any)
                (PP (P of)
                    (NP (D the)
                        (ADJP (ADJ ordinary) (ADJ human))
                        (NS distempers))))
            (BEP is)
            (PP (P of)
                (NP (D the) (N body))))))
    (. .))
(ID BOETHRI-1785,161.361))
```

Successfully, the improved algorithm achieved a recall of 0.97 (152/156=0.97), a precision of 0.23 (152/640=0.23) and an F1=0.37. It is important to note here that whereas the overgeneration of examples leads to precision mistakes (i.e. generating 'noise' in the data), undergeneration leads to recall mistakes (since the more restrictive an algorithm, the fewer relevant examples will be retrieved). However, moderate overgeneration is not crucial for the present study, as I have manually filtered all the examples of PAE retrieved automatically. It should also be noted that precision was also lowered due to some wrong analyses in the parsed files. Here is an example that was wrongly parsed as an instance of PAE in the PPCMBE:

(97) I did not mean to reproach you, nor meant anything but respect and impatience to know how you *did*. JOHNSON-1775,2,27.511

>   (IP-INF (TO to)
>   (VB know)
>   (CP-QUE (WADVP-1 (WADV how))
>   (C 0)
>   (IP-SUB (ADVP *T*-1)
>   (NP-SBJ (PRO you))
>   **(DOD did)**
>   **(VB *))))))))**

(..))
(ID JOHNSON-1775,2,27.511))

There was yet another issue that arose with regard to how examples of PAE had been coded in the PPCMBE, since inconsistencies in the annotation were found. Whereas some examples of PAE after a modal auxiliary had already been annotated by adding the tag *VB **, others had not. Below I include two examples from the very same file that illustrate this fact:

(98) *I said all I could* to lessen your merit. AUSTEN-180X,171.240

((IP-MAT (NP-SBJ (PRO I))
       (VBD said)
       (NP-OB1 (Q all)
             (CP-REL (WNP-1 0)
                   (C 0)
                   (IP-SUB (NP-OB1 *T*-1)
                         (NP-SBJ (PRO I))
                         (MD could)))
(ID AUSTEN-180X,160.14))

Compare the annotation of the previous example with the one below:

(99) and have endeavoured to give something like the truth with as little
incivility as I could, AUSTEN-180X,171.240

((IP-MAT (CONJ and)
        (NP-SBJ *con*)
        (HVP have)
        (VBN endeavoured)
        (IP-INF (TO to)
            (VB give)
            (NP-OB1 (Q+N something)
                (ADJP (ADJ like)
                    (NP (D the) (N truth))))
            (PP (P with)
              (NP (QP (ADVR as) (Q little))
                (N incivility)
                (PP (P as)
                  (CP-CMP (WNP-1 0)
                    (C 0)
                    (IP-SUB (NP-MSR *T*-1)
                        (NP-SBJ (PRO I))
                        (MD could)
                        (VB *))))))
        (, ,)
(ID AUSTEN-180X,171.240))

Finally, there were also some cases in which the speech had been interrupted and the programme interpreted the sentence as involving ellipsis after a modal auxiliary:

(100) No, *I'll* – Yes, I'll read, first, and walk, afterwards.
      COLMAN-1805,47.905

((IP-MAT (, -)
    (INTJ No)
    (, ,)
    (NP-SBJ **(PRO $I))**
    (MD $'ll)
    (CODE {TEXT:I'll})
    (BREAK 0)
    (. -))
(ID COLMAN-1805,47.905))

2.2.4 The database and the variables

The examples of PAE obtained after the manual and the automatic analyses were stored in a database and sorted by (i) genre, (ii) period and a number of co-textual and structural variables like the (iii) type of anaphora – anaphoric, cataphoric, exophoric, (iv) mismatches in polarity, aspect, voice, modality and tense between the antecedent and the ellipsis site, (v) antecedent and ellipsis clause types – declarative, interrogative, imperative, (vi) lexical and syntactic distance between the antecedent and the ellipsis site, (vii) the type of focus of the ellipsis site – auxiliary choice, subject choice, both auxiliary and subject choice, object choice and so on. Figure 1 shows a screenshot of the layout of the database:

i. ID

As can be observed, examples are stored by means of an ID number which is provided in the PPCMBE, in this case 'ANON-1711,11.105'. This ID contains information about the file where the example of PAE was found, such as its author (in this case it is an anonymous text) and the year when it was published (1711).

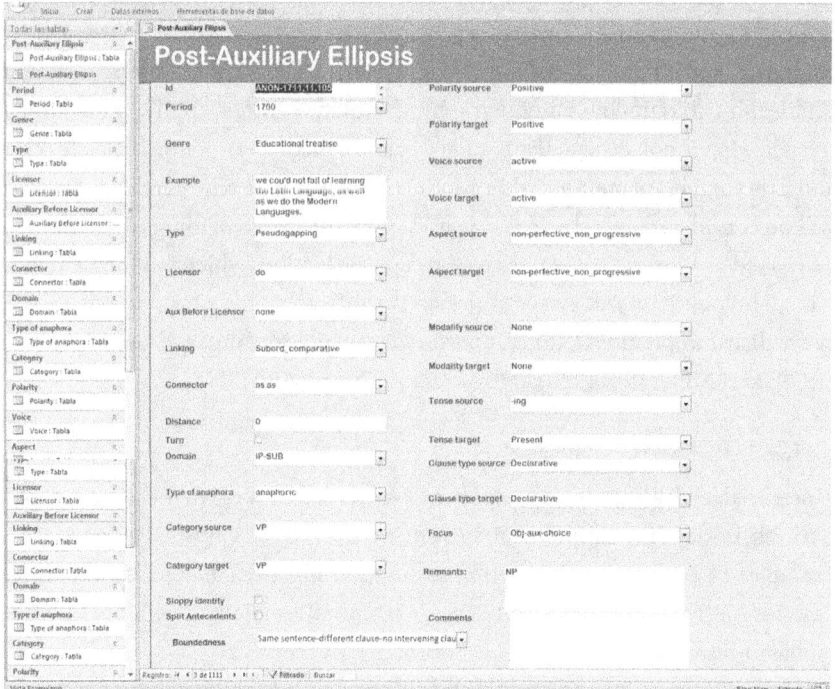

Figure 1 PAE database layout.

ii. Period
Examples of PAE have been classified according to the period in which they were attested. The period under study in this volume is Late Modern English, which ranges from 1700 to 1914. Thus, examples were sorted arbitrarily as belonging to the following five periods: 1700–50, 1751–1800, 1801–50, 1851–82 and 1883–1914. This variable will provide us with information regarding any possible variations in the patterns of PAE in Modern English. With the exception of the studies by Warner (1993, 1997) and Gergel (2009), previous empirical research on ellipsis (see Section 1.2) has focused on Present-Day English. As already mentioned, this monograph provides new data on PAE in Modern English, first, in order to carry out an analysis of this strategy in a significantly large parsed corpus which is annotated also for ellipsis, and, second, in an attempt to determine whether our data can be taken as evidence of diachronic variation between Modern and Present-Day English.

iii. Genre
This variable seeks to provide the genre distribution of PAE examples with respect to the eighteen genres represented in the PPCMBE: Diary, Drama comedy, Non-private letters, Private letters, Trial proceedings, Sermon, Philosophy, Biography autobiography, Biography other, Bible, Educational treatise, Handbook other, History, Law, Science medicine, Fiction, Science other and Travelogue. As mentioned in Section 2.2.2, the first nine genres mentioned will be considered speech-related genres, whereas the remaining nine ones will be treated as writing-related genres (except for Fiction, which will be treated as a mixed type). I am not aware of previous studies that have tried to analyse the genre distribution of PAE for this period of the English language (see Biber et al. (1999) and Miller (2011, 2014) for Present-Day English).

iv. Type
This variable classifies the examples of PAE as either VPE or PG. See Chapter 3 for an in-depth description of each of these types of ellipsis. Here are some examples of VPE and PG, where a distinction has been made between those cases of VPE and PG in which licensors *have* and *be* allow the ellipsis of either verbal or non-verbal material:

    (101) I shall send the parcel as soon as I *can*. JOHNSON-1775,2,5.109
             [VPE, verbal material elided after licensor *can*]

(102) the interest felt in its concerns should be diminished; and in this sense it *is*, WELLESLEY-1815,846.251 [VPE, verbal material elided after licensor *be*]

(103) They were very civil to me, as they always *are*; AUSTEN-180X,160.17 [VPE, non-verbal material elided after licensor *be*]

(104) Have we not agreed, added she, that the good are happy, and the wicked miserable? — We *have*. BOETHRI-1785,155.300 [VPE, verbal material elided after licensor *have*]

(105) Bare. Indeed, Mrs. Liddy, I have a very great Opinion of you; and to let you see I *have*, will entrust you with a Secret, DAVYS-1716,32.269 [VPE, non-verbal material elided after licensor *have*]

(106) they cou'd not fail of Learning it, as well as they *do* English. ANON-1711,5.28 [PG, verbal material elided after licensor *do*]

(107) whereas pity is more justly due to the oppressors; who ought therefore to be conducted to judgment, as the sick *are* to the physicians. BOETHRI-1785,161.351 [PG, verbal material elided after licensor *be*]

(108) their propensity to vice is really as much a disease of the mind, as any of the ordinary human distempers *is* of the body. BOETHRI-1785,161.361 [PG, non-verbal material elided after licensor *be*]

(109) Lou. Were I sure you would follow, as I would *have* you, DAVYS-1716,35.369 [PG, verbal material elided after licensor *have*]

(110) He has no more notion, my dear Tom, of a modern 'good match', than Eve *had* of pin-money. COLMAN-1805,23.154 [PG, non-verbal material elided after licensor *have*]

The novelty of this study is that it analyses the frequency, properties and distribution per genres of these ellipsis types in Late Modern English.

v. Licensor

As mentioned earlier, licensors are those elements that allow ellipsis. In this case, the licensors of PAE are modal auxiliaries, auxiliaries *be*, *have* and *do* and infinitival marker *to*. The original form of the licensors as they appear in the corpus has been stored, for example, *is*, *are*, *ain't*, *durst* or *shouldest*. Here are some examples (in italics):

(111) Cool and undaunted courage to resist oppression, is the character of this nation; but wanton cruelty *is not*. WOLLASTON-1793,21.161

(112) Phipps: I don't observe an alternation in your lordship's appearance. Lord Goring: You *don't*, Phipps? WILDE-1895,73.939

(113) he stood as near the Shore as he *durst* with the Ship, DEFOE-1719,207.238

(114) you would have awakened them as you *have* me. FIELDING-1749,3,10.382

(115) all nut-bearing trees may be safely grafted upon each other, as *may* also the plum-bearing trees. GRAFTING-1780,25.215

(116) – yes, and a wery good place it is to live in, *ain't* it? DICKENS-1837,545.23

(117) Because thou hast hearkened to what thy Wife said, and eat of the Tree which I commanded thee that thou *shouldest not*. PURVER-OLD-1764,3,1G.120

As mentioned in Section 2.2.1.3, in Present-Day English PG is not licensed by infinitival marker *to*, as opposed to what happens in cases of VPE. As Miller (2014) puts forward, no instances of PG licensed by *to* have been found in corpora. With the exception of Bos and Spenader (2011) and Miller (2014), there are no corpus studies which have paid attention to the licensors of PAE and it would be interesting to check which licensors of PAE were possible in Modern English, their frequency and their distribution per ellipsis types.

vi. Auxiliary(ies) before licensor

In Section 2.2.1.3 it was mentioned that whereas VPE in Present-Day English can be licensed by more than one auxiliary, PG as a general rule cannot (see Levin 1986, Hoeksema 2006 and Miller 2014). This is illustrated in examples (118) and (119) respectively, repeated here for convenience:

(118) I saw it and obviously so did Arnold, but nobody else *could have*. [BNC]

(119) Speaker A: Cream rinse makes my hair get dirty faster. Speaker B: ??It *may have* ø mine ø once, too.

As already mentioned in Section 2.2.1.3, Levin (1986) reports only one case of PG where there are two auxiliaries involved:

(120) I processed everybody's check last week, but I *must not've* ø yours.

This variable, therefore, was included in order to check whether the same principle holds for an earlier period of the language.

vii. Syntactic linking

This variable seeks to find out what kind of syntactic relation holds between the antecedent clause(s) and the clause which contains the ellipsis site. These are the categories used to classify the examples: none, coordination and subordination. Figure 2 represents the types of syntactic linking under study.

In those cases where no syntactic relation is established, the antecedent and the ellipsis site appear in different sentences, as in tag questions, CP-questions or sentences delimited by punctuation boundaries (see (121) to (123) respectively). On the other hand, in cases of coordination, clauses are joined thanks to the conjunctions *and, or, but* (see (124) below). Finally, I have included the following cases of subordination: comparative (including equatives and *as*-appositives, as in (125) and (126)), relative (free, bound (including cases of antecedent-contained deletion), see (127)) and adverbial (temporal, concessive, cause, manner, conditional and so forth, see (128)).

(121) I can recollect nothing more to say. When my letter is gone, I suppose I shall. AUSTEN-180X,175.335 [none]

(122) One wouldn't say so from the sort of hats they wear, would one? WILDE-1895,64.673 [none, tag question]

(123) Phipps: I don't observe an alternation in your lordship's appearance. Lord Goring: You don't, Phipps? WILDE-1895,73.939 [none, CP question]

(124) That I had received such from Edward also I need not mention; *but* I do, AUSTEN-180X,187.622 [coordination]

(125) If therefore we did but hear others talk Latin, and endeavour'd to understand them, and talk with them, *as* much *as* we do to understand and talk with those who speak in the Modern Tongues. ANON-1711,11.105 [comparative subordination].

(126) It were ridiculous to assert, that a Man upon Reflection hath the same Kind of Approbation of the Appetite of Hunger, or the

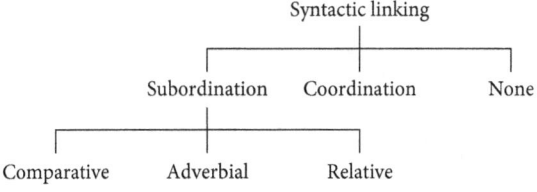

Figure 2 Syntactic linking.

Passion of Fear, *as* he hath of Good-will to his Fellow-creatures. BUTLER-1726,262.245 [comparative subordination, known as as-*appositives* in Hardt and Rambow (2001) and Nielsen (2005)].

(127) did you see the Lenox make all the Sail she could to get up with them, while Day-light lasted? AUSTEN-180X,171.240 [antecedent-contained deletion, where 'the target clause is embedded in the source clause, by virtue of a relative clause' (Bos and Spenader 2011: 469). Notice that the target clause is *she could*, which is part of the VP in the source clause. The deleted material is not a VP but only the transitive verb *make*].

(128) They can by no means, therefore, be members of happiness; for *if* they were, happiness might be said to be made up of one member, BOETHRI-1785,116.162 [adverbial subordination]

The type of syntactic linking that holds between the antecedent(s) of ellipsis and the target of ellipsis has been studied by Hardt and Rambow (2001), Nielsen (2005) and Bos and Spenader (2011) for Present-Day English. Here I extend these works by analysing the type of linking in PAE constructions in Late Modern English.

viii. Boundedness

The type of syntactic linking established between the source and the target of ellipsis can also be classified with respect to the type of boundedness exhibited, that is, according to whether the antecedent and the ellipsis site take place in different sentences or within the same sentence with the ellipsis site in a different clause. Figure 2 on syntactic linking has been completed by adding the information related to boundedness (see Figure 3).

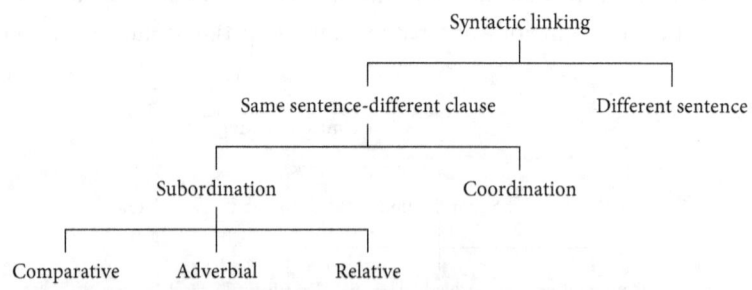

Figure 3 Syntactic linking and boundedness.

Simplifying, the clause is taken here as the maximal projection comprising a verb group and its arguments and satellites, while the sentence is understood as a unit showing suprasegmental independence. The data will be sorted following a three-way distinction: same sentence-different clause with no intervening clauses in between the source and the target of ellipsis; same sentence-different clause with one or more intervening clauses between the antecedent and the ellipsis site; and different sentence, where the source and the target of ellipsis appear in different sentences (there is no syntactic relation established between them). This information will be of particular importance for the section on distance and turn. This is so because, on the one hand, it will help us to check the syntactic complexity evinced by examples of PAE and its interaction with lexical distance (the distance existing between the antecedent and the ellipsis site in number of words, see Section *xi* for more details) and, on the other hand, it will allow us to calculate the frequency of changes of turn, as these are only possible when the antecedent and the ellipsis site occur in different sentences (see Section *xii* for further information).

ix. Connector
Related to the variable on syntactic linking, the purpose is to classify the different connectors that serve as links between the antecedent clause(s) and the clause that has been the target of ellipsis. For example, *and, or, nor, but* (coordinating conjunctions), *as, than, as ... as, because, although, where, when* and *if* (subordinating conjunctions).

x. Distance in number of clauses (IPs)
This variable encodes sentential distance, that is, it measures distance between the antecedent clause(s) and the target of ellipsis, in number of clauses (coded with the label *IP* in the corpus). To such an end, the parsing of the PPCMBE has been used. This measure will provide us with an insight into the degree of syntactic complexity of the material between the antecedent clause(s) and the elliptical clause. As in Hardt and Rambow's (2001) and Nielsen's (2005) studies, a value of 0 means that the VPs are in the same sentence. Here are some examples, where values 0, 1 and 2 have been assigned to distance in number of IPs between the antecedent clause(s) and the target of ellipsis respectively (intervening clauses have been underlined):

(129) *He has got as far as he can*, WILDE-1895,62.628

((IP-MAT (NP-SBJ (PRO He))
    (HVP has)
    (VBN got)
    (NP-MSR (ADJP (ADVR as) (ADJ far))
        (PP (P as)
            (CP-CMP (WNP-1 0)
                (C 0)
                (IP-SUB (NP-MSR *T*-1)
                    (NP-SBJ (PRO he))
                    (MD can)))))
    (.,))
(ID WILDE-1895,62.628))

(130) a change of key could affect people as <u>they said</u> it did. BENSON-190X,123.586

        (IP-SUB (NP-SBJ (D a)
                (N change)
                (PP (P of)
                    (NP (N key))))
        (MD could)
        (VB affect)
        (NP-OB1 (NS people))
        (PP (P as)
          (CP-ADV (WADVP-1 0)
             (C 0)
             (IP-SUB (NP-SBJ (PRO they))
                (VBD said)
                (CP-THT (C 0)
                    (IP-SUB (ADVP *T*-1)
                      (NP-SBJ (PRO it))
                      (DOD did)
                      (VB *))))))))
    (..))
(ID BENSON-190X,123.586))

(131) *It follows*, then, that <u>we must admit that renown is not different from the other three</u>. '*It does*,' said I. BOETHJA-1897,96.30

```
((IP-MAT-SPE (' '
         (NP-SBJ-1 (PRO It))
         (VBP follows)
         (, ,)
         (ADVP (ADV then))
         (, ,)
         (CP-THT-SPE-1 (C that)
              (IP-SUB-SPE (NP-SBJ (PRO we))
                   (MD must)
                   (VB admit)
                   (CP-THT-SPE (C that)
                        (IP-SUB-SPE (NP-SBJ (N renown))
                             (BEP is)
                             (NEG not)
                             (ADJP (ADJ different)
                                  (PP (P from)
                                       (NP (D the) (OTHER other) (NUM three))))))))
         (' ')
         (. .))
(ID BOETHJA-1897,96.29))

((IP-MAT (' '
(IP-MAT-SPE (NP-SBJ (PRO It))
         (DOP does)
         (VB *))
         (' ')
         (, ,)
         (VBD said)
         (NP-SBJ (PRO I))
         (. .))
(ID BOETHJA-1897,96.30))
```

A word of caution is in order here. In example (131), two instances of IPs are said to occur:

```
((IP-MAT (' '
(IP-MAT-SPE (NP-SBJ (PRO It))
```

In these cases, only one IP will be counted, not two.

xi. Distance in number of words
This variable aims at measuring distance between the antecedent clause(s) and the ellipsis site, in words (in the same vein as in Hardt and Rambow 2001 and Nielsen 2005). This measure will balance the previous measure of syntactic distance, since there can be cases where clauses are very long and therefore the antecedent clause(s) and the ellipsis site are far away in number of words but with no intervening IPs (as in (132)). The reverse is also true: there are cases where the antecedent clause(s) and the target of ellipsis are very close in number of words but separated by several IPs (see (133)):

(132) it cannot be *very material*, as far as regards mental discipline, whether *it is by inflexion or by auxiliaries*. BAIN-1878,371.189

Here there are no intervening IPs between the antecedent clause (*it cannot be very material*) and the ellipsis site (*it is by inflexion or by auxiliaries*), but there are nine words of distance between the two. Compare this example with (133), where the same amount of words intervenes between the antecedent clause and the elliptical sentence but in this case there are two IPs in between:

(133) *I can recollect nothing more to say.* When my letter is gone, I suppose I *shall*. AUSTEN-180X,175.335

xii. Turn
This variable describes whether the antecedent clause and the ellipsis site have taken place within the same turn or not, that is, whether there is a change of speaker. As is well known, VPE is an instance of PAE that can apply across sentence boundaries. The distribution of PG, however, is more constrained in this sense. Therefore, this variable will try to provide us with the frequency with which examples of PAE appear in a different turn with respect to their antecedent clause(s). Here are some examples that illustrate ellipsis within the same turn (134) and in a different turn (135):

(134) Latin may be learn'd after this Method. And since it *may*, ANON-1711,15.152 I wonder much that this Method shou'd not be preferr'd.
(135) Herb. (R.) Nonsense, my love, I wouldn't insult him by mentioning such a thing.
Mrs. C. *Wouldn't you?* BROUGHAM-1861,21.758

In the description of the variables syntactic linking and boundedness it was mentioned that the antecedent and the ellipsis site could appear in different sentences, that is, in contexts where no syntactic relation is established between them. It is precisely in this type of syntactic context that changes of speaker apply. In other words, a change of turn is only applicable in contexts where the source and the target of ellipsis belong to different sentences. In Figure 4 you will find an illustration of syntactic linking and boundedness and their relevance for the type of turn exhibited by the examples of PAE.

In addition, it should be noted that although tag questions are constructions of their own which have specific characteristics (see variable *xxxi*), for the sake of classification they have been treated as constructions where the antecedent and the ellipsis site are said to belong to different sentences and occur within the same turn, as illustrated in (136):

(136) That is a great comfort, *is it not?* WILDE-1895,66.726

In CP-questions, on the other hand, the antecedent and the ellipsis site also appear in different sentences but can occur either within the same turn or in another turn, as shown in (137) and (138), respectively:

(137) and felt it was my duty to counteract it. *Did I?* BROUGHAM-1861,20.734
(138) Phipps: I don't observe an alternation in your lordship's appearance. Lord Goring: *You don't*, Phipps? WILDE-1895,73.939

xiii. Domain
This variable pays attention to the syntactic domain where the ellipsis site takes place, as analysed in the PPCMBE. Taking into account the annotation of this

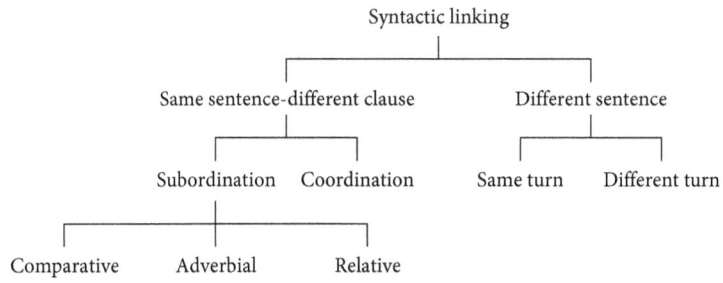

Figure 4 Syntactic linking and boundedness and their relevance for type of turn.

corpus, five possible syntactic contexts have been found in the examples of PAE from this period: IP-MAT (matrix clause) (139), IP-SUB (subordinate clause) (140), IP-IMP (imperative clause) (141), CP-QUE-TAG (tag questions) (142), and CP-questions (143). Here are some examples of each of these syntactic domains:

(139) and I tried to thank him, *but could not*; BENSON-190X,115.325

((IP-MAT (CONJ and)
    (NP-SBJ (PRO I))
    (VBD tried)
    (IP-INF (TO to)
        (VB thank)
        (NP-OB2 (PRO him)))
    (. ,))
(ID BENSON-190X,115.324))

((IP-MAT (CONJ but)
    (NP-SBJ *con*)
    (MD could)
    (NEG not)
    (. ;))
(ID BENSON-190X,115.325))

(140) Fortunately I don't know what bimetallism means. And I don't believe *anybody else does either*. WILDE-1895,57.485

((IP-MAT (CONJ And)
    (NP-SBJ (PRO I))
    (DOP $do)
    (NEG $n't)
    (CODE {TEXT:don't})
    (VB believe)
    (CP-THT (C 0)
        (IP-SUB (NP-SBJ (Q+N anybody) (ELSE else))
        (DOP does)
        (VB *)
        (CONJ either)))
    (. .))
(ID WILDE-1895,57.485))

(141) Bur. Don't take on so – *don't you, now!* COLMAN-1805,33.483

    (IP-IMP-PRN (DOI $do)
        (NEG $n't)
        (CODE {TEXT:don't})
        (NP-SBJ (PRO you)))
    (, ,)
    (ADVP-TMP (ADV now))
    (. !))
(ID COLMAN-1805,33.483))

(142) We shall not be at Worthing so soon as we have been used to talk of, *shall we?* (AUSTEN-180X,169.204)

((IP-MAT (NP-SBJ (PRO We))
    (MD shall)
    (NEG not)
    (BE be)
    (PP (P at)
      (NP (NPR Worthing)))
    (ADVP-TMP (ADVP (ADVR so))
     (ADV soon)
    (PP (P as)
       (CP-CMP (WADVP-1 0)
          (C 0)
          (IP-SUB (ADVP-TMP *T*-1)
            (NP-SBJ (PRO we))
            (HVP have)
            (BEN been)
            (ADJP (VAN used)
              (IP-INF (TO to)
                (VB talk)
                (PP (P of)
                  (NP *))))))))
    (, ,)
    (CP-QUE-TAG (IP-SUB (MD shall)
      (NP-SBJ (PRO we))))
    (. ?))
(ID AUSTEN-180X,169.204))

(143) and felt it was my duty to counteract it. *Did I?*
     BROUGHAM-1861,20.734

((IP-MAT (CONJ and)
    (NP-SBJ *con*)
    (VBD felt)
    (CP-THT (C 0)
        (IP-SUB (NP-SBJ-1 (PRO it))
            (BED was)
            (NP-OB1 (PRO$ my) (N duty))
            (IP-INF-1 (TO to)
                (VB counteract)
                (NP-OB1 (PRO it)))))
    (. .))
(ID BROUGHAM-1861,20.733))

((CP-QUE (IP-SUB (DOD Did)
    (NP-SBJ (PRO I))
    (VB *))
(. ?))
(ID BROUGHAM-1861,20.734))

xiv. Type of anaphora

As mentioned in Section 1.2, there can be three types of 'phoric' or referential relations between ellipses and their antecedents: anaphoric, cataphoric or exophoric. Anaphoric ellipses are those in which the ellipsis site appears after an earlier antecedent (see (144)). On the other hand, cataphoric ellipses are those in which the ellipsis site occurs before its antecedent (as in (145)). Both anaphoric and cataphoric ellipses are known as endophoric anaphora, since they refer to a linguistic antecedent. Exophoric ellipses, in turn, have no linguistic antecedent available (Miller and Pullum 2014) and have been excluded from this piece of research, which focuses on cases of endophoric ellipsis exclusively.

(144) Popery we see has *arisen* just as it was foretold it *would* arise.
     WOLLASTON-1793,12.78

(145) For if as many as *cou'd* meet conveniently shou'd *meet* together every Night. ANON-1711,16.161

As pointed out in Section 2.2.1.3, it seems to be the case that the distribution of the types of anaphora is not the same in VPE and PG since cataphoric examples are possible in VPE (146), but not in PG (147) (Hardt 1993: 18):

(146) Although I don't know if Tom *does* ~~write magazines~~, I know Harry writes magazines.
(147) *Although I don't know if Tom *does* ~~write~~ books, I know Harry writes magazines.

This difference in the distribution of the types of anaphora with regard to both VPE and PG has not been systematically studied in corpora, though see Bos and Spenader (2011) and Miller (2014) for corpus studies on Present-Day English. This study extends these previous works by analysing this aspect in Modern English.

xv. Category of the source of the ellipsis
This variable checks the category of the element(s) of the antecedent clause(s) that serves as antecedent(s) for the elided clause. The following are the possible values assigned to this variable: antecedents may be APs, NPs, PPs, AdPs, VPs or non-constituents.

(148) as if she were *grateful for it*! I verily believe she *is* ~~*grateful for it*~~! YONGE-1865,169.272 [antecedent: AP; ellipsis site: AP]
(149) schoolmasters should be *celibates*, or rather that housemasters should be ~~*celibates*~~, BENSON-1908,79.372 [antecedent: NP; ellipsis site: NP]
(150) Herb. Pshaw, that's *of no consequence*. Dr. S. Oh, I thought it was ~~*of consequence*~~; BROUGHAM-1861,13.445 [antecedent: PP; ellipsis site: PP]
(151) he's *here*, isn't he ~~*here*~~? BROUGHAM-1861,20.713 [antecedent: AdP; ellipsis site: AdP]
(152) I *think*, don't you ~~*think*~~? that there may be another attraction. (YONGE-1865,176.459) [antecedent: VP; ellipsis site: VP]
(153) I can *walk*, and I can *chew gum*. Gerry can ~~*walk and chew gum*~~ too, but not at the same time. [Webber (1978); in Hardt (1992a, 1993)] [antecedent: non-constituent; ellipsis site: VP]
(154) *This problem was to have been looked into*, but obviously nobody did ~~*look into this problem*~~. [Merchant (2008a: 169)] [antecedent: non-constituent; ellipsis site: VP]

As can be observed, in cases of split antecedents (153) (see *xvii* below for a description of this phenomenon) and passive–active voice mismatches (154) (see *xxi* for more details) the antecedent would be a string that does not shape a constituent, whereas what is elided would be a VP (an instance of coordinated VPs in the case of (153)). This has been investigated in Bos and Spenader (2011) and Miller and Hemforth (2014).

xvi. Category of the target of ellipsis
The same values as in *xv* have been assigned for the category of the target of the ellipsis site: APs, NPs, PPs, AdPs, VPs or non-constituents. Examples of the category of the elided element are already present in the previous examples (148) through (154).

xvii. Split antecedents
This phenomenon, also known as 'combined antecedents' in Hardt (1992a), refers to cases of VPE in which the antecedent is the result of the combination of two or more separate VPs. Here are some examples:

(155) Wendy is eager to *sail around the world* and Bruce is eager to *climb Kilimanjaro*, but neither of them can because money is too tight. [Webber 1978; in Hardt (1992a, 1993)]
(156) So I say to the conspiracy fans: *leave him alone. Leave us alone.* But they won't. [Hardt (1990: 227)]

Crucially, as Hardt (1993: 30) points out, 'a combination of the two VP's [sic] is required, the reading wouldn't be permitted by syntactically copying either of the preceding VP's to the ellipsis site'. The meaning of the ellipsis sites of these two examples would be 'they won't leave him alone or leave us alone' and 'neither of them can sail around the world or climb Kilimanjaro'.

xviii. Sloppy identity
As already mentioned in Chapter 1, when ellipsis is resolved a number of non-equivalences between the source clauses and their elliptical counterparts may emerge. Therefore, in these cases identity between the source and the target of ellipsis is not absolute. This phenomenon has been extensively studied in Fiengo and May (1994), who have coined this phenomenon 'vehicle change' (see also Ross 1969; Sag 1976; Williams 1977; Hardt 1993; Lasnik 1995; Murguia 2004). In this volume, the notion of sloppy identity is used in two ways (as in Murguia 2004): on the one hand, to refer to those cases where a pronoun (or other

variable) in the source clause is interpreted differently in the elliptical clause (see example (157), where both the strict and the sloppy readings are possible); on the other hand, to categorize those cases of partial syntactic identity where there are differences in the syntactic realization of certain elements, for instance, the alternation of *some/any*, *you/me*, *my/your* between the antecedent and the ellipsis site (see (158)–(160)):

(157) Max saw his mother, and Oscar did too.
 a. Max saw Max's mother, and Oscar saw Oscar's mother. [sloppy]
 b. Max saw Max's mother, and Oscar saw Max's mother. [strict]
 [Murguia (2004: 24)]
(158) Max didn't talk to *anyone*, but Oscar did ~~talk to someone~~. [Murguia (2004: 37)]
(159) Mabel Chiltern: I wish I had brought *you* up!. Lord Goring: I am so sorry you didn't ~~bring me up~~. WILDE-1895,55.425
(160) I know how to crane *my* neck, but you don't know how to ~~crane your neck~~. [Ross (1969: 250)]

Thus, four subtypes of sloppy identity have been distinguished: (i) a pronoun in the antecedent is interpreted differently in the ellipsis site, (ii) sloppy pronouns, (iii) sloppy polarity, and (iv) sloppy possessives, as instantiated in examples (161)–(164) from our corpus respectively:

(161) General Kruse$_i$, of the Nassau service, likewise conducted *himself*$_i$ much to my satisfaction; as did General Trip$_j$ ~~conduct himself$_j$ much to my satisfaction~~, commanding the heavy brigade of cavalry, WELLESLEY-1815,860.457
(162) Herbert, will you answer *me* one question ingenuously? Herb. Yes, uncle, if I can ~~answer you one question ingenuously~~. BROUGHAM-1861,15.544
(163) Q. Were there *any* police officers with the magistrates?
 A. There were ~~some police officers with the magistrates~~. WATSON-1817,1,166.2202
(164) Mr. Wetherell. Did you give *your* note to Mr. Hone's publication?
 A. No, indeed, I did not ~~give my note to Mr. Hone's publication~~. WATSON-1817,1,163.2112

Sloppy identity has only been studied empirically in Nielsen (2005) and Bos and Spenader (2011) for Present-Day English. I extend these studies by analysing examples of sloppy identity in Modern English.

xix. Polarity of the source of ellipsis
This variable aims at providing information about the polarity of the antecedent clause(s) of ellipsis. The possible values would be positive, negative and explicit polar alternative, illustrated in (165)–(167) respectively:

(165) I *will submit* to your pleasure as I would if you should sentence me to death. REEVE-1777,17.410
(166) Poets *ought not to be read* in the Method which they are, ANON-1711,22.225
(167) Q. *Were you or not desired* to attend there by any person. A. I was not: WATSON-1817,1,157.1990

As shown in example (167), the antecedent expresses both positive and negative polarity, where the speaker is asking his/her interlocutor to choose one of the possible options.

It should be noted that examples involving negative polarity items like *no*, *never* or *nothing*, as in (168)-(170), have been treated as examples of negative polarity:

(168) I could make *no* answer; but hope you do. CARLYLE-1835,2,300.673
(169) In a little I believe I shall be fully convinced that happiness is rather in a sedate than in a flashy life, and shall *never* think it necessary for the entertainment of company, as I now habitually do, BOSWELL-1776,46.353
(170) we have *nothing* to consult about, have we, William? BROUGHAM-1861,10.345

xx. Polarity of the target of ellipsis
This variable, in turn, focuses on determining the polarity of the ellipsis site. The same values for polarity as before have been assigned: positive (171), negative (172) and explicit polar alternative (173).

(171) Fortunately I don't know what bimetallism means. And I don't believe anybody else *does* either. WILDE-1895,57.485
(172) Welshmen and cattle could go where invaders *could not*. BRADLEY-1905,206.123
(173) Q. Did not the Strafford, soon after the Enemy were put to Flight, enter into Action again with the Spanis Vice-Admiral? A. I can n't say whether she *did or not*. HOLMES-TRIAL-1749,16.250

As in *xix*, the presence of negative polarity items is an indicator of negative polarity, as in (174)-(176):

(174) John. Indeed, sir, I can't tell. Shuff. *No* more can I. COLMAN-1805,20.44

(175) Formerly, they would have ask'd to who. Shuff. We *never* do, now; COLMAN-1805,23.145

(176) but he did not dare to receive me. *Nor* did any one else; WESLEY-174X,12.49

Importantly, it should also be noted that cases like (177) below, where formally the polarity of the example of ellipsis is positive but the meaning negative, have been treated as instances of negative polarity:

(177) Lady C. He does me honour. Sir G. Aside, laughing. The devil he *does*! COLLIER-1835,13.337

In (177) the meaning of the statement *the devil he does* is opposite to what is actually conveyed, that is, it contrasts in polarity with its antecedent even if its form is positive. Three similar examples have been attested in our corpus (and all belong to the same text).

xxi. Voice of the source of ellipsis
This variable determines whether the antecedent of the ellipsis site is either active, as in (178), or passive, as in (179):

(178) every man *had built* because he wished to ~~build~~. THRING-187X,225.271

(179) and therefore it *cannot be learn'd* by Conversation, as the Modern Languages are ~~learned~~; ANON-1711,12.125

xxii. Voice of the target of ellipsis
Just like in *xxi*, this variable checks whether the voice of the target of ellipsis is active or passive, as in (178) and (179) above respectively, where *build* in the active voice and *learned* in the passive voice have been elided, respectively. The importance of checking this variable lies in the fact that it has been assumed in the literature that while mismatches in voice between the antecedent and the ellipsis site are possible in VPE, this would not be true of cases of PG (see Merchant 2008a). This aspect of PAE constructions has been understudied

empirically before, and certainly it has not been studied at all in Late Modern English.

xxiii. Aspect of the source of ellipsis
This variable pays attention to the type of aspect of the antecedent of the ellipsis. These are the possible values for aspect: non-perfective-non-progressive (180), non-perfective-progressive (181), perfective-progressive (182) and perfective-non-progressive (183):

> (180) 'There's no place *I want to see* as much as Scotland' said Rachel. 'Oh, yes! Young ladies always do.' YONGE-1865,164.134
> (181) and he *was leaning* out of window as far as he could. DICKENS-1837,561.418
> (182) But, before the Decree for his Return, he *had not been wanting* to stir up the Grecians, as much as he could, to defend their Liberty. HIND-1707,317.219
> (183) But we *have proved* that one is the very same thing as good. 'We have.' BOETHJA-1897,114.249

xxiv. Aspect of the target of ellipsis
This variable seeks to determine the aspect of the target of ellipsis. The same values as in *xxiii* have been assigned to the targets of ellipsis, that is, non-perfective-non-progressive, non-perfective-progressive, perfective-non-progressive and perfective-progressive. The first three types of aspect have been attested in my corpus (184)-(186), but not the fourth one (perfective-progressive):

> (184) We shall not be at Worthing so soon as we have been used to talk of, *shall* we? AUSTEN-180X,169.204
> (185) Q. was the person speaking when you got to the field? A: I believe he *was not*. WATSON-1817,1,182.2646
> (186) tho' it was as thoroughly dress'd after being cut for Eastwell, as it *had been* for the Ashford Assembly. AUSTEN-180X,163.71

Aspect (of either the source of the ellipsis or the target of ellipsis) has not been taken into account in corpus-based studies on ellipsis.

xxv. Modality of the source of ellipsis
This variable determines the presence or absence of modal auxiliaries in the antecedent of ellipsis. All possible modal auxiliaries in English have been stored,

such as *can, will, may, shall, ought (to)*, and so on. It should be mentioned that I have grouped auxiliaries like *should, could, might* and *would* with *shall, can, may* and *will*, respectively, in order to avoid interference with the variable tense (see *xxvii* below for more details).

(187) Latin *may* be learn'd after this Method. And since it may, ANON-1711,15.152

(188) Even the delicate associations with words *can* be expounded through our own language; just as they must be to the pupil who is studying the original. BAIN-1878,366.96

(189) our Children *wou'd* talk Latin according to the Method I have mention'd, as well as their's did. ANON-1711,5.30

xxvi. Modality of the target of ellipsis
This variable determines the presence or absence of modal auxiliaries in the ellipsis site. The same values as in *xxv* apply. Here are some examples:

(190) Honour may arise from them; good *cannot*. SOUTHEY-1813,177.72

(191) One wouldn't say so from the sort of hats they wear, *would* one? WILDE-1895,64.673

(192) You will remember what I said to you, *won't* you? WILDE-1895,56.445

With the exception of Bos and Spenader (2011) no corpus studies have checked the frequency of modal auxiliaries in elliptical constructions, although its importance is highlighted in, for example, Miller and Pullum (2014), as they show a correlation between different types of focus in PAE constructions and the presence of mismatches in modality. See variable *xxxi* below for more details.

xxvii. Tense of the source of ellipsis
This variable describes the tense or lack thereof of the antecedent of ellipsis. These are the possible values: present, past (for tensed elements) and *–ing*, *–en*, *to* infinitive and plain form[19] (for untensed elements). Below all of these types are illustrated:

(193) she *fries* better than she did. [present]

(194) I *said* all I could to lessen your merit. AUSTEN-180X,171.240 [past]

(195) and *looking* at the very first group of people he sees there, with the same interest as Mr Pickwick did. DICKENS-1837,547.69 [*–ing*]

(196) and dip it in the spawn of Frogs, *beaten* as you would the whites of eggs, ALBIN-1736,4.75 [*-en*]

(197) and have endeavoured *to give* something like the truth with as little incivility as I could, AUSTEN-180X,171.240 [*to* infinitive]

(198) *Run away* from a good father, as you did. COLMAN-1805,41.743 [bare form]

As advanced in *xxv*, if the verb that serves as the antecedent is immediately preceded by a modal auxiliary, the only values that have been assigned have been present and past, as tense would be marked in the modal auxiliary in question. Here are some examples:

(199) We *shall* not be at Worthing so soon as we have been used to talk of, shall we? AUSTEN-180X,169.204 [present]

(200) we *shou'd* as easily and perfectly learn it as we do English. ANON-1711,8.70 [past]

xxviii. Tense of the target of ellipsis

In the case of the tense of the target of ellipsis, the only values that have been assigned are present, past and infinitival marker *to*, as it is the licensors of ellipsis (that is, the auxiliaries that license ellipsis) that have been judged with respect to tense. This is illustrated in the examples below:

(201) Q. Do you see there either of the persons whom you saw at Greystoke Place? A. No, I *do* not. WATSON-1817,1,114.919 [present]

(202) Q. Did Mr. Hunt come afterwards? A. Yes, he *did* afterwards. WATSON-1817,1,113.873 [past]

(203) Mr. Gurney. I wish the warders would just move their heads. Mr. Wetherell. If he can find them out himself he *may*, WATSON-1817,1,114.921 [present]

(204) Upon this Lord Aylesford was sent for to court and a list of justices was given him to put in. He pretended he *would*, but put in but seven. RYDER-1716,176.447 [past]

(205) He has not answered. I hope he will have the good sense not *to*. THRING-187X,218.59 [infinitival marker *to*]

No corpus studies have studied the role of tense in PAE constructions, so it constitutes a relevant contribution in this analysis.

xxix. Clause type of the source of ellipsis
This variable determines the type of clause of the antecedent clause(s), an issue which has not been addressed before in empirical studies. Three different types of clauses have been considered: declarative, interrogative and imperative. This will provide us with information about the frequency of the type of clause that serves as antecedent for ellipsis in PAE constructions. Here are some examples:

(206) this matter *does not depend on my brother's consent*, and even if it did, Ermine's own true position is that which is most honourable to her. YONGE-1865,178.507 [declarative]

(207) But dost not thou allow that all which is good is *good by participation in goodness*? 'It is.' BOETHJA-1897,111.197 [interrogative]

(208) Dr. S. *Cross over to the other*. Mrs. H. Alas I cannot! BROUGHAM-1861,29.1066 [imperative]

It is important to note that tag questions, which are constructions that contain a statement followed by a short question (normally marking a contrast in polarity), have not been considered under this variable. Put differently, I have not treated them as being composed of an antecedent which is declarative, followed by an ellipsis site which is interrogative; instead, they have been treated as constructions of their own.

xxx. Clause type of the target of ellipsis
The aim of this variable is to establish the type of clause of the target of ellipsis. The same values as in *xxix* have been used: elliptical clauses can be declarative, interrogative or imperative (also leaving tag questions aside), as instantiated in (209)-(211):

(209) I am afraid Lord Brancaster knew a good deal about that. *More than his poor wife ever did.* WILDE-1895,65.700 [declarative]

(210) for as there is no concord betwixt the virtuous and the wicked ; so neither can the vicious agree with one another. *And how should they?* BOETHRI-1785,176.447 [interrogative]

(211) Bur. Nay, consider what confusion! – pluck up a courage; *do*, now! COLMAN-1805,35.544 [imperative]

This variable will allow us to determine the frequency of the type of clause of the ellipsis site in PAE constructions.

xxxi. Focus of the target of ellipsis

This variable addresses certain discourse conditions on the use of PAE which have been tackled by Kehler (2000, 2002); Kertz (2010, 2013); Miller (2011, 2014); Miller and Pullum (2014); Miller and Hemforth (2014). Following Kertz (2008), Miller (2011) and Miller and Pullum (2014), I have distinguished two central uses of PAE: auxiliary choice and subject choice, and propose that the following conditions should be met (Miller and Pullum 2014: 12):

> Type 1: Auxiliary choice
>
> FORMAL CHARACTERISTICS: The subject of the antecedent is identical with the subject of the PAE construction and the auxiliary is (at least weakly) stressed, signaling a new choice of tense, aspect, modality, or (in the most overwhelmingly frequent case) polarity.
>
> DISCOURSE REQUIREMENT: A choice between the members of a jointly exhaustive set of alternative situations must be highly salient in the discourse context, and the point of the utterance containing the PAE is strictly limited to selecting one member of that set.
>
> Type 2: Subject choice
> FORMAL CHARACTERISTICS: The subject of the antecedent is distinct from the subject of the PAE construction, and stressed if it is a pronoun.
>
> DISCOURSE REQUIREMENT: A particular property must be highly salient in the discourse context, and the point of the utterance containing the PAE must be strictly limited to identifying something or someone possessing that property.

These two different types of focus are exemplified below in (212) and (213), respectively:

(212) Q. Did you see the Boat come from the Cornwal? A. I *did not*.
    HOLMES-TRIAL-1749,48.824 [auxiliary choice]

(213) and yet no Man for many Years has Writ finer Latin than *he* did.
    ANON-1711,14.146 [subject choice]

There can also be cases where focus can express both subject and auxiliary choice, as in (214) below:

(214) that it cannot be so quickly learn'd as the *Modern Tongues are*.
    ANON-1711,12.126 [subject-auxiliary choice]

In sum, these would be all the values for focus assigned to cases of VPE: auxiliary choice, subject choice and subject-auxiliary choice.

With regard to cases of PG, Miller (2014: 78) argues that noncomparative PG constructions also seem to follow certain discourse conditions which are described below:

> Type 1: Object choice
>
> FORMAL CHARACTERISTICS: The subject of the antecedent is identical to that of the PG construction but the object is distinct, and stressed if it is a pronoun.
>
> DISCOURSE REQUIREMENT: Both the referent of the remnant and a particular open proposition $p(x)$ must be highly salient in the discourse context, and the point of the utterance containing the PG must be limited to identifying something or someone satisfying $p(x)$ and such that it forms a contrastive focus with the referent of the correspondent of the remnant in the antecedent.
>
> Type 2: Subject and object choice
>
> FORMAL CHARACTERISTICS: The subject and object of the antecedent are distinct from those of the PG construction and both are stressed if they are pronouns.
>
> DISCOURSE REQUIREMENT: Both the referents of the remnant and subject and a particular doubly open proposition $p(x,y)$ must be highly salient in the discourse context, and the point of the utterance containing the PG must be limited to identifying a pair satisfying $p(x,y)$ and such that they form a pair of contrastive foci with the referents of the correspondent of the remnant and the subject of the antecedent.

Since PG always contains contrastive objects (see (215) below), Miller (2014), following the terminology in Miller and Pullum (2014), calls these cases 'obj-choice', that is, object choice (which would be the symmetric of subject choice VPE, where two subjects are contrasted, as in (213) above). The contrastive objects appear in italics:

> (215) Mr. Serjeant Copley. How did you read *it* over? A. The same as I would *any thing else*. WATSON-1817,1,100.586 [object choice]

As mentioned earlier, PG may involve both subject choice and object choice, that is, both the subject and object of the antecedent would be in contrast with those of the pseudogapped clause, as in (216) below.

(216) It were ridiculous to assert, that a Man upon Reflection hath the same Kind of Approbation of the Appetite of Hunger, or the Passion of Fear, as he hath of Good-will to his Fellow-creatures. BUTLER-1726,262.245 [subject-object choice]

Furthermore, there could also be a triple contrast on subjects, objects and auxiliaries, in which case the PG construction would involve secondary auxiliary choice (contrastive elements appear in italics) (Miller 2014: 77):

(217) Yes, *you* my [=*might*, PhM] love *your baby* and *your toddler* to death – *I did mine* – but that doesn't mean to say a child can fulfill all the needs of an adult, [subject-object-auxiliary choice]

Summing up, these will be the possible values for focus in cases of PG: object choice, subject-object choice, object-auxiliary choice and subject-object-auxiliary choice.

Tag questions have not been considered here for focus since these are constructions in which the subject of the target of the ellipsis and that of the antecedent are always the same (as evinced in (218) and (219) below). Therefore focus distinctions cannot be applied to them in the same sense as they would be for standard cases of VPE, as in these cases it would always involve auxiliary choice focus (because subjects are identical in the antecedent and in the ellipsis site):

(218) 'We$_i$ judge happiness to be good, *do we$_i$ not?*' BOETHJA-1897,106.146 [negative tag]

(219) Dr. S. You$_i$ wouldn't have her say it in earnest, *would you$_i$?* BROUGHAM-1861,11.361 [positive tag]

These tag questions where there is a contrast in polarity with respect to its antecedent are referred to as 'reversed polarity tags' by Huddleston and Pullum (2002: 892). However, there can also be cases where the polarity of the antecedent and that of the tag question remains the same, as in (220):

(220) I$_i$ mistrusted he had something on his mind, and was resolved to find it out; *did I$_i$?* BROUGHAM-1861,20.720 [constant polarity tag]

This type of tag question is known as 'constant polarity tag' (Huddleston and Pullum 2002: 892). Reversed polarity tags are much more frequent than constant polarity tags (which would be a marked case), and the latter occur predominantly with a positive antecedent (see Huddleston and Pullum 2002: 892).

The novelty of the present study lies in the fact that there are no corpus studies that have studied the focus of the target of ellipsis in cases of PAE in Modern English.

xxxii. Remnants

As mentioned in Sections 1.1 and 2.2.1.2 of the present volume, PG is characterized by the presence of a contrastive remnant that survives ellipsis. In the literature it is usually mentioned that the most frequent types of remnants are NPs, ProNPs and PPs, as illustrated in (221)-(223) below, respectively:

(221) we cou'd not fail of learning the Latin Language, as well as we do *the Modern Languages*. ANON-1711,11.105

(222) If all the People in the Inn were not asleep, you would have awakened them as you have *me*. FIELDING-1749,3,10.382

(223) I'll stick to him, as close as your ladyship does *to your saddle*. COLLIER-1835,17.550

To these types of remnants, I have added two other types that appear not to have been mentioned in the literature: infinitival VP remnant and Adverbial Phrase, respectively, illustrated in (224) and (225):

(224) they were as sure to hit us, as we were *to hit a Bird in a Tree with small Shot*. DEFOE-1719,207.236

(225) and appear as green at the utmost limit of their territory as they do *far down*. RUSKIN-1835,1,25.631

As mentioned in Section 2.1, only Miller (2014) has carried out a large-scale corpus investigation of the NP remnant in PG for Present-Day English (using the COCA corpus). In his study, he investigated the distribution of the NP remnant in comparative and noncomparative PG constructions. In this volume I extend this study by analysing a previous stage of the language.

In the following chapter the results of the data analysis of PAE in Modern English will be presented, which will allow a qualitative analysis of the diachronic evolution of both VPE and PG.

3

A corpus-based analysis of Post-auxiliary Ellipsis in Modern English

In this chapter I analyse the results of the empirical study of PAE in Modern English. As will be shown, the different variables under study have been divided into three main groups: core defining variables of PAE (grammatical and semantic/discursive), usage variables (diachronic evolution and genre distribution of PAE) and processing variables (syntactic and lexical distance between the source and the target of ellipsis). The discussion of the results will pave the way for a qualitative analysis of both VPE and PG and for the conclusions of this piece of research.

3.1 Core defining variables

This section will pay attention to those variables that shape PAE both from a grammatical and semantic/discursive point of view. As far as grammatical variables go, I will take into account (i) the type of licensors that allow the occurrence of PAE, (ii) the presence or absence of auxiliaries before the licensors of PAE, (iii) the type of syntactic relation established between the source and the target of ellipsis (coordination, subordination, none, etc.), (iv) the syntactic domain where ellipsis takes place (matrix clause, subordinate clause, tag question, etc.), (v) the category of the source of ellipsis and that of the target (NP, VP, AP, non-constituent, etc.), (vi) the presence or absence of split antecedents, (vii) the types of remnants of PG (their category and syntactic function in the clause) and, finally, (viii) auxiliary-related variables (where I will also analyse whether there are any mismatches between the source and the target of ellipsis with respect to polarity, voice, aspect, modality and tense). As far as the semantic and discursive variables are concerned, I will focus on the study of (i) the type of clause of the source and the target of ellipsis (declarative, interrogative, imperative and tag question), (ii) the type of anaphora (anaphoric and cataphoric), (iii) the type of focus (subject choice, auxiliary choice, object choice, etc.), (iv) sloppy identity (pronoun and polarity mismatches) and (v) turn (change in the speaker between the source and the target of ellipsis).

3.1.1 Grammatical variables

i. Licensors of PAE in Late Modern English
As mentioned in Section 2.2.4, only few corpus studies such as Bos and Spenader (2011) and Miller (2014) have paid attention to the licensors of PAE. In this study I have tried to fill in the gap by presenting data from an earlier period of the language in order to see whether diachronic variation is at work or not. As can be observed in Tables 2 and 3, auxiliary *do* (with all its possible variants like *does*, *did* and *dost*) is the most frequent licensor in both PG (38.37 per cent) and VPE (36.20 per cent) in my data, followed by auxiliary *be* (33.72 per cent in PG and 26.82 per cent in VPE). However, whereas the third most frequent licensor in PG is auxiliary *have* (15.12 per cent), modal auxiliaries (*can*, *could*, *shall*, *should*, *may*, *might*, etc.) occupy that position in VPE (31.32 per cent). This amounts to saying that modal auxiliaries are the least frequent licensors in PG (12.79 per cent). No examples have been attested with infinitival marker *to* as a licensor of PG, which is in line with Levin's (1986) and Miller's (2014) studies. As mentioned in Section 2.2.1.3, in Present-Day English PG, unlike VPE, is not licensed by infinitival marker *to* (see Miller 2014: 88). The example from Levin (1986: 54) is repeated here for convenience in (1):

(1)   Speaker A: Van Gogh's work is beginning to impress me.
      Speaker B: *It's starting *to* ø me, too / Well! It's finally starting *to* ø.

As plotted in Tables 2 and 3, the data from Modern English confirm that *to* was not a possible licensor of PG in this period either. Finally, the two least frequent licensors of VPE are auxiliary *have* (5.46 per cent) and infinitival marker *to* (0.78 per cent), respectively.

The different tokens of each of the licensors are presented in Table 2, whereas in Table 3 the total figures for licensors *be*, *have*, *do* and modal auxiliaries are summarized.

Let us now compare our data with those reported in Bos and Spenader (2011) for VPE in Present-Day English. As mentioned in Section 2.1, they focused on the analysis of VPE in twenty-five sections of the *Wall Street Journal* from

Table 2 Licensors of PAE in Late Modern English

LICENSORS	PG Abs. Freq.	%	VPE Abs. Freq.	%	TOTAL PAE Abs. Freq.	%
be	29	33.72	269	26.24	298	26.82
have	13	15.12	56	5.46	69	6.21
do	33	38.37	371	36.20	404	36.36
may/might	0	0	26	2.54	26	2.34
can/could	1	1.16	163	15.90	164	14.76
will/would	8	9.30	76	7.41	84	7.56
must	1	1.16	11	1.07	12	1.08
ought	0	0	9	0.88	9	0.81
shall/should	1	1.16	34	3.32	35	3.15
dare to	0	0	1	0.10	1	0.09
need	0	0	1	0.10	1	0.09
to	0	0	8	0.78	8	0.72
TOTAL	86		1,025		1,111	

Table 3 Licensors of PAE in Late Modern English (main types)

LICENSORS	PG Abs. Freq.	%	VPE Abs. Freq.	%	TOTAL PAE Abs. Freq.	%
be	29	33.72	269	26.24	298	26.82
have	13	15.12	56	5.46	69	6.21
do	33	38.37	371	36.20	404	36.36
modals	11	12.79	321	31.32	332	29.88
to	0	0	8	0.78	8	0.72
TOTAL	86		1,025		1,111	

the Penn Treebank. Since their study is based on a written genre, it would be reasonable to compare their results with my subcorpus of writing-related genres (see Section 3.2.2 for more details on genre distribution in my database). In Tables 4 and 5, I provide the figures from both Bos and Spenader's study (2011) and this piece of research:

Interestingly enough, if we compare Bos and Spenader's results with ours, we observe that the order of frequency of the licensors is practically the same, the only difference being the percentages of each of the licensors. More specifically, auxiliary *do* is a trigger for ellipsis on around 44 per cent of the occasions in Bos and Spenader's (2011) study, and on 35.56 per cent in ours. Then, the second most frequent licensor is auxiliary *be*, occurring 22 per cent of the times in their study and 31.11 per cent in this investigation. Modal auxiliaries, on the other

Table 4 Licensors of VPE in Present-Day English in Bos and Spenader's (2011) Study

LICENSORS	Abs. Freq.	%
do	213	43.83
be	108	22.22
have	43	8.85
can/could	40	8.23
will/would	40	8.23
to	29	5.97
may/might	5	1.03
should	7	1.44
must	1	0.21
TOTAL	486	

Table 5 Licensors of VPE in Writing-Related Genres in Late Modern English

LICENSORS	Abs. Freq.	%
do	48	35.56
be	42	31.11
can/could	27	20.00
may	5	3.70
will/would	5	3.70
have	4	2.96
should	3	2.22
to	1	0.74
TOTAL	135	

hand, occupy the third position and have a frequency of 19.14 per cent in Bos and Spenader's (2011) work and 29.63 per cent in the present study. Following, auxiliary *have* acts as a trigger for VPE in around 9 per cent of the cases in their work and in 2.96 per cent in ours. Finally, *to* licenses VPE in 5.97 per cent of the cases in Bos and Spenader's (2011) work and in 0.74 per cent in ours. Notice, though, that the percentage of *to* as a licensor of VPE in Present-Day English seems to be over 8 times higher than in Late Modern English.

Nevertheless, one should be cautious about the interpretation of the previous figures. In the light of the data presented in Tables 4 and 5, it could be concluded that auxiliaries *do* and *be* are the most frequent licensors of PAE in Late Modern English. However, if we take into account the influence of an independent factor such as the total occurrence of these licensors in the whole corpus, we reach a different conclusion. The relative frequency of each of the licensors (presented in Table 6) reveals that modal auxiliaries are by far the most frequent licensors of PAE in Late Modern English (19.54). Licensor *be* is shown to be the second

Table 6 Relative Frequencies of the Licensors of PAE in Late Modern English

LICENSORS	Abs. Freq.	Token Frequency	R.f./1,000
be	298	37,727	7.90
have	69	11,642	5.93
modals	332	16,995	19.54
to	8	15,335	0.52

most frequent licensor (7.90), although it licenses PAE in less than half of the times when compared with modal auxiliaries. This licensor is followed closely by licensor *have* (5.93). However, a caveat is in order here, namely that there might be cases where auxiliary *have* could not possibly be a licensor of PAE, as pointed out by Miller (p.c.). This is illustrated in (2) for example, where causative *have* does not permit ellipsis:

(2) *I had him leave the house. I feel awfully sorry, but I had.

This means that figures are probably higher for the relative frequency of auxiliary *have*, which would license PAE on more occasions. As far as infinitival marker *to* is concerned, one can observe that relative frequencies confirm that it is by far the most uncommon licensor of PAE in the period under analysis in this volume (0.52).

In Graph 1 the relative frequencies of the licensors of PAE in Late Modern English are represented.

Finally, the relative frequency of auxiliary *do* could not be calculated in the same terms as the other licensors just mentioned, as *do* normally licenses the

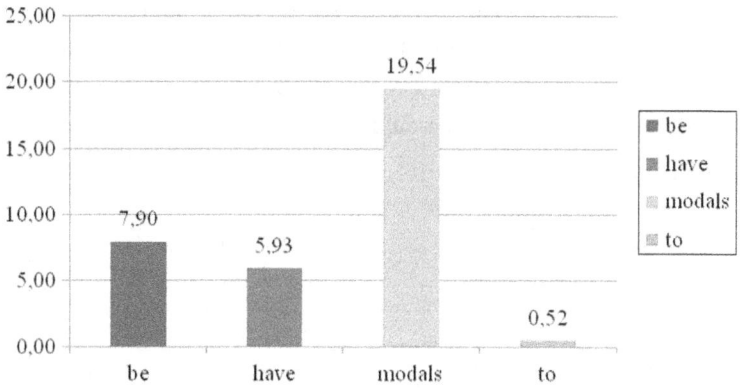

Graph 1 Representation of the relative frequencies of the licensors of PAE in Late Modern English.

ellipsis of main verbs in the past or present tense (underlined), as in (3) and (4) below:

(3) If the Church of Rome <u>approves of</u> and <u>countenances</u> monastic vows, or <u>enjoins</u> celibacy on certain orders in her communion; the Church of God *does* not. WOLLASTON-1793,40.317

(4) Lady Markby shaking her head: Ah! I am afraid Lord Brancaster <u>knew</u> a good deal about that. More than his poor wife ever *did*. WILDE-1895,65.700

Therefore, the relative frequency of auxiliary *do* as a licensor of PAE (404) was calculated with respect to the total number of main verbs in either present or past tense (72,254), which yielded a relative frequency of 5.59 per every 1,000 instances – in fact, if the relative frequency of auxiliary *do* had been calculated against the total number of occurrences in the corpus (4,498), the result would be 90.04. Notice, though, that these figures for *do* are only approximate, as there could be cases where the antecedent of ellipsis contains a modal auxiliary, and therefore there would be no main verbs in either present or past tense involved, as in (5):

(5) Marlow. Or you *may clap* them on a plate by themselves. I *do*. GOLDSMITH-1773,28.262

Once again, it would be interesting to compare the relative frequencies of our study with those of Bos and Spenader's (2011) work for VPE in Present-Day English. Tables 7 and 8 provide the figures from their study and those from the writing-related genres of our study.[1]

In the light of their data, one can observe that modal auxiliaries are also the most frequent triggers of VPE (7.48), though this frequency is slightly higher than the one attested in Modern English (5.50). The second and third most frequent licensors in their work would be auxiliary *have* (3.82) and *be* (3.52), respectively, while the reverse is true in our study: auxiliary *be* (2.55) licenses

Table 7 Relative Frequencies of the Licensors of VPE in Bos and Spenader's (2011) Study

LICENSORS	Abs. Freq.	Token Frequency	R.f./1,000
modals	93	12,427	7.48
have	43	11,249	3.82
be	108	30,124	3.59
to	29	29,868	0.97

Table 8 Relative Frequencies of the Licensors of VPE in Writing-Related Genres in Late Modern English

LICENSORS	Abs. Freq.	Token Frequency	R.f./1,000
modals	39	7,094	5.50
be	42	16,473	2.55
have	5	4,022	1.24
to	1	6,752	0.15

ellipsis more often than auxiliary *have* (1.24). Regarding licensor *to*, the data show that it has increased its frequency over six times in Present-Day English (0.97) if compared with Late Modern English (0.15) but is still by far the least frequent trigger of PAE. Finally, Bos and Spenader (2011) report that auxiliary *do* has a relative frequency of 68.64, but in their case this figure is calculated with respect to the total number of occurrences of auxiliary *do* in the corpus. I have already pointed out the problems that arise from this methodological decision. In fact, if that figure were taken as a measure in the present analysis, auxiliary *do* would also be the most frequent trigger of VPE in writing-related genres (58.11).

In summary, then, it could be concluded that modal auxiliaries are the most frequent licensors of VPE in both (Late) Modern English and Present-Day English in the light of the comparison between our study and that of Bos and Spenader (2011). Besides, the least frequent licensor of VPE in both periods has also been found to be the same: infinitival marker *to*, which seems to increase its frequency over six times in Present-Day English. With regard to auxiliary *be*, it seems to have increased its frequency slightly in the transition from Late Modern to Present-Day English. Finally, auxiliary *have* also seems to have trebled its frequency in Present-Day English. Of course, these conclusions should be taken as preliminary in the face of the small range of data available for Present-Day English, as the data from Bos and Spenader's (2011) study all belong to the *Wall Street Journal* sections of the Penn Treebank, and this might bias the data. It therefore remains an open question whether the tendencies observed here with respect to the licensors of VPE are true of Present-Day English.

It would also be interesting to have a look at the distribution of the licensors of PAE in both writing and speech-related genres. We have already shown the distribution of the licensors in VPE in writing-related genres. Let us have a look at their distribution in speech-related genres.

Table 9 also shows that auxiliary *do* is clearly the most frequent licensor of VPE in speech-related genres. Then, modal auxiliaries comprise almost 30 per cent of the cases, followed by auxiliaries *be* (24.84 per cent) and *have*

Table 9 Licensors of VPE in Speech-Related Genres in Late Modern English

LICENSORS	Abs. Freq.	%
do	300	38.22
be	195	24.84
can/could	119	15.16
will/would	54	6.88
have	49	6.24
shall/should	24	3.06
may/might	20	2.55
must	10	1.27
ought	8	1.02
to	6	0.76
TOTAL	785	

(6.24 per cent) and infinitival marker *to* (0.76), respectively. But let us have a look at the relative frequency of these licensors in order to check whether the same tendency is observed.

In this case, the relative frequency of the licensors of VPE in speech-related genres coincides with the percentages of the absolute frequencies presented in Table 9. As can be observed, modal auxiliaries are by far the most common triggers of VPE in these text types (29.73). This figure is over five times higher than the one present in writing-related genres (5.50). Auxiliary *be* is the second most frequent licensor of VPE (11.55) and again, its presence is over four times more common in speech-related genres. The same is true of auxiliary *have* (8.19) and infinitival marker *to* (0.85), whose frequencies are 1.24 and 0.15 in writing-related genres, respectively (six times higher in speech-related texts). Finally, auxiliary *do* has a relative frequency of 100.94 (300/2,972), but once again, methodological problems arise if this figure is taken into account. If one calculates the number of verbs in the present and past tense with respect to the number of times auxiliary *do* acts as a trigger of VPE in speech-related genres, this would be the result: 8.74 (300/34,288).

Table 10 Relative Frequencies of the Licensors of VPE in Speech-Related Genres in Late Modern English

LICENSORS	Abs. Freq.	Token Frequency	R.f./1,000
modals	235	7,904	29.73
be	195	16,877	11.55
have	49	5,985	8.19
to	6	7,044	0.85

As far as the distribution of the licensors of PG per type of genre is concerned, it has been found that auxiliaries *do* and *be* are by far the most frequent licensors in writing-related genres (42.86 per cent), comprising over 85 per cent of the total (see Table 11). These are followed by modal auxiliaries *will* and *would* (14.29 per cent). Notice, however, that auxiliary *have* does not license PG in written texts.

With regard to the licensors of PG in speech-related genres, Table 12 shows that auxiliaries *do* and *be* are again the most frequent (34.62 per cent and 28.85 per cent, respectively). However, auxiliary *have* occupies the third position this time with a percentage of 21.15, followed by modal auxiliaries (*will*, *would*, *could*, *must* and *shall*) which comprise 15.38 per cent of the cases.

Let us have a look at the relative frequencies of the licensors of PG in both types of genres. As can be inferred from Table 13, auxiliary *be* is the most common licensor of PG (0.53), followed by modal auxiliaries (0.38). As mentioned earlier, no instances of auxiliary *have* as a licensor of PG in writing-related genres have been attested. With respect to auxiliary *do*, if its frequency was compared against the total number of tokens of auxiliary *do*, its relative frequency would be 1.28 (and therefore it would be the most common licensor of PG). However, if the frequency of *do* was compared against the total number of verbs in the present and past tense, its relative frequency would be 0.35 (and it would occupy the third position).

Table 11 Licensors of PG in Writing-Related Genres in Late Modern English

LICENSORS	Abs. Freq.	%
do	9	42.86
be	9	42.86
will/would	3	14.29
have	0	0
TOTAL	21	

Table 12 Licensors of PG in Speech-Related Genres in Late Modern English

LICENSORS	Abs. Freq.	%
do	18	34.62
be	15	28.85
have	11	21.15
will/would	5	9.62
could	1	1.92
must	1	1.92
shall	1	1.92
TOTAL	52	

Table 13 Relative Frequencies of the Licensors of PG in Writing-Related Genres in Late Modern English

LICENSORS	Abs. Freq.	Token Frequency	R.f./1,000
be	9	16,877	0.53
modals	3	7,904	0.38
have	0	5,985	0.00

Interestingly, the reverse situation is observed in the relative frequencies of PG in speech-related genres. The relative frequencies are so similar among the most frequent categories of licensors that the differences plotted in Table 14 do not lead to significant conclusions. Interestingly, according to the data provided in Table 14, auxiliary *have* is the most frequent licensor (1.84), followed by modal auxiliaries (1.01) and auxiliary *be* (0.89). Therefore, auxiliary *have* was not attested as a licensor of PG in the writing-related genres and is shown to be the most common licensor of PG in speech-related ones. As for auxiliary *do*, if its frequency was compared against the total number of tokens of auxiliary *do*, its relative frequency would be 6.06 and it would then be the most common trigger of PG. Nevertheless, if the frequency of *do* was compared against the total number of verbs in the present and past tense, its relative frequency would be 0.52 (that is, it would be the least frequent licensor of PG in speech-related genres).

As a final remark, it is also worth pointing out that some licensors have been attested in Late Modern English that are no longer used in Present-Day English, as can be seen in (6)-(9) (in italics):

(6) he stood as near the Shore as he *durst* with the Ship. DEFOE-1719,207.238

(7) Thou mayest freely eat of every Tree of the Garden; Excepting that of the Knowledge of Good and Evil, of which thou *shalt* not. PURVER-OLD-1764,2,1G.80

Table 14 Relative Frequencies of the Licensors of PG in Speech-Related Genres in Late Modern English

LICENSORS	Abs. Freq.	Token Frequency	R.f./1,000
have	11	5,985	1.84
modals	8	7,904	1.01
be	15	16,877	0.89

(8) Thou mayest freely eat of every Tree of the Garden; Excepting that of the Knowledge of Good and Evil, of which thou shalt not: for on the Day thou *dost*, thou shalt quite die. PURVER-OLD-1764,2,1G.81

(9) Because thou hast hearkened to what thy Wife said, and eat of the Tree which I commanded thee that thou *shouldest* not. PURVER-OLD-1764,3,1G.120

It should be noted, though, that except for example (6), which belongs to the Fiction genre and contains an example of the modal auxiliary *dare to* in past tense, the other examples belong to the Bible genre. Consequently, these licensors instantiate archaic uses of auxiliary *do* and modal auxiliaries *shall* and *should* which had kept their inflectional endings from a previous stage of the English language. One can conclude then that they were not common licensors of PAE in Late Modern English.

A further remark seems in order here as regards the modal auxiliary *ought to*, which only licenses PAE and, more precisely, VPE, without *to* on nine occasions, illustrated in (10)-(11):

(10) I am afraid I do not keep my promise and purpose to you so well as I *ought* in the writing way; CARLYLE-1835,2,271.258

(11) Enable me to begin it and end it as I *ought*. HAYDON-1808,1,27.679

A careful analysis of all of the examples of *ought* as a licensor of VPE reveals that the common feature that they share is that they all occur in speech-related genres such as Trial proceedings, Drama comedy, Private letters and Diary, and in a mixed genre such as Fiction (see Section 3.2.2 for more details on the division of speech versus writing-related genres). Since no examples of *ought* as a licensor of PAE have been attested in writing-related genres, it remains to be investigated whether this type of licensor is only typical of speech-related genres or whether it is a mere chance that no examples have been attested in the writing-related ones.

In summary, then, the relative frequency of the licensors of PAE has revealed that modal auxiliaries are the most common trigger of PAE in Late Modern English (19.54), followed by auxiliaries *be* (7.90) and *have* (5.93), and (much more marginally) infinitival marker *to* (0.52), respectively. Notice, however, that no instances of infinitival marker *to* as a trigger of PG have been attested, in line with empirical works on PG in Present-Day English like Miller (2014). The relative frequencies of the licensors of VPE in both speech and writing-related genres have revealed that their frequency is the following (in decreasing order): modal auxiliaries, *be*, *have* and infinitival marker *to*. It has also been shown that the relative frequency of VPE in writing-related genres in Late Modern English is the same as the one reported in Bos and Spenader's (2011) study for VPE in Present-Day English. In the case of PG, the relative frequencies of the licensors in writing-related genres show that the pattern followed is (in decreasing order) auxiliary *be*, modal auxiliaries and auxiliary *have*, and that the opposite trend is true in speech-related genres, although those empirical differences between text types are not statistically significant. Finally, it has also been reported that our data contain examples of licensors of PAE which are no longer used in Present-Day English, such as *shouldest*, *shalt*, *dost*, *durst* and *ought*. A close analysis of these licensors has shown that, with the exception of *durst* (the past tense of *dare to*) and *ought*, the examples of these licensors belong to the Bible genre and constitute archaic uses of auxiliary *do* and modal auxiliaries *shall* and *should*. Finally, *ought* has only been attested in speech-related genres.

ii. Auxiliary before licensor

As put forward in Section 2.2.1.3, VPE in Present-Day English can be licensed by more than one auxiliary, while PG as a general rule cannot (see Levin 1986; Hoeksema 2006; and Miller 2014, for example). This contrast is illustrated with the examples repeated here for convenience in (12)-(13):

(12) I saw it and obviously so did Arnold, but nobody else *could have*.
[BNC Corpus]
(13) Speaker A: Cream rinse makes my hair get dirty faster.
Speaker B: ??It *may have* ø mine ø once, too. [Levin 1986: 54]

I have investigated this variable in order to check potential differences between Late Modern and Present-Day English. Tables 15 and 16 provide the results for VPE and PG.

As observed in Table 15, the cases with an auxiliary before a licensor represent 8.14 per cent of the total of examples of PG. Regarding VPE, Table 16 shows that the percentage of auxiliaries before a licensor goes down to 4.39 per cent (almost half as much as PG). This result is not in line with the situation we find in Present-Day English, as put forward in Levin (1986) and Miller (2014), where these scholars claim that, whereas there can be auxiliaries before a licensor in VPE, in PG generally this is not possible. In fact, Levin (1986: 54) only reports one such case of PG, repeated in (14), while Miller (2014) does not report any in his large-scale corpus study of PG:

(14) I processed everybody's check last week, but I *must not've* ø yours.

Table 15 Auxiliary before Licensor in PG

AUXILIARY	PG	
	Abs. Freq.	%
none	79	91.86
have	3	3.49
must	2	2.33
would	2	2.33
TOTAL	86	

Table 16 Auxiliary(ies) before Licensor in VPE

AUXILIARY	VPE	
	Abs. Freq.	%
none	980	95.61
have	8	0.78
could	7	0.68
ought to	6	0.58
can	3	0.29
shall	3	0.29
should	3	0.29
would	3	0.29
would have	3	0.29
should have	2	0.20
may	1	0.10
must	1	0.10
need	1	0.10
could have	1	0.10
might	1	0.10
might have	1	0.10
will	1	0.10
TOTAL	1,025	

In the following examples I show the occurrences of PG in my database which involve the presence of two auxiliaries (in italics):

(15) But had not known that the British Government was anxious to do as the French Ministers *would have* them. TROLLOPE-1882,183.436

(16) Lou. Were I sure you would follow, as I *would have* you, I should not care how soon I led up the Dance; DAVYS-1716,35.369

(17) The Parliamentarian army of the South was as completely wiped out in September as the Royalist army of the North *had been* in July. OMAN-1895,392.263

(18) he was more cruel and treacherous to his poor Hungarian subjects, than ever the Turk *has been* to the Christians. MONTAGU-1718,79.26

(19) Tho' it was as thoroughly dress'd after being cut for Eastwell, as it *had been* for the Ashford Assembly. AUSTEN-180X,163.71

(20) Or, if there is any thing to which they have a tendency and impulse, it *must be* to the supreme and all-sufficient good. BOETHRI-1785,124.260

(21) Even the delicate associations with words can be expounded through our own language; just as they *must be* to the pupil who is studying the original. BAIN-1878,366.96

As can be observed, the only combinations of two auxiliaries found in PG are the following: *would have, had been* and *must be*. Notice also that all of these combinations (with the exception of (20)) take place in cases of comparative PG (see the following subsection on syntactic linking for a description of what has been termed in the literature as '*as*-appositives', treated in this study as a type of comparative construction).

In the case of VPE, as illustrated in Table 16, the array of combinations is more varied, ranging from just one auxiliary before the licensor (as in (22)-(24)) to two auxiliaries before the licensor (as in (25)-(27)):

(22) A. They could not have disabled the Cornwal so much as she *had been*, HOLMES-TRIAL-1749,27.469

(23) Men are as apt to publish what is not worth saying as women *can be*. YONGE-1865,175.409

(24) But in a little time I hope to do all you *would have*. JOHNSON-1775,2,9.177

(25) its doctrinal positions and subtle distinctions are at this moment better understood through translators and commentators, writing in English, French, and German, than they *could have been* to Bentley, Porson, or Parr. BAIN-1878,362.49

(26) we are nearly in all respects the same persons as we *should have been* without this knowledge, FROUDE-1830,2,44.290

(27) That the wicked, who suffer the chastisement which they merit, are happier than they *would have been*, BOETHRI-1785,154.295

As was the case with the examples of PG, all the combinations where there are two auxiliaries before the licensor occur in comparative VPE, as instantiated in (25)-(27). Nevertheless, when only a single auxiliary precedes the licensor of VPE, more syntactic contexts come into play. Although in the vast majority of cases, they take place in comparative constructions (68.42 per cent), as instantiated in (22)-(23), my database contains examples in contexts of coordination (18.42 per cent), instances where no syntactic relation holds between the source and the ellipsis site (10.53 per cent), and also in one example of relative subordination (2.63 per cent), as in (24).

In summary, it has been found that the percentage of auxiliaries before a licensor is almost twice as high in PG than in VPE in Late Modern English, although this difference is not statistically significant ($\chi^2(1)=1.5$, p=0.22). This is not in keeping with what would have been expected in Present-Day English (see Levin 1986 and Miller 2014), that is, VPE can be licensed by more than one auxiliary while PG as a general rule cannot. In addition, it has been shown that PG permits the presence of a single auxiliary before the licensor and almost exclusively in comparative contexts. As far as VPE is concerned, it allows the presence of either one or two auxiliaries before the licensor of ellipsis, and this exclusively in comparative contexts. Those cases in which there is only one auxiliary before the licensor of VPE are attested in comparatives in the vast majority of cases, followed by coordination, by contexts in which no syntactic relation holds between the source and the target of ellipsis and, much more marginally, in relative subordination.

iii. Syntactic linking

This section will aim at determining what kind of syntactic relation is established between the antecedent clause(s) and the clause which contains the ellipsis site. This aspect has also been studied in corpus-based studies like Hardt and Rambow (2001), Nielsen (2005) and Bos and Spenader (2011) for the Present-Day English period. Here I extend these works by analysing the type of syntactic linking in PAE constructions in Modern English. A graphical representation of the types of syntactic linking under study and their classification is provided in Figure 5.

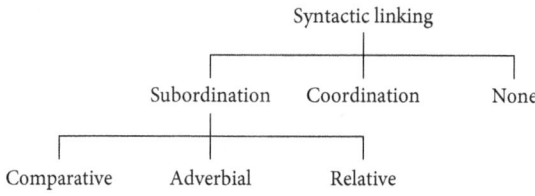

Figure 5 Syntactic linking.

If you recall from Section 2.2.4, these are the categories that have been used in order to classify the examples: none, coordination and subordination. First, in those cases where no syntactic relation is established, the antecedent and the ellipsis site appear in different sentences, as in tag questions, CP-questions or sentences delimited by punctuation boundaries (see (28)-(30)). Second, in cases of coordination, clauses are joined thanks to the conjunctions *and*, *or* and *but* (see (31)). Finally, I have considered the following cases of subordination: comparative (including equatives and *as*-appositives, see (32) and (33), respectively), relative (including cases of antecedent-contained deletion, see (34)) and adverbial (temporal, concessive, cause, manner, conditional, and so on, see (35)).

(28) I can recollect nothing more to say. When my letter is gone, I suppose I shall. AUSTEN-180X,175.335 [none]

(29) One wouldn't say so from the sort of hats they wear, would one? WILDE-1895,64.673 [none, tag question]

(30) Phipps: I don't observe an alternation in your lordship's appearance. Lord Goring: You don't, Phipps? WILDE-1895,73.939 [none, CP question]

(31) That I had received such from Edward also I need not mention; *but* I do, AUSTEN-180X,187.622 [coordination]

(32) If therefore we did but hear others talk Latin, and endeavour'd to understand them, and talk with them, *as* much *as* we do to understand and talk with those who speak in the Modern Tongues. ANON-1711,11.105 [comparative subordination].

(33) It were ridiculous to assert, that a Man upon Reflection hath the same Kind of Approbation of the Appetite of Hunger, or the Passion of Fear, *as* he hath of Good-will to his Fellow-creatures. BUTLER-1726,262.245 [comparative subordination][2]

(34) take *all the Ways you can* to destroy them. MAXWELL-1747,23.239 [antecedent-contained deletion]

(35) They can by no means, therefore, be members of happiness; for *if* they were , happiness might be said to be made up of one member, BOETHRI-1785,116.162 [adverbial subordination]

As repeatedly mentioned in this volume, VPE has been claimed to have the capacity to occur in both coordination and subordination contexts. However, the distribution of PG seems to be much more restrictive and the literature on the topic has usually pointed out that this construction is favoured in comparative contexts. The focus of this section, then, will be to try to dilucidate the types of syntactic linking that have been attested in both PG and VPE in Modern English. Let us start by describing the situation in cases of PG, shown in Table 17.

As shown in Table 17, PG predominates in *as*-appositives, also known as equatives, since they comprise over 40 per cent of the total (see (36)). Following, comparatives other than equatives (i.e. with connectors such as *than*, for example) represent almost 34 per cent of the cases (as in (37)). Altogether, then, comparative constructions are present in almost 74 per cent of the cases PG. Interestingly enough, the antecedent and the target of ellipsis occur in different sentences on 15.12 per cent of the occasions, that is, there is no syntactic linking (as in (38)). Much more marginally, PG has also been attested in contexts of coordination (4.65 per cent, as in (39)) and several types of subordination: concessive (2.33 per cent, as in (40)), cause (1.16 per cent, as in (41)), conditional (1.16 per cent, as in (42)) and relative (1.16 per cent, as in (43)).

(36) and the hills dip down beneath them *as* they would beneath water. RUSKIN-1835,1,12.325

(37) A skilled florist will produce a finer effect with a few inexpensive blossoms *than* an unskilled one will with a cartload of choice material. WEATHERS-1913,1,8.192

(38) My question was, whether you had any conversation about the bills? A. No; about Mr. Castle, I had. WATSON-1817,1,99.550

(39) this was a request I would have refused any other man; *but* could not one from whom I have gained so much. HAYDON-1808,1,33.839

(40) but did not admire the strain of its poetry in general, *though* I did its morality. BOSWELL-1776,49.475

Table 17 Syntactic Linking in PG

SYNTACTIC LINKING	Abs. Freq.	%
as-*appositive*	35	40.70
subordination comparative	29	33.72
none	13	15.12
coordination	4	4.65
subordination concessive	2	2.33
subordination cause	1	1.16
subordination conditional	1	1.16
subordination relative	1	1.16
TOTAL	86	100.00

(41) *Since* the Law was given by Moses, Grace and Truth was by Jesus Christ. PURVER-NEW-1764,1,1J.32

(42) *if* there is any thing to which they have a tendency and impulse, it must be to the supreme and all-sufficient good. BOETHRI-1785,124.260

(43) I have been always in the habit of treating my own Horses much after the same manner *that* I would myself. SKEAVINGTON-184X,27. C2.413

The previous results have been summarized in Table 18, where *as*-appositives and comparatives have been grouped together, as well as all the types of subordination with adverbial meaning (cause, concessive and conditional).

Table 18 reveals, as mentioned earlier, that the vast majority of cases of PG are composed by comparative constructions (over 74 per cent), followed by those cases where there is no syntactic linking (15.12 per cent), coordination (4.65 per cent), adverbial subordination (4.65 per cent) and relative subordination (1.16 per cent). Tables 19 and 20 show the data concerning the types of connectors found in coordinate and subordinate clauses, respectively.

Three types of coordinating conjunctions (*and*, *but* and *or*) have been attested in PG in the few examples of coordination. As regards subordinate clauses, comparative connectors are the most frequent: *as* (48.57 per cent), *as ... as* (27.14 per cent), *than* (12.86 per cent) and *so as* (1.43 per cent). This implies that *as*-appositives constitute the most frequent type of comparatives,

Table 18 Summary of Syntactic Linking in PG

SYNTACTIC LINKING	Abs. Freq.	%
subordination comparative	64	74.42
none	13	15.12
coordination	4	4.65
subordination adverbial	4	4.65
subordination relative	1	1.16
TOTAL	86	100.00

Table 19 Connectors in Coordinate Clauses in PG

CONNECTOR	Abs. Freq.	%
and	1	25.00
but	2	50.00
or	1	25.00
TOTAL	4	100.00

Table 20 Connectors in Subordinate Clauses in PG

CONNECTOR	Abs. Freq.	%
as	34	48.57
as as	19	27.14
than	9	12.86
none	4	5.71
so as	1	1.43
that	1	1.43
though	1	1.43
whereas	1	1.43
TOTAL	70	100.00

followed by equatives (thanks to connectors such as *as ... as* and *so ... as*) and *than*-comparatives. Altogether, they comprise 90 per cent of the subordinating conjunctions attested in PG.

Let us now compare the results just presented with those reported in Hoeksema's (2006) and Miller's (2014) studies. On the one hand, Hoeksema's (2006) corpus data consisted of 227 examples of PG, which included 21 examples of naturally occurring data from Levin's dissertation. He found that 87 per cent of the examples of PG occurred in comparative subordination, followed by 4 per cent in coordination and 4 per cent in other types of subordination (adverbial and relative). As can be observed, his results are very much in line with ours, where comparative subordination represents nearly 75 per cent of the examples and coordination and adverbial subordination account both for nearly 5 per cent of the data. Notice, however, that no instances of PG where there is no syntactic linking between the source and the target of ellipsis are reported, while in this study this lack of syntactic linking is present in over 15 per cent of the cases. On the other hand, Miller (2014) focused his research on cases of PG with NP remnants. He reported that only forty-seven of the cases under analysis (3.3 per cent) were instances of noncomparative PG, but he did not deal with the type of syntactic linking established between the source and the target of ellipsis. In our study, however, we found nine such cases out of thirty examples of PG with NP remnants. Regarding comparative PG, Miller (2014) reported 1,368 cases, which would represent 96.7 per cent of the examples of PG with NP remnants that he found in the COCA. His results, therefore, exhibit a stronger bias towards comparative structures than previous studies like Hoeksema (2006) (87 per cent) and Sharifzadeh (2012) (90 per cent). If compared with this piece of research, the twenty-one cases out of thirty of instances of comparative PG with

NP remnants represent 70 per cent of the examples. Consequently, PG with NP remnants is indeed a construction that has a preference for comparative contexts, especially so in Present-Day English, since its percentage is significantly higher if compared with the same data from Late Modern English. Of course, it would be interesting to compare my results with data from Present-Day English taking into account all of the types of remnants attested in PG in order to gain more insights on the syntactic behaviour of PG and its diachronic evolution.

Miller (2014) also analyses the distribution of comparative and noncomparative PG with NP remnants by types of genre in the COCA corpus and he found that noncomparative PG is typical of the spoken register (combining the figures from purely spoken speech with reported speech), rendering 91.7 per cent of the cases of noncomparative PG. The proportion here is in line with this finding, as 8/9 cases of noncomparative PG have been found in speech-related genres (see Section 3.2.2 for more details on the types of genres considered as speech and writing-related genres). As for comparative PG, Miller (2014) found that it occurs in all registers of COCA but is especially frequent in fiction (30.11 per cent) and magazines (29.53 per cent). Furthermore, comparative PG with NP remnants in the spoken register represents 13.37 per cent of the cases. If one compares these data with those in my database, speech-related genres represent 57.14 per cent while writing-related ones render 42.8 per cent of the examples. Therefore, it seems that comparative PG was more frequent in the spoken register in Late Modern English than it is in Present-Day English. Once again, it should be noted that this preliminary conclusion would need further research.

With respect to VPE, the results presented in Table 21 show that in over half of the instances there is no syntactic linking between the antecedent and the ellipsis

Table 21 Syntactic Linking in VPE

SYNTACTIC LINKING	Abs. Freq.	%
none	516	50.34
subordination comparative	185	18.05
as-appositive	138	13.46
subordination relative	74	7.22
coordination	57	5.56
subordination conditional	34	3.32
subordination cause	11	1.07
subordination temporal	7	0.68
subordination concessive	2	0.20
subordination manner	1	0.10
TOTAL	1,025	100.00

site. That is, the source and the target of ellipsis occur in different sentences (see examples (44) and (45)). This lack of syntactic linking is, therefore, the most common situation with VPE. Comparative subordination (18.05 per cent; see (47) and (48)) and *as*-appositives (13.46 per cent, as in (46)) are the second and third most frequent types when syntactic linking is observed. The fourth most frequent type in VPE is relative subordination, yielding 7.22 per cent of the cases (see (49)). Coordination represents only 5.56 per cent of the total (see (50)). Much less frequent are cases of conditional (3.32 per cent, as in (51)), causal (1.07 per cent, as in (52)), temporal (0.68 per cent, as in (53)), concessive (0.20 per cent, as in (54)) and manner (0.10 per cent, as in (55)) subordination.

(44) I am afraid Lord Brancaster knew a good deal about that. More than his poor wife ever did. WILDE-1895,65.700

(45) He won't take any interest in politics then, will he? WILDE-1895,63.650

(46) I felt in general that I was as a little Schoolboy, who had laboriously written out his Copy *as* he could, CARLYLE-1835,2,288.505

(47) No one, except myself, knows Robert better *than* you do. WILDE-1895,52.365

(48) But they did us no hurt, only gaped, and stared, and hallowed *as* loud *as* they could. WESLEY-174X,17.141

(49) I am very glad you tell me *all you do* about Sir A. Buchanan. VICTORIA-186X,1,206.465

(50) I tried to thank him, *but* could not. BENSON-190X,115.325

(51) *If* the Church of Rome pretends to sacrifice him afresh in their mass; the Church of Christ does not.WOLLASTON-1793,40.312

(52) Can one ever hope you will make a figure, when you only fight *because* it was right you should? WALPOLE-174X,5,20.473

(53) Q. You left Spa Fields *when* the other persons did. WATSON-1817,1,128.1319

(54) A public schoolmaster, of gentle boys, I mean, who has particularly studied the subject, and has succeeded in maintaining purity among his boys, to a degree, I believe that no other Public School does, *though* many do a great deal. NIGHTINGALE-189X,420.11

(55) As He employed the poor, the illiterate, 'unlearned and ignorant men', 'the foolish things of the world, and the weak things of the world, and base things of the world, and things despised, yea, things' accounted *as if* they were not. PUSEY-186X,302.318

Table 22 Summary of Syntactic Linking in VPE

SYNTACTIC LINKING	Abs. Freq.	%
none	516	50.34
subordination comparative	323	31.51
subordination relative	74	7.22
coordination	57	5.56
subordination adverbial	55	5.37
TOTAL	1,025	100.00

Table 22 sums up the results for syntactic linking in VPE. One can conclude that in most of the instances of VPE there is no syntactic linking between the source and the target of ellipsis, yielding 50.34 per cent of the total, which contrasts with the percentage of PG (15.12 per cent). The second most important type of syntactic linking is represented by comparative subordination, comprising 31.51 per cent of the examples of VPE. Notice that although the percentage of comparative constructions is high in VPE, it is almost 2.5 times higher in PG (74.42 per cent). Far less common are cases of relative subordination (7.22 per cent), coordination (5.56 per cent) and adverbial subordination (5.37 per cent). Interestingly, while the percentage of relative subordination is higher in VPE than in PG (7.22 per cent versus 1.16 per cent), that of the last two types of linking mentioned is almost the same as that found in PG (4.65 per cent in both cases).

Furthermore, it has been found that almost 73 per cent of the examples of relative subordination are instances of bound relative clauses (as in (56)), while the remaining 27 per cent are instances of free relative clauses (as in (57)). Out of those examples of bound relative clauses, over 33 per cent were instances of antecedent-contained deletion, as in (58):

(56) Q. You say you took *the best note you could* of what passed? WATSON-1817,1,163.2122

(57) He does *what he can* for Carter. JOHNSON-1775,2,21.388

(58) he would not look upon us as Enemies, but do us *all the Service he could*. OFFICER-1744,210.13

As for the types of connectors attested in coordinate clauses, provided in Table 23, in around 50 per cent of the cases the connector would be the conjunction *and*, followed by *but* (42.11 per cent). Much more marginally, the conjunctions *nor* and *or* are present in around 7 per cent of the cases altogether.

As was the case with PG, connectors in subordinate clauses abound in VPE and, not surprisingly (due to the big difference in number), are more varied than

Table 23 Connectors in Coordinate Clauses in VPE

CONNECTOR	Abs. F`req.	%
and	29	50.88
but	24	42.11
nor	3	5.26
or	1	1.75
TOTAL	57	100.00

in PG. As can be observed in Table 24, comparative connectors are also the most frequent ones: *as* (28.98 per cent), *as ... as* (21.46 per cent), *than* (14.82 per cent) and *so ... as* (4.65 per cent). This means that the most frequent type of comparative construction would be the *as*-appositive, followed by equatives (connected by means of *as ... as* and *so ... as*) and comparative structures connected via *than*. If you recall, the same pattern was found for comparatives in PG. Overall, they comprise around 70 per cent of the subordinating conjunctions attested in VPE, whereas this percentage goes up to 90 per cent in PG.

Table 24 Connectors in Subordinate Clauses in VPE

CONNECTOR	Abs. Freq.	%
as	131	28.98
as as	97	21.46
than	67	14.82
none	41	9.07
if	34	7.52
so as	21	4.65
what	16	3.54
which	9	1.99
for	6	1.33
when	5	1.11
whether	5	1.11
because	4	0.88
that	4	0.88
where	3	0.66
though	2	0.44
after	1	0.22
as if	1	0.22
like	2	0.44
till	1	0.22
whom	1	0.22
why	1	0.22
TOTAL	452	100.00

Let us now compare these results on syntactic linking with those reported in Bos and Spenader (2011). Since their study focuses on instances of VPE in the twenty-five sections of the *Wall Street Journal*, I will provide the figures found for VPE in writing-related genres in Late Modern English (see Table 25) for the sake of comparison. However, it must be noted that there were some cases in which the types of syntactic linking reported in Bos and Spenader (2011) could not be easily translated into the classification followed in this study, and therefore the figures provided for their work must be considered only approximately (see Table 26). For example, in the case of pattern 9 from their study '[$_{src}$ NP VP] (.|,and|or) (even) if [$_{tgt}$ NP AUX]', which they illustrate with the example *It isn't yet clear whether the 200-ruble limit will be lifted. If it isn't, the black market for dollars probably will continue to thrive*), I had to leave out the twenty-one cases of VPE they report. This was so because it was difficult to decide whether this type of pattern could be classified as a case of coordination (since it allows the

Table 25 Syntactic Linking in VPE in Writing-Related Genres

TYPE OF LINKING	Abs. Freq.	%
as-*appositives*	43	31.85
subordination comparative	41	30.37
none	17	12.59
subordination relative	14	10.37
coordination	13	9.63
subordination conditional	5	3.70
subordination cause	1	0.74
subordination temporal	1	0.74
TOTAL	135	100.00

Table 26 Syntactic Linking in Bos and Spenader's (2011) Study

TYPE OF LINKING	Abs. Freq.	%
as-*appositives*	108	25.06
subordination comparative	107	24.83
none	83	19.26
coordination	58	13.46
subordination relative	31	7.19
subordination temporal	15	3.48
subordination conditional	8	1.86
subordination manner	8	1.86
subordination concessive	7	1.62
subordination cause	6	1.39
TOTAL	431	100.00

presence of optional coordinating conjunctions such as *and* and *or*), conditional subordination (due to the presence of the conjunction *if*) or no syntactic linking at all (given that this pattern allows a punctuation boundary such as a full stop before the conjunction *if*, as in the example that they provide for this type of pattern). This means that these twenty-one cases could, depending on the type of connector or punctuation mark chosen, fall into three different types of syntactic linking in the present investigation. For this reason, it was decided that it would be safer to leave them out. Besides, I have only taken into account those cases of VPE whose triggers are the same as in this study. This has implied leaving out those examples whose triggers were *do so, do the opposite, do the same* and *do likewise*.

As can be observed, the results of this study are very much in line with those provided in Bos and Spenader (2011): *as*-appositives (31.85 per cent in our study versus 25.06 per cent in theirs) and comparatives (30.37 per cent versus 24.83 per cent) predominate in both studies. Comparative structures, therefore, yield 62.22 per cent of the examples in my database, while they represent 49.88 per cent in Bos and Spenader's study. The third position is also common to the two studies: in 12.59 per cent of the cases there is no syntactic linking between the source and the target of ellipsis in my data, while this percentage goes up to 19.26 per cent in theirs. Then, the fourth and the fifth positions switch in the two accounts: in my study, relative subordination (10.37 per cent) occupies the fourth position and coordination (9.63 per cent) the fifth one, while the reverse is true in theirs: coordination appears in the fourth position (13.46 per cent) and relative subordination (7.19 per cent) in the fifth one, although these differences are not statistically so dissimilar. Following, all types of adverbial subordination represent a total of 5.18 per cent in our study and 10.21 per cent in theirs. In conclusion, the comparison of the data from both studies suggests that the first three types of linking are the same in both studies, that is, *as*-appositives, comparatives and lack of syntactic linking. The other differences are not so pronounced: while coordination, adverbial subordination and relative subordination occupy the last positions (in decreasing order of frequency) in Bos and Spenader's study, the order is slightly different in mine (relative subordination, coordination and adverbial subordination). It would be interesting to check how much these figures would change if one included those twenty-one examples which could have fallen into three different types of linking according to the classification followed in this volume. In addition, in their analysis of Sections 5 and 6 from the Penn Treebank and a balanced corpus that they created with positive examples of VPE, Hardt and Rambow (2001: 4) found that the different forms of subordination favour VPE while the absence of a direct relation disfavours its presence. Interestingly enough, if only the results from the analysis of Sections 5 and 6 from the Penn Treebank are taken into account, their results are similar to mine: VPE occurs more frequently in comparative subordination (6/15), followed by *as*-appositives (4/15), other subordination (2/1), coordination (2/15) and none (1/15). Once again, comparative structures predominate. The main difference between the results in Hardt and Rambow's (2001), Bos and Spenader's (2011) and this study would be that the first reported that the lack of syntactic linking disfavours VPE, while this type of linking is the third most frequent in Bos and Spenader's (2011) work and in this piece of research.

One final remark should be made with respect to syntactic linking which has already been clearly pointed out by Bos and Spenader (2011) and could be extended to our study on PAE in Late Modern English mutatis mutandis:

> In contrast to the expectations raised by formal work, our frequency results are surprising in two ways: we found types that make up a considerably greater proportion of VPE cases than theoretical work suggests, and types discussed frequently in the theoretical work that are extremely infrequent or non-existent in the data annotated. For example, comparative and equative constructions were frequent with VPE, 193 cases, or 31 per cent of the total number of examples. Theoretical papers on VPE seldom use these constructions to illustrate processes in ellipsis yet these constructions seem to facilitate the use of VPE. Actually, the standard example of VPE in theoretical work consists of two sentences conjoined with *and*, where the second sentence is marked by the presupposition trigger *too*. In such examples, the event in the target clause is linked presuppositionally with the source clause event. But among the 554 examples found, there were only five cases with *too*: three cases where the source–target pattern includes *too*, and two additional examples with *too* marking the source – target connection, while not being part of the connection itself. The dominance of this type of example in the theoretical literature gives the impression that presuppositional marking is perhaps an essential part of VPE licensing, and indeed work like Rooth (1992) and Bos (1994) use the identification of focus and redundancy communicated by focus particles like *too* as a part of their resolution algorithm. Because the Wall Street Journal texts are written, it is somewhat surprising to find so few overt markers of redundancy if its recognition is instrumental in ellipsis interpretation. [Bos and Spenader (2011: 487)]

In our study, as mentioned above, comparative constructions (including *as*-appositives and equatives) represent over 60 per cent of the total instances of VPE, which highlights the importance of such constructions as typical syntactic contexts that favour VPE. By contrast, only one example has been found where VPE contains the presupposition trigger *too* (*Cha. Why, you must have trembled for your life when mounted. Hec. I believe I did too*, COLLIER-1835,8.138), in line with the results reported in Bos and Spenader's (2011) paper. These facts alone demonstrate that empirical studies on ellipsis should not be underestimated, as they have been proved of high importance to test the theoretical validity of the different hypotheses put forward by theoretical studies.

iv. Syntactic domain

The syntactic domain where the ellipsis site takes place has also been object of study in this investigation. Five possible syntactic contexts have been found in the examples of PAE from this period taking into account the annotation of the PPCMBE, that is, IP-MAT (matrix clause), IP-SUB (subordinate clause), IP-IMP (imperative clause), CP-QUE (CP-questions) and CP-QUE-TAG (tag questions), illustrated in (59)-(63), respectively:

(59) Mabel Chiltern: Don't forget. Lord Goring: Of course I shan't. WILDE-1895,55.431

((*IP-MAT* (META (NP (NPR Lord) (NPR Goring))
         (, :))
    (PP (P Of)
       (NP (N course)))
    (NP-SBJ (PRO I))
    (MD $sha)
    (NEG $n't)
    (CODE {TEXT:shan't})
    (. .))
  (ID WILDE-1895,55.431))

(60) and dip it in the spawn of Frogs, beaten *as you would the whites of eggs*, ALBIN-1736,4.75

(RRC (VAN beaten)
      (PP (P as)
         (CP-ADV (WADVP-1 0)
             (C 0)
             (IP-SUB (ADVP *T*-1)
                 (NP-SBJ (PRO you))

                    (MD would)
                    (VB *)
                    (NP-OB1 (D the)
                              (NS whites)
                              (PP (P of)
                                  (NP (NS eggs))))))))
(ID ALBIN-1736,4.75)

(61) *Do*, send the cloaths if you send them in a wheelbarrow.
     JOHNSON-1775,2,33.645

((*IP-IMP*-SPE (IP-IMP-SPE (DOI Do))
        (, ,)
        (CODE {COM:sic})
        (VBI send)
        (NP-OB1 (D the) (NS cloaths))
        (PP (P if)
            (CP-ADV-SPE (C 0)
                        (IP-SUB-SPE (NP-SBJ (PRO you))
                                    (VBP send)
                                    (NP-OB1 (PRO them)))))
        (PP (P in)
            (NP (D a) (N wheelbarrow)))
        (. .))
(ID JOHNSON-1775,2,33.645))

(62) Lord Fitz. And I must go and walk my three miles, this morning. Sir
     Simon. *Must you, my lord*? COLMAN-1805,46.878

        ((CP-QUE (META (CODE <font>)
                  (NP (NPR Sir) (NPR Simon))
                  (, .)
                  (CODE <$$font>))
                  (IP-SUB (MD Must)
                          (NP-SBJ (PRO you)))
                  (, ,)
                  (NP-VOC (PRO$ my) (N lord))
                  (. ?))
        (ID COLMAN-1805,46.878))

(63) You married a man with a future, *didn't you?* WILDE-1895,58.503

(*CP-QUE-TAG* (IP-SUB (DOD $did)
                    (NEG $n't)
                    (CODE {TEXT:didn't})
                    (NP-SBJ (PRO you))
                    (VB *)))
           (. ?))
(ID WILDE-1895,58.503))

The importance of the study of the syntactic domain where ellipsis takes place lies in the fact that it allows one to check the level of syntactic complexity that may exist between the antecedent and the ellipsis site. In other words, there may be cases where the syntactic linking existing between the source and the target of ellipsis is one of coordination, but the ellipsis site is further embedded in a subordinate clause, as in (64):

(64) I could make no answer; *but hope you do.* CARLYLE-1835,2,300.673

The syntactic domain where cases of PAE take place is shown in Table 27.

In the light of the data gathered in Table 27, the ellipsis site in instances of PAE occurs in syntactic domains of subordination in the vast majority of cases (64.36 per cent). These are followed by syntactic domains of coordination, which represent nearly 30 per cent of the examples. The contexts of tag questions (4.41 per cent), CP-questions (1.71 per cent) and imperatives (0.54 per cent) are much more marginally represented in the corpus and they have only been found in cases of VPE. Notice that PG only occurs in two types of syntactic domains: subordinate (83.72 per cent) and matrix clauses (16.28 per cent), while VPE has been attested in a wider variety of syntactic domains: subordinate clauses (62.73 per cent), matrix clauses (30.05 per cent), tag questions (4.78 per cent), CP-questions (1.85 per cent) and imperative clauses (0.59 per cent). Therefore, it

Table 27 Syntactic Domain of Ellipsis in PAE Constructions

SYNTACTIC DOMAIN	PG		VPE		PAE	
	Abs. Freq.	%	Abs. Freq.	%	Abs. Freq.	%
IP-SUB	72	83.72	643	62.73	715	64.36
IP-MAT	14	16.28	308	30.05	322	28.98
CP-QUE-TAG	0	0.00	49	4.78	49	4.41
CP-QUE	0	0.00	19	1.85	19	1.71
IP-IMP	0	0.00	6	0.59	6	0.54
TOTAL	86		1,025		1,111	

should be highlighted that ellipsis sites are attested in subordinate clauses in the vast majority of cases, even more so in the case of PG when compared with VPE.

Let us now pay attention to the interaction between syntactic linking and syntactic domain in cases of PAE. The data regarding PG are provided in Table 28.

As mentioned earlier, over 80 per cent of the instances of PG take place within the syntactic domain of subordination, while around 16 per cent do so within that of matrix clauses. The most frequent pattern is one where the type of syntactic linking established between the source and the target of ellipsis is comparative subordination and, at the same time, the ellipsis site occurs within the domain of subordination, yielding over 74 per cent of the examples of PG attested. The second most frequent combination is instantiated by cases where there exists no syntactic relation between the antecedent and the ellipsis site and, in addition, the ellipsis sites occur within the domain of a matrix clause, accounting for approximately 10 per cent of the total. However, notice that the fact that the type of syntactic linking established between the source and the target of ellipsis is one of coordination does not necessarily imply that the ellipsis site will be found within the syntactic domain of a matrix clause. In fact, two cases have been found where the ellipsis site appears within a domain of subordination, rendering 2.32 per cent of the total, as shown in the following examples:

(65) Court. Do you remember before the Cornwal's Boat came on Board you, if you was going in a parallel Line with the Enemy, *or whether you were more to Windward*, or more from the Wind, than they were?
HOLMES-TRIAL-1749,73.1372

(66) Q. Had you no preventer Braces? A. I believe we had at the lower Yards, *but don't know whether we had at Topsail-Yards or not*.
HOLMES-TRIAL-1749,67.1248

Table 28 Syntactic Linking and Syntactic Domain in PG

SYNTACTIC LINKING	SYNTACTIC DOMAIN					
	IP-SUB		IP-MAT		TOTAL	
	Abs. Freq.	%	Abs. Freq.	%	Abs. Freq.	%
coordination	2	2.78	2	14.29	4	4.65
none	4	5.56	9	64.29	13	15.12
subord. comparative	64	88.89	0	0.00	64	74.42
subord. relative	1	1.39	0	0.00	1	1.16
subord. adverbial	1	1.39	3	21.43	4	4.65
TOTAL	72	83.72	14	16.28	86	100.00

In these examples the antecedents (*was going in a parallel Line with the Enemy* and *we had at the lower Yards*, respectively) and the ellipsis sites are connected via the coordinating conjunction *or* but they occur within a syntactic domain of subordination, introduced in both cases by the complementizer *whether*.

Importantly, there are also three cases where the syntactic linking established between the antecedent and the ellipsis site would be adverbial subordination but the ellipsis site appears within the matrix clause, rendering 3.48 per cent of the total (the subordinating conjunctions where one can find the antecedents of the ellipsis sites appear in italics (*since, tho* and *if*), while the licensors of PG appear in italics within the matrix clauses delimited by square brackets):

(67) *Since* the Law was given by Moses, [Grace and Truth *was* g̶i̶v̶e̶n̶ by Jesus Christ]$_{IP-MAT}$. PURVER-NEW-1764,1,1J.32

(68) for *tho* I have not s̶t̶u̶d̶i̶e̶d̶ equally, [I *have* studied regularly]$_{IP-MAT}$. HAYDON-1808,1,30.764

(69) *if* there is any thing to which they have a tendency and impulse, [it *must be* a̶ ̶t̶e̶n̶d̶e̶n̶c̶y̶ ̶a̶n̶d̶ ̶i̶m̶p̶u̶l̶s̶e̶ to the supreme and all-sufficient good]$_{IP-MAT}$. BOETHRI-1785,124.260

It has been shown that in the vast majority of cases of PG there is one-to-one correspondence between the type of syntactic linking between the antecedent and the ellipsis site and the domain of the ellipsis site. In other words, in contexts of subordination, the ellipsis site normally appears within a subordinate clause, and in cases of coordination or no syntactic linking, the ellipsis site usually takes place in matrix clauses. Let us now have a look at the situation in VPE, whose data are provided in Table 29.

In the light of the data, VPE takes place in subordinate clauses in the vast majority of cases, representing over 60 per cent of the cases. VPE in matrix clauses is half as frequent, yielding around 30 per cent of the total. In this respect, VPE resembles PG, though the percentage of ellipsis in subordinate clauses in the former is lower (60 per cent versus 80 per cent, respectively). Notice, also, that there are three more syntactic domains where ellipsis takes place that are not evinced in cases of PG: tag questions (4.78 per cent), CP-questions (1.85 per cent) and IP-imperatives (0.59 per cent), though their representation is much more marginal and altogether they only represent around 7 per cent of the instances of VPE. These three domains have been found in contexts where there is no syntactic relation between the source and the target of ellipsis. But let us now pay attention to the most frequent combinations that arise in VPE once syntactic linking and syntactic domain have been cross-tabulated. The most

Table 29 Syntactic Linking and Syntactic Domain in VPE

SYNTACTIC LINKING	SYNTACTIC DOMAIN													
	IP-SUB		IP-MAT		CP-QUE-TAG		CP-QUE		IP-IMP		TOTAL	
	Abs. Freq.	%	Abs. Freq.	%	Abs. Freq.	%	Abs. Freq.	%	Abs. Freq.	%	Abs. Freq.	%
coordination	33	5.13	24	7.79	0	0.00	0	0.00	0	0.00	57	5.56
none	166	25.82	276	89.61	49	100.00	19	100.00	6	100.00	516	50.34
subord. comparative	323	50.23	0	0.00	0	0.00	0	0.00	0	0.00	185	18.05
subord. relative	74	11.51	0	0.00	0	0.00	0	0.00	0	0.00	74	7.22
subord. adverbial	47	7.31	8	2.60	0	0.00	0	0.00	0	0.00	193	18.83
TOTAL	643	62.73	308	30.05	49	4.78	19	1.85	6	0.59	1,025	100.00

frequent pattern is comparative subordination with the ellipsis site being found within a subordinate clause, which represents over 30 per cent of the examples. This is followed by those cases where the antecedent and the ellipsis site appear in different sentences (i.e. there is no syntactic relation between them) and the ellipsis site is found within the domain of a matrix clause, rendering almost 27 per cent of the total. These two most frequent patterns were the same in PG. Next, the third most frequent combination attested has been one where the antecedent and the ellipsis site appear in different sentences and, at the same time, the ellipsis site is in a subordinate clause, yielding over 16 per cent of the total. Here are some examples (the syntactic domain of ellipsis appears in between square brackets and the licensor of ellipsis in italics):

(70) I didn't dare to make the smallest repartee, I need hardly tell you. [If I had ~~dared to make the smallest repartee~~]$_{IP-SUB}$, it would have stopped the music at once. WILDE-1895,57.476

(71) Q. Can you see him in court? A. I cannot say [that I *do* ~~see him in court~~]$_{IP-SUB}$. WATSON-1817,1,94.398

As was the case with PG, there are some cases of VPE whose type of linking is coordination but their ellipsis sites appear within a domain of subordination (3.21 per cent), as in these examples:

(72) Q. Did you hear any body, *and* [if you *did* ~~hear any body~~]$_{IP-SUB}$, who was it proposed any amendment to that? WATSON-1817,1,128.1312

(73) He continued praising God as often as he could speak, *and* [when he could not ~~speak~~]$_{IP-SUB}$, his Eyes were fixt upwards. WESLEY-174X,37.640

In the previous examples, the antecedents and the targets of ellipsis are coordinated via the conjunction *and*, but the latter appear within a syntactic domain of subordination introduced by the subordinating conjunctions *if* and *when*, respectively.

In addition, as in PG, there are also a few cases where the antecedent and the ellipsis site are linked via adverbial subordination but the ellipsis site appears within a matrix clause (0.78 per cent of the total), illustrated in the following example:

(74) *if* the second boy can not correct the first, [the third or fourth *may* ~~correct the first~~]$_{IP-MAT}$. LANCASTER-1806,60.377

In summary, it has been reported that the ellipsis site in instances of PAE occurs in syntactic domains of subordination in the vast majority of cases (64.36 per cent, and this percentage goes up to over 80 per cent in PG). These are followed by syntactic domains of coordination, which represent nearly 30 per cent of the examples. Those instances where the ellipsis takes place in contexts of tag questions (4.41 per cent), CP-questions (1.71 per cent) and imperatives (0.54 per cent) are much more marginally represented in the corpus under study, as they have only been found in cases of VPE. In addition, when one pays attention to the interaction between the type of syntactic linking and the type of syntactic domain evinced in instances of PAE, it has been discovered that in the vast majority of cases of PAE there exists a one-to-one correspondence between the type of syntactic linking established between the antecedent and the ellipsis site and the domain where the ellipsis site occurs. Thus, in contexts where the type of syntactic linking is one of subordination, the ellipsis site normally appears within the domain of a subordinate clause, while in cases of coordination or no syntactic linking, the ellipsis site usually appears within the domain of a matrix clause. However, it has been found that both in PG and in VPE there may be cases where this correspondence is not met. For instance, there are examples where the antecedent and the ellipsis site appear in different sentences and, at the same time, the ellipsis site is embedded in a subordinate clause. Moreover, there are also cases where the antecedent and the ellipsis site are coordinated, but the ellipsis site appears further embedded. Finally, it has also been found that there might be cases where the antecedent and the ellipsis site are linked via adverbial subordination but the ellipsis site appears within a matrix clause.

v. Category of the source of ellipsis versus category of the target of ellipsis
This section will analyse the category of the element(s) that serve(s) as antecedent(s) for the elided clause. This has also been studied empirically by Bos and Spenader (2011). Other empirical works on the identity between the category of the source and that of the target of ellipsis have been carried out in the field of psycholinguistics (Arregui et al. 2006; Kim et al. 2011; Miller and Hemforth 2014), as mentioned in Section 1.2.4.

If you recall, the following types of categories have been distinguished in the present study: antecedents may be APs, NPs, PPs, AdPs, VPs or non-constituents (in cases of split antecedents and passive–active voice mismatches the antecedent would be a string that does not form a constituent). Table 30 shows the results for the categories of the source of ellipsis in PG and VPE.

Table 30 Category of the Source of Ellipsis

CATEGORY SOURCE	PG Abs. Freq.	%	VPE Abs. Freq.	%	TOTAL PAE Abs. Freq.	%
VP	62	72.09	795	77.56	857	77.14
AP	12	13.95	98	9.56	110	9.90
NP	9	10.47	93	9.07	102	9.18
PP	3	3.49	31	3.02	34	3.06
AdP	0	0.00	5	0.49	5	0.45
Non-constituent	0	0.00	3	0.29	3	0.27
TOTAL	86		1,025		1,111	

As can be gathered from Table 30, PG possesses a verbal antecedent in the vast majority of cases (72.09 per cent). More marginally, non-verbal antecedents also occur: APs (13.95 per cent), NPs (10.47 per cent) and PPs (3.49 per cent), and they represent altogether over a quarter of the examples. These non-verbal types of PG have not been discussed in the literature, which enhances the importance of this corpus study. By contrast, cases of non-verbal antecedents in VPE have been coined in the literature either as 'Predicate Phrase Ellipsis' (van Craenenbroeck and Merchant 2013) or as 'Predicative Ellipsis' (Bos and Spenader 2011). Below, I include examples of all the types of antecedents attested in PG:

(75) I have been always in the habit of $[treating]_{VP}$ my own Horses much after the same manner that I would myself; SKEAVINGTON-184X,27.C2.413

(76) Lady Chiltern: Robert is as $[incapable]_{AP}$ of doing a foolish thing as he is of doing a wrong thing. WILDE-1895,54.391

(77) My question was, whether you had $[any\ conversation]_{NP}$ about the bills? A. No; about Mr. Castle, I had. WATSON-1817,1,99.550

(78) the Enemy being at that Time $[at\ a\ greater\ Distance\ from\ us]_{PP}$ than they were at any Time before that I saw them. HOLMES-TRIAL-1749,75.1408

As far as the category of the antecedents in VPE is concerned, in Table 30 one observes that the distribution is the same as in PG: VP antecedents prevail, as they comprise 77.56 per cent of the total. As was the case with PG, these verbal antecedents are followed by non-verbal ones: APs (9.56 per cent), NPs (9.07 per cent), PPs (3.02 per cent) and AdPs (0.49 per cent), respectively. Overall, these non-verbal antecedents are present in 22.15 per cent of the times. Notice, however, that in VPE there are two types of antecedents that have not been attested in PG: AdPs and non-constituents, although it should be noted that they are very marginally represented in VPE. In (79)-(84), I provide examples of the types of antecedents of VPE in my database:

(79) but I need not [*stay*]$_{VP}$ now, need I? YONGE-1865,160.36

(80) Life is never [*fair*]$_{AP}$, Robert. And perhaps it is a good thing for most of us that it is not. WILDE-1895,41.63

(81) My father tells me that even I have [*faults*]$_{NP}$. Perhaps I have. WILDE-1895,47.238

(82) Q. Were you [*at the Merlin's Cave*]$_{PP}$, in a room there? A. I was. WATSON-1817,1,123.1161

(83) Q. That was [*afterwards*]$_{AdP}$ – two months after you had printed those bills, was it not? WATSON-1817,1,92.331

(84) Bur. [Pray, now, master, don't say any more! come, be a man! get on your things; and face the bailiffs, that are rummaging the goods]$_{Non-constituent}$. Job. I can't, John; I can't. COLMAN-1805,35.540

We are now in a position to check whether there exists categorial identity between the sources and the targets of ellipsis. On the one hand, it has been found that there are no mismatches between the categories of the source and those of the target of ellipsis in PG. This implies, therefore, that no cases of nominal antecedents like the ones reported in Hardt (1992a, 1993) for VPE have been attested in Late Modern English:

(85) Today there is little or no OFFICIAL *harassment of lesbians and gays* by the national government, although autonomous governments might. [Hardt (1993: 35); emphasis in the original]

On the other hand, one case of categorial identity mismatch has been attested in VPE in the period under study, which represents only 0.09 per cent of the total:

(86) Q. [*Did you make any answer to it, or did you give it him?*]$_{Non-constituent}$ A. No, I did not [make any answer to it or give it him]$_{VP}$; WATSON-1817,1,85.137

If you recall from Section 2.2.4, example (86) constitutes a case of VPE that contains split antecedents (see subsection *vi* below for more details), where two different sentences are coordinated and serve as the source of ellipsis. In the reply to this question, two coordinated VPs, and not two coordinated sentences, are elided: 'make any answer to it or give it him'. In the light of the examples of

PAE attested in our corpus, it seems that syntactic identity between the source and the target of ellipsis is required in Late Modern English (with the exception of example (86)). This finding is in line with Bos and Spenader's (2011) for VPE in Present-Day English.

As already advanced in Sections 2.2.1 and 2.2.4, licensors *be* and *have* are special in the sense that they may trigger the ellipsis of both verbal and non-verbal material in PG and VPE. So far, no theoretical or empirical works on PG have ever mentioned the possibility of omitting non-verbal material. Our data reveal that the ellipsis of non-verbal material is possible in both PG and VPE, and not only in VPE. Let us have a look at the categories of the target of ellipsis triggered by licensors *be* and *have* in PG first.

As can be gathered from Table 31, in PG auxiliary *be* triggers ellipsis of non-verbal material in over 65 per cent of the cases. Ellipsis of APs is the most frequent (41.38 per cent), followed by NPs (13.79 per cent) and PPs (10.34 per cent) (see examples (87)-(89)). Ellipsis of verbal material, therefore, represents almost 35 per cent of the total (as in (90)). In the case of auxiliary *have*, one can observe that ellipsis of verbal material predominates in PG (61.54 per cent), while ellipsis of NPs yields 38.46 per cent of the total (illustrated in examples (91) and (92), respectively).

(87) Mrs. H. My dear uncle, I'm glad to see you! As I am [*glad*]$_{AP}$, my little darling pet, to see you, BROUGHAM-1861,17.598

(88) if there is any thing to which they have a tendency and impulse, it must be [*a tendency*]$_{NP}$ to the supreme and all-sufficient good. BOETHRI-1785,124.260

(89) tho' the former seemed to be as much for Uniformity and Subscriptions in their own Way, as their Antagonists were [*for Uniformity*]$_{PP}$ in theirs. KIMBER-1742,260.C1.55

(90) the Morality of That is no more determined by one Part, than the Beauty or Deformity of This is [*determined*]$_{VP}$ by one single Feature. YONGE-1865,166.201

(91) for tho I have not studied equally, I have [*studied*]$_{VP}$ regularly. HAYDON-1808,1,30.764

(92) He has no more notion, my dear Tom, of a modern 'good match', than Eve had [*a notion*]$_{NP}$ of pin-money. COLMAN-1805,23.154

Now, let us compare these data with those attested in VPE, shown in Table 32.

One can observe almost the same tendency as in PG: ellipsis of non-verbal material after licensor *be* predominates, representing 68.15 per cent of the cases.

Table 31 Category of the Target of Ellipsis Triggered by Auxiliaries *Be* and *Have* in PG

	be		have	
CATEGORY TARGET	Abs. Freq.	%	Abs. Freq.	%
NP	4	13.79	5	38.46
VP	10	34.48	8	61.54
AP	12	41.38	0	0.00
PP	3	10.34	0	0.00
TOTAL	29		13	

Table 32 Category of the Target of Ellipsis Triggered by Auxiliaries *Be* and *Have* in VPE

	be		have	
CATEGORY TARGET	Abs. Freq.	%	Abs. Freq.	%
NP	93	27.68	16	29.09
VP	107	31.85	39	70.91
AP	99	29.46	0	0.00
PP	32	9.52	0	0.00
AdP	5	1.49	0	0.00
TOTAL	336		55	

Hence, ellipsis of verbal material happens on 31.85 per cent of the occasions (see (97)). As was the case with PG, APs are the most frequent non-verbal elided categories (29.46 per cent), followed closely by NPs (27.68 per cent) and more marginally by PPs (9.52 per cent) and AdPs (1.49 per cent) (see (93)-(96), respectively). Notice that ellipsis of AdPs has not been attested in PG. Regarding licensor *have*, once again it licenses ellipsis of verbal material in the vast majority of cases (70.91 per cent), whereas ellipsis of NPs is attested in 29.09 per cent of the cases (see (98)-(99)).

(93) He at first appeared very languid, as indeed he was [*very languid*]$_{AP}$. DODDRIDGE-1747,19.154

(94) Q. That it was not the French tri-coloured flag? A. It was not [*the French tri-coloured flag*]$_{NP}$. WATSON-1817,1,167.2240

(95) Q. Was Mr. Raynsford in a situation to hear Hunt's speech? A. I should think he was [*in a situation to hear Hunt's speech*]$_{PP}$. WATSON-1817,1,120.1090

(96) A.I really believe it was afterwards, but I am not sure whether it was [*afterwards*]$_{AdP}$ or not. HOLMES-TRIAL-1749,60.1093

(97) was the person speaking when you got to the field? A. I believe he was not [*speaking when I got to the field*]$_{VP}$. WATSON-1817,1,182.2646

(98) Q. Have you seen the bill since you handed it over to the Grand Jury at Hicks's Hall? A. No, I have not [*seen the bill since I handed it over to the Grand Jury at Hicks's Hall*]$_{VP}$. WATSON-1817,1,93.362

(99) When we have a Minister of Horticulture, as the French and Belgians have [*a Minister of Horticulture*]$_{NP}$, then perhaps the horticultural trade will receive as much consideration as agriculture does in connection with the rating of the land. WEATHERS-1913,1,1.9

Finally, comparison between the results obtained in the present study and those reported in Bos and Spenader's (2011) work will be offered here. In Table 34, the results with regard to the category of the source in VPE are divided into three different groups: those triggered by licensor *be*, those by *have* and those by other licensors.

In Bos and Spenader's (2011) study it has been found that VPE triggered by licensors other than *be* and *have* predominates, representing 68.9 per cent of the

Table 33 Category of the Source in Bos and Spenader's (2011) Study

CATEGORY SOURCE	VPE+be Abs. Freq.	%	VPE+have Abs. Freq.	%	Other VPE Abs. Freq.	%	TOTAL VPE Abs. Freq.	%
AdP	0	0.00	0	0.00	0	0.00	0	0.00
AP	48	44.44	0	0.00	0	0.00	48	9.88
NP	20	18.52	0	0.00	0	0.00	20	4.12
PP	4	3.70	0	0.00	0	0.00	4	0.82
VP	36	33.33	43	100.00	335	100.00	414	85.19
TOTAL	108	22.22	43	8.85	335	68.93	486	100.00

Table 34 Category of the Source in Writing-Related Genres in Late Modern English

CATEGORY SOURCE	VPE+be Abs. Freq.	%	VPE+have Abs. Freq.	%	Other VPE Abs. Freq.	%	TOTAL Abs. Freq.	%
AdP	0	0.00	0	0.00	0	0.00	0	0.00
AP	19	45.24	0	0.00	0	0.00	19	14.07
NP	6	14.29	3	75	0	0.00	9	6.67
PP	2	4.76	0	0.00	0	0.00	2	1.48
VP	15	35.71	1	25	89	100.00	105	77.78
TOTAL	42	31.11	4	2.96	89	65.93	135	100.00

cases of VPE. In addition, VPE licensed by auxiliary *be* comprises about 22 per cent of the examples, followed by VPE licensed by auxiliary *have* (8.85 per cent). In the light of the data provided in Table 34, the same tendency has been found in our study, as VPE triggered by licensors other than *be* and *have* is also the most frequent by far (65.93 per cent). It should be highlighted, however, that the percentage of VPE triggered by auxiliary *be* is slightly higher (31.11 per cent) in Late Modern English and that of VPE triggered by licensor *have* is three times less frequent (2.96 per cent) when compared with the data from Present-Day English.[3]

If one pays attention to the category of the source licensed by auxiliary *be*, it is clear that both studies illustrate the same tendency: verbal antecedents represent 33.33 per cent of the cases in Present-Day English and 35.71 per cent in Late Modern English (in writing-related genres). Therefore, non-verbal antecedents comprise 66.67 per cent of the total in Bos and Spenader (2011) and 64.29 per cent in the present monograph. Within non-verbal antecedents triggered by *be*, APs are the most frequent in both studies (44.44 per cent in their work versus 45.24 per cent in ours), followed by NPs (18.52 per cent in theirs versus 14.29 per cent in ours) and PPs (3.70 per cent in theirs versus 4.76 per cent in ours). Notice that no AdPs in the source of ellipsis have been attested in both investigations (that is, in writing-related genres, since it has been shown before that they are attested in speech-related genres in my database).

The situation changes when one focuses on VPE triggered by auxiliary *have*, where one finds that only verbal antecedents have been attested in Bos and Spenader's (2011) paper. This is not true of writing-related genres in this study, where their representation is much more marginal, as mentioned earlier, and the NP antecedents are more common than the verbal ones.

In conclusion, it has been shown that almost the same exact tendencies and proportions have been attested regarding the category of the sources of ellipsis in Late Modern English and in Present-Day English. As a result, then, verbal antecedents triggered by licensors other than *be* and *have* predominate, followed by VPE licensed by auxiliary *be*, and VPE licensed by auxiliary *have*. The only significant difference lies in the fact that licensor *have* seems to trigger ellipsis three times more frequently in Present-Day English than in the previous period of the English language. Also, auxiliary *have* has been reported to possess only verbal antecedents in Bos and Spenader's (2011) investigation, while in my study the NP sources seem to be more frequent (though both verbal and non-verbal antecedents are marginally represented in the writing-related genres of our study). Overall, therefore, it seems that there have not been significant changes with respect to the category of the source of VPE in the transition from Late Modern English to Present-Day English. What is more, on the one hand, it has been found that there is categorial identity between the source and the target of ellipsis in PG. On the other hand, one case of categorial identity mismatch has been attested in VPE in the period under study due to the existence of split antecedents. As a consequence, in the light of the examples of PAE attested in my corpus study, it seems that syntactic identity between the source and the target of ellipsis is required in Late Modern English (with the exception of the example of split antecedents just mentioned). This finding is in line with Bos and Spenader's (2011) for VPE in Present-Day English.

vi. Split antecedents

As mentioned in Section 2.2.4, those examples with 'split antecedents' are also known as 'combined antecedents' in Hardt (1990). Hardt includes in this category cases of VPE in which the antecedent is the result of the combination of two or more separate VPs.

(100) I *can walk*, and I *can chew gum*. Gerry *can* too, but not at the same time. [Hardt (1990: 277); originally in Webber (1978)]

In (100) the meaning of the ellipsis site would be 'Gerry can walk and chew gum too'. Split antecedents, as Hardt (1990: 277) points out, present 'a problem for most accounts of VP ellipsis, since there is no syntactic object consisting of the combination of two separate VP's'.

I investigated whether split antecedents were possible in Modern English, and the findings are given in Table 35.

As can be observed, only three examples of split antecedents have been attested in the present corpus study, which amounts to only 0.29 per cent of the cases of VPE and, hence, 0.27 per cent of the total cases of PAE. As predicted by

Table 35 Split Antecedents in Late Modern English

SPLIT ANTECEDENTS	PG		VPE		PAE	
	Abs. Freq.	%	Abs. Freq.	%	Abs. Freq.	%
Absence	86	100.00	1,022	99.71	1,108	99.73
Presence	0	0.00	3	0.29	3	0.27
TOTAL	86		1,025		1,111	

the literature on PG, no instances of split antecedents have been found. The three instances of split antecedents found are the following:

(101) Q. Did you make any answer to it, or did you give it him? A. No, I did not; WATSON-1817,1,85.137

(102) Bur. Pray, now, master, don't say any more! come, be a man! get on your things; and face the bailiffs, that are rummaging the goods. Job. I can't, John; I can't. COLMAN-1805,35.539

Note that in (102) there are two licensors of VPE (*I can't*) which receive their interpretation from the previous split antecedents. It is interesting to note that all these three examples of split antecedents occur in dialogues. Hence, the split antecedents appear in a different turn, that is, a change of speaker is involved. Another common property that they share is that they all belong to speech-based genres such as Trial proceedings (101) and Drama comedy (102).

So far, only Nielsen (2005) and Bos and Spenader (2011) have studied split antecedents empirically. While the latter found no examples of split antecedents in their study, Nielsen (2005) reports that split antecedents occur in 0.30 per cent of cases, in line with the finding presented in this monograph (0.29 per cent). Therefore, split antecedents were as uncommon in Late Modern English as they appear to be nowadays.

vii. Remnants of PG

As mentioned at different points in this volume (Sections 1.1, 2.2.1 and 2.2.4), PG is characterized by the presence of a contrastive remnant which is not affected by ellipsis (though some exceptions to this general rule have been found, as will become clear later). I will provide a classification of the remnants of PG found according to their category and function in the clause/phrase where they occur. In the literature it is usually assumed that the types of remnants present in PG are NPs, ProNPs and PPs. However, as can be observed in Table 36, I have found four additional types of remnants, which have never been considered before: Infinitival VPs (103), AdPs (104), double NPs (105) and CPs (106). These four types comprise 8.15 per cent of the remnants of PG in the period under study. Here are some of the examples attested:

(103) Mrs. H. My dear uncle, I'm glad to see you! As I am, my little darling pet, [*to see you*]$_{\text{Inf. VP}}$, believe me. BROUGHAM-1861,17.598

(104) and appear as green at the utmost limit of their territory as they do [*far down*]$_{\text{AdP}}$. RUSKIN-1835,1,25.631

Table 36 Category of the Remnant of PG in Late Modern English

REMNANT CATEGORY	PG	
	Abs. Freq.	%
PP	50	58.14
NP	20	23.26
ProNP	9	10.47
Infinitival VP	3	3.49
AdP	2	2.33
NP NP	1	1.16
CP	1	1.16
TOTAL	86	

(105) God also called the Light Day, as he did [*the Darkness*]$_{NP}$ [*Night*]$_{NP}$. PURVER-OLD-1764,1,1G.14

(106) Q. Did we not engage closer before Sun-set, and after it was Dark, than we did [*when we were in a Line of Battle*]$_{CP}$? HOLMES-TRIAL-1749,78.1471

In the light of Table 36, it is clear that PPs are the remnants of PG in most of the cases (58.14 per cent), followed by NPs (24.42 per cent; notice that double NPs have been included in this figure) and ProNPs (10.47 per cent). This amounts to saying that in almost 60 per cent of the cases, we have a prepositional-based remnant in PG, whereas in around 35 per cent it is noun based. Some instances are presented in (107)-(109):

(107) I did not think you would have held out against her. 'Not when I had [*against you*]$_{PP}$.?' YONGE-1865,168.266

(108) I know they will watch her as a Fox would [*a Poultry-Yard*]$_{NP}$. DAVYS-1716,48.836

(109) the Prisoner paid the Men of his own Company himself, as all the Captains of Companies did [*theirs*]$_{ProNP}$. TOWNLEY-1746,21.71

Notice that three cases (3.48 per cent) have been found where the antecedent (underlined) has no overt object corresponding to the remnant:

(110) Even the delicate associations with words <u>can be expounded</u> through our own language; just as they must be [*to the pupil who is studying the original*]$_{PP}$. BAIN-1878,366.96

(111) that you know one <u>loves</u>, right or wrong, as one does [*one's nurse*]$_{NP}$. WALPOLE-174X,5,4.31

(112) Lou. Were I sure you would <u>follow</u>, as I would have [*you*]$_{ProNP}$, I should not care how soon I led up the Dance; DAVYS-1716,35.369

This subtype of PG has only been treated in Miller (2014: 81). He puts forward that 'the antecedent has a null anaphor as object, the reference of which is provided explicitly in the discourse context'. In his large-scale corpus study of PG, he found 13 occurrences of this subtype of comparative PG (0.95 per cent), which follow the same syntactic pattern as our examples: they are cases of *as*-appositives. One of the examples he provides is quoted below (Miller 2014: 81):

(113) My echoes are no longer tormentors but friends, and when one of them dies (as, inevitably, they have begun to) I <u>mourn</u> a little, as I would [*a sister*]$_{NP}$. (Fic)

If you recall, it could also be the case that the remnant of PG is composed of the objects of prepositions (Levin 1986; Gengel 2013; Miller 2014), known as 'deprepositionalized remnants' (Miller 2014: 81). In his corpus study, Miller (2014: 81) found 115 examples of deprepositionalized remnants (8.12 per cent). However, no instances of deprepositionalized remnants were found in my database. Further research seems in order here so as to check whether or not deprepositionalized remnants were an innovation of the Present-Day English period.

Let us now have a look at the different functions of the remnants of PG both at the clausal and phrasal levels. As shown in Table 37, the remnants of PG involve clausal functions in the vast majority of cases (76.75 per cent), be they adverbials (40.70 per cent) or objects of the clause (36.05 per cent) (see examples (114)-(115) and (116)-(117), respectively).

(114) for her desire of secrecy was prompted by the resolution to leave him unbound, whereas his wish for publicity was [*with the purpose of binding himself*]$_{Adverbial}$. YONGE-1865,166.201

Table 37 Syntactic Function of the Remnant of PG in Late Modern English

REMNANT FUNCTION	Abs. Freq.	%
Clausal functions		
Adverbial	35	40.70
Object	31	36.05
Phrasal functions		
Complement of N	12	13.95
Complement of A	8	9.30
TOTAL	86	

(115) that we ourselves differ from others, just as much as they do [*from us*]$_{\text{Adverbial}}$ BUTLER-1726,245.137

(116) If all the People in the Inn were not asleep, you would have awakened them as you have [*me*]$_{\text{D.O.}}$. FIELDING-1749,3,10.382

(117) I take it to be undoubtedly certain, that he, who can correct Latin when it is writ as all School-masters do [*their Boy's Exercises*]$_{\text{D.O.}}$ can correct it when it is spoke. ANON-1711,16.163

Notice that I have not made a distinction between optional (as in (114)) and obligatory adverbial elements (like prepositional complements, as in (115)) and have grouped them under the same label. In the case of objects, I have also included example (118), which is the only one that contains an indirect object:

(118) Even the delicate associations with words can be expounded through our own language; just as they must be [*to the pupil who is studying the original*]$_{\text{I.O.}}$. BAIN-1878,366.96

In 23.25 per cent of the cases, the remnants of PG involve phrasal functions: the remnants attested are either complements of nouns (13.95 per cent) or complements of adjectives (9.30 per cent). Here are some examples:

(119) He has no more <u>notion</u>, my dear Tom, of a modern 'good match,' than Eve had [*of pin-money*]$_{\text{Complement of N}}$. COLMAN-1805,23.154

(120) their propensity to vice is really as much a <u>disease</u> of the mind, as any of the ordinary human distempers is [*of the body*]$_{\text{Complement of N}}$. BOETHRI-1785,161.361

(121) Lady Chiltern: Robert is as <u>incapable</u> of doing a foolish thing as he is [*of doing a wrong thing*]$_{\text{Complement of A}}$. WILDE-1895,54.391

(122) philosophy is only <u>fitted</u> for speculative, as mathematical and classical studies are [*for practical*]$_{\text{Complement of A}}$, teaching. WHEWELL-1837,10.57

Finally, Miller (2014) reports a difference in the distribution of pronominal and NP remnants depending on whether PG occurs in comparative or in noncomparative constructions. He found that whereas in noncomparative PG pronominal remnants are highly predominant (74.5 per cent), the opposite is true of comparative PG, which has been found to contain NP remnants in the vast majority of cases (86.5 per cent). Our data for the remnants of comparative PG corroborate his findings: NP remnants represent 80 per cent of the total. However, in the case of noncomparative PG, the distribution of NP and ProNP remnants is almost the same: 55.56 per cent NP remnants versus 44.44 per cent ProNP remnants. This contrasts sharply with Miller's findings, where the tendency is more clearly marked towards a preference for pronominal remnants (75 per cent).

As a summary, I have provided a classification of the remnants of PG found according to their category and function in the clause/phrase where they occur. On the one hand, it has been shown that, apart from the categorial types of remnants usually mentioned in the literature such as NPs, PPs and ProNPs, four new types have been attested: infinitival VPs, AdPs, double NPs and CPs. Whereas prepositional-based remnants predominate (approx. 60 per cent), noun-based ones represent around 35 per cent of the cases, followed by the additional types attested (8.15 per cent), which had not been considered before. It has also been found that there might be cases of PG where there is no overt object in the antecedent corresponding to the remnant (3.48 per cent). In addition, notice that I have not found any cases of deprepositionalized remnants, while Miller (2014) reports that they represented 8.4 per cent of his database. Further research would be needed in order to check whether deprepositionalized remnants were an innovation of the Present-Day English period. As far as the syntactic function of the remnants of PG is concerned, it has been found that they involve clausal functions in the vast majority of cases (76.75 per cent), be they adverbials (40.70 per cent) or objects of the clause (36.05 per cent). Therefore, in 23.25 per cent of the cases, the remnants of PG involve phrasal functions, either as complements of nouns (13.95 per cent) or as complements of adjectives (9.30 per cent).

viii. Auxiliary-related variables

This section analyses the role of auxiliary-related variables such as polarity, voice, aspect, modality or tense and whether any mismatches have been attested with respect to these variables between the source and the target of ellipsis in instances of PAE. If you recall from Section 1.2.2, the importance of the above-mentioned variables was pointed out by Halliday and Hasan (1976). I will start the discussion by focusing on the data regarding polarity.

- Polarity in PAE

The polarity status of the source and the target of ellipsis in PG and VPE will be described to check whether there exist any mismatches between the polarity of the source and that of the ellipsis site. In Tables 38 and 39, the data concerning PG are provided.

As can be inferred from Tables 38 and 39, in PG the target of ellipsis is positive in 97.67 per cent of the total dataset. What is more, the polarity of both the source

Table 38 Polarity of the Source and Polarity of the Target of Ellipsis in PG

	POLARITY TARGET							
	explicit polar alternative		negative		positive		TOTAL	
POLARITY SOURCE	Abs. Freq.	%	Abs. Freq.	%	Abs. Freq.	%	Abs. Freq.	%
negative	0	0.00	0	0	9	10.71	9	10.47
positive	1	100.00	1	100.00	75	89.29	77	89.53
TOTAL	1	1.16	1	1.16	84	97.67	86	100.00

Table 39 Mismatches in Polarity between the Source and the Target of Ellipsis in PG

	POLARITY TARGET							
	Explicit Polar Alternative		Negative		Positive		TOTAL	
POLARITY SOURCE	Abs. Freq.	%	Abs. Freq.	%	Abs. Freq.	%	Abs. Freq.	%
Negative	0	0.00	0	0	9	10.71	9	10.47
Positive	1	100.00	1	100.00	0	0.00	2	2.33
TOTAL	1	1.16	1	1.16	9	10.47	11	12.79

and the target of ellipsis in PG is positive in the vast majority of cases (87.20 per cent), see example (123). This means that, in general, there are no mismatches between the source and the target of ellipsis with respect to polarity in PG. The remaining 12.80 per cent constitute cases of polarity mismatch between the source and the target of ellipsis: the most common mismatch is instantiated by negative source-positive target, which represents 10.46 per cent of the cases (see (124)). Then, there are two more types of mismatches which are much more marginally represented in PG: positive source-explicit polar alternative target (which comprises 1.16 per cent of the total, as in (125)) and positive source-negative target (which also comprises 1.16 per cent of the total, as in (126)).

(123) Mr. Serjeant Copley. How *did* you *read* it *over*? A. The same as I would any thing else. WATSON-1817,1,100.586

(124) but *did not admire* the strain of its poetry in general, though I *did* its morality. BOSWELL-1776,49.475

(125) Q. Had you no preventer Braces? A. I believe we *had* at the lower Yards, but don't know whether we *had* at Topsail-Yards *or not* but I believe not, HOLMES-TRIAL-1749,67.1248

(126) this was a request I *would have refused* any other man; but *could not* one from whom I have gained so much. HAYDON-1808,1,33.839

Let us now concentrate on the description of the types of polarity of the source and the target of ellipsis attested in VPE, shown in Tables 40 and 41.

As was the case with PG, the target of ellipsis is positive in the majority of cases (78.34 per cent), followed by negative targets (20.78 per cent) and, much more marginally, explicit polar alternative targets (0.87 per cent). In addition, in 61.85 per cent of the examples both the source of ellipsis and its target are positive. Therefore, once again polarity matching also predominates in VPE (see example (127)). If one adds that negative polarity in both the source and the ellipsis site constitutes 4.48 per cent of the cases (see (128)), then the previous figure goes up to 66.33 per cent of the total. The mismatches attested in VPE have the following patterns (in decreasing order of frequency): negative source-positive target (16.20 per cent) (as in (129)), positive source-negative target (16.20 per cent)

Table 40 Polarity of the Source and Polarity of the Target of Ellipsis in VPE

	POLARITY TARGET							
	Explicit Polar Alternative		Negative		Positive		TOTAL	
POLARITY SOURCE	Abs. Freq.	%	Abs. Freq.	%	Abs. Freq.	%	Abs. Freq.	%
Explicit Polar Alternative	0	0	1	0.47	3	0.37	4	0.39
Negative	2	22.22	46	21.60	166	20.67	214	20.88
Positive	7	77.78	166	77.93	634	78.95	807	78.73
TOTAL	9	0.87	213	20.78	803	78.34	1,025	100.00

Table 41 Mismatches in Polarity between the Source and the Target of Ellipsis in VPE

	POLARITY TARGET							
	Explicit Polar Alternative		Negative		Positive		TOTAL	
POLARITY SOURCE	Abs. Freq.	%	Abs. Freq.	%	Abs. Freq.	%	Abs. Freq.	%
Eexplicit Polar Alternative	0	0	1	0.10	3	0.29	4	0.39
Negative	2	0.20	0	0.00	166	16.20	168	16.39
Positive	7	0.68	166	16.20	0	0.00	173	16.88
TOTAL	9	0.88	167	16.29	169	16.49	345	33.66

(as in (130)), positive source-explicit polar alternative target (0.68 per cent) (see (131)), explicit polar alternative source-positive target (0.29 per cent) (see (132)), negative source-explicit polar alternative target (0.20 per cent) (see (133)) and explicit polar alternative source-negative target (0.10 per cent) (see (134)). Interestingly enough, in the case of the two most common mismatches, that is, negative source-positive target and vice versa, their frequency is exactly the same in VPE.

(127) The Classical Languages *train* the mind as nothing else *does*. BAIN-1878,366.109

(128) Q. You *did not endeavour* to see what it was? A. No, I *did not*. WATSON-1817,1,181.2619

(129) but this matter *does not depend on* my brother's consent, and even if it *did*, Ermine's own true position is that which is most honourable to her. YONGE-1865,178.507

(130) He continued praising God as often as he *could speak*, and when he *could not*, his Eyes were fixt upwards. WESLEY-174X,37.640

(131) A. I really believe it *was* afterwards, but I am not sure whether it *was, or not*. HOLMES-TRIAL-1749,60.1093

(132) but I am not quite positive whether it *was* then *or not*, but I believe it *was*.

(133) Q. *Did not* the Strafford, soon after the Enemy were put to Flight, *enter* into Action again with the Spanis Vice-Admiral? A. I can n't say whether she *did or not*. HOLMES-TRIAL-1749,16.250

(134) Q. *Were you or not desired* to attend there by any person. A. I *was not*. WATSON-1817,1,157.1990

Within these cases of VPE, we have included cases of tag questions that may be biasing the data, as they unmarkedly involve contrasts in polarity between the source and the target of ellipsis. Let us check the distribution of the types of polarity in tag questions, presented in Table 42.

The proportions of both negative (53.06 per cent) and positive polarity targets (46.93 per cent) in tag questions are almost the same. In 80 per cent of the cases, there is mismatch in polarity between the source and the target of ellipsis: positive source-negative target represents 53.06 per cent of the examples (see (135)), while negative source-positive target represents 26.53 per cent of the total (see (136)). The remaining 20.40 per cent constitute cases of tag questions with marked polarity, where both the source and the ellipsis site are instances of positive polarity (as in (137)).

Table 42 Polarity of the Source and Polarity of the Target of Ellipsis in Tag Questions

	POLARITY TARGET					
	Negative		Positive		TOTAL	
POLARITY SOURCE	Abs. Freq.	%	Abs. Freq.	%	Abs. Freq.	%
Negative	0	0.00	13	56.52	13	26.53
Positive	26	100.00	10	43.48	36	73.47
TOTAL	26	53.06	23	46.93	49	100.00

(135) I *think*, *don't you*? that there may be another attraction. YONGE-1865,176.459

(136) and that *is not* far, *is it*? WILDE-1895,62.629

(137) Q. You *believe* now it was Hooper's, *do you*? WATSON-1817,1,170.2313

If one subtracts the cases of tag questions from the data presented in Table 41, it would be possible to check the influence that they exert on the patterns of polarity attested in VPE.

In the light of Table 43, we observe that the targets of ellipsis are still positive in the vast majority of cases, although its percentage has slightly risen to almost 80 per cent of the cases. These are followed by negative targets, whose proportion has decreased from 20.78 per cent to 19.15 per cent. Finally, explicit polar alternative targets go up from 0.87 per cent to 0.92 per cent, but their percentage remains very low. Before, it was mentioned that in 61.85 per cent of the examples, both the source of ellipsis and its target involved positive polarity. Now that tag questions have been excluded, this percentage goes up to approximately 64 per cent of the total. It can be confirmed, then, that the most common pattern

Table 43 Polarity of the Source and Polarity of the Target of Ellipsis in VPE

	POLARITY TARGET							
	Explicit Polar Alternative		Negative		Positive		TOTAL	
POLARITY SOURCE	Abs. Freq.	%	Abs. Freq.	%	Abs. Freq.	%	Abs. Freq.	%
Explicit Polar Alternative	0	0.00	1	0.53	3	0.38	4	0.40
Negative	2	22.22	46	24.60	153	19.62	201	20.60
Positive	7	77.78	140	74.87	624	80.00	771	79.00
TOTAL	9	0.92	187	19.15	780	79.91	976	100.00

as regards polarity in VPE is one where there are no mismatches between the source and the target of ellipsis and both are positive. Negative polarity in both the source and the ellipsis site constitutes 4.71 per cent of the cases. Therefore, in 68.71 per cent of the examples of VPE there are no mismatches between the source and the target of ellipsis. In Table 44, I offer the final percentages of the patterns of mismatches attested in VPE (in decreasing order of frequency): negative source-positive target (15.69 per cent), positive source-negative target (14.26 per cent), positive source-explicit polar alternative target (0.72 per cent), explicit polar alternative source-positive target (0.31 per cent), negative source-explicit polar alternative target (0.21 per cent) and explicit polar alternative source-negative target (0.10 per cent). These percentages confirm the data presented before: the proportions of the two most common mismatches, that is, negative source-positive target and vice versa are slightly lower than before. Also, the percentage of negative source-positive target is somewhat higher than that of positive source-negative target. However, as mentioned above, these two patterns shared the same percentage in Table 41. Finally, the percentages of the least common patterns remained almost unchanged.

As a summary, then, it has been found that in the vast majority of cases there are no mismatches in terms of polarity between the source and the target of ellipsis in PAE. Within these cases, the most common type of polarity attested by far is positive polarity in PG and VPE. What is more, positive polarity is the only one attested in PG when no mismatches exist between the source and the target of ellipsis (87.20 per cent). As for VPE, 64 per cent of the examples exhibit positive polarity in both the source of ellipsis and the ellipsis site and only 4.71 per cent of them negative polarity. In conclusion, then, mismatches represent only 12.80 per cent of the examples of PG and almost a third of the total in VPE (31.29 per cent).

Table 44 Mismatches in Polarity between the Source and the Target of Ellipsis in VPE

POLARITY SOURCE	POLARITY TARGET							
	Explicit Polar Alternative		Negative		Positive		TOTAL	
	Abs. Freq.	%	Abs. Freq.	%	Abs. Freq.	%	Abs. Freq.	%
Explicit Polar Alternative	0	0.00	1	0.10	3	0.31	4	0.41
Negative	2	0.21	0	0.00	153	15.69	155	15.90
Positive	7	0.72	139	14.26	0	0.00	146	14.97
TOTAL	9	0.92	140	14.36	156	16.00	305	31.29

- Voice in PAE

It has also been of particular interest for the present study to analyse the types of voice in PAE to check the most common patterns found as well as the impact of theories like the ones presented in Sag (1976); Kehler (2000, 2002); Merchant (2008a) and Kertz (2008, 2013). Let us first consider the data gathered in Table 45, where one can observe that the active voice predominates in the target of ellipsis in PG, since it comprises almost 90 per cent of the examples found. What is more, in over 87 per cent of the cases, the voice of both the source and the target of ellipsis is active, which means that only around 10 per cent of the instances have passive voice in the target of ellipsis in this type of PAE. The VPE data, presented in Table 46, point towards the same direction since the active voice predominates in the target of ellipsis (93.76 per cent), although the percentage is slightly higher with respect to PG. Also, the most common pattern attested in VPE regarding voice is one where both the source and the target of ellipsis are active, yielding over 93 per cent of the total. Thus, the percentage of passive voice in the target of ellipsis in VPE only represents 6.24 per cent of the examples, which is slightly lower than in PG. In sum, active voice prevails

Table 45 Voice of the Source and the Target of Ellipsis in PG

	VOICE TARGET					
	Active		Passive		TOTAL	
VOICE SOURCE	Abs. Freq.	%	Abs. Freq.	%	Abs. Freq.	%
Active	75	97.40	0	0.00	75	87.21
None	1	1.30	0	0.00	1	1.16
Passive	1	1.30	9	100.00	10	11.63
TOTAL	77	89.53	9	10.47	86	100.00

Table 46 Voice of the Source and the Target of Ellipsis in VPE

	VOICE TARGET					
	Active		Passive		TOTAL	
VOICE SOURCE	Abs. Freq.	%	Abs. Freq.	%	Abs. Freq.	%
Active	957	99.58	6	9.38	963	93.95
None	3	0.31	0	0.00	3	0.29
Passive	1	0.10	58	90.63	59	5.76
TOTAL	961	93.76	64	6.24	1,025	100.00

in both the source and the target of ellipsis of both types of PAE, representing around 90 per cent of the examples found.

Let us now consider the mismatches in voice found for cases of PAE. Since as early as Sag (1976), the possibility of finding voice mismatches between the source and the target of ellipsis has become of interest (see Section 1.2.4 for experimental evidence from the field of psycholinguistics). Sag (1976) contended that voice mismatches in ellipsis resulted in ungrammatical examples, which led him to propose that syntactic identity needed to hold between the source and the target of ellipsis. However, Dalrymple et al. (1991); Hardt (1992b, 1993); and Kehler (2000, 2002), among others, provided some examples of ellipsis where voice mismatches were acceptable and served as counterevidence of Sag's (1976) theory:

(138) A lot of this material *can be presented* in a fairly informal and accessible fashion, and often I do ~~present it in a fairly informal and accessible fashion~~. [Dalrymple et al. (1991); originally in Chomsky (1982)]

(139) The ice cream *should be taken* out of the freezer, if you can ~~take it out of the freezer~~. [heard in conversation] [Hardt (1993: 37)]

(140) This problem *was to have been looked into*, but obviously nobody did ~~look into the problem~~. [heard in conversation] [Kehler (2000: 548)]

The examples of acceptable voice mismatch mentioned in the literature had been found in corpora or corresponded to naturally occurring data. However, an alternative account of ellipsis in which the latter is licensed by semantics rather than by syntax (Dalrymple et al. 1991) would predict the acceptability of the previous examples of passive/active mismatch, but also that in (141), which is obviously unacceptable. As mentioned in Kertz (2008: 83), canonical examples of unacceptable mismatch in ellipsis follow a formula, like in example (141), where a passive antecedent and an intended active target have been paired:

(141) #The material *was skipped* by the instructors and the TA's did ~~skip the material~~ too.

(142) The instructors *skipped* the material, and the TA's did ~~skip the material~~ too. [Kertz (2008: 283)]

Notice that (142), where both the antecedent and the target of ellipsis are active, yields a grammatical example of ellipsis. Since both syntactic and semantic approaches about the type of identity that needs to be established between the source and the target of ellipsis do not account for the whole range of data, there emerged other proposals, presented in Kehler (2000, 2002) and Kertz (2008, 2013). Kehler (2000, 2002) attempted to account for the data by resorting to discourse structure instead of syntactic structure. More specifically, Kehler (2000, 2002) contended that examples could be sorted by the type of coherence relation established between the source and the target of ellipsis. In his opinion, those cases of unacceptable voice mismatch are the result of a 'Resemblance' coherence relation, where the similarity between the parallel events described in the two clauses is emphasized, as illustrated in example (141). When this type of coherence relation is established between two clauses, the two events described are interpreted as independent and receive a symmetric reading. In contrast, he argues that the coherence relation established between the two clauses in cases of acceptable voice mismatch would be 'Cause-Effect', where what is highlighted is the beginning and end states of the events reported in the two clauses, as in example (140). In this case, the first event is interpreted as the cause of the second event, that is, there is an asymmetric reading. This leads Kehler to argue that syntactic identity is only required in cases of Resemblance coherence, but not in cases of Cause-Effect coherence. To support his theory, he offers several examples of voice mismatches gathered from corpora or spontaneous speech, where the coherence relation is Cause-Effect. Convincingly, he presents these examples together with constructed ones where a Resemblance coherence relation is operative, which demonstrates that acceptability decreases as one changes the type of coherence:

(143) This problem was to have been looked into, but obviously nobody did *look into this problem*.
(144) #This problem was looked into by John, and Bob did *look into the problem* too.
(145) Of course this theory could be expressed using SDRSs, but for the sake of simplicity we have chosen not to *express this theory using SDRSs*.
(146) This theory was expressed using SDRSs by Smith, and Jones did *express this theory using SDRSs* too. [Kehler (2000: 548ff)]

However, Kertz (2008, 2013) makes still another proposal in order to account for the data concerning the acceptability of the voice mismatches presented thus far. Concretely, she contends that the crucial difference between the cases of acceptable and unacceptable ellipsis is due to information structure, and not to syntactic or discourse structure. In her view, 'cases of unacceptable mismatch tend to focus the subject argument of the target clause, while cases of acceptable mismatch focus the auxiliary verb' (Kertz 2008: 284).

In her view, there exists an informational structural constraint that imposes that contrastive arguments should be preferentially aligned in the syntax, that is, they must appear in the same argument position. This implies that 'sensitivity to mismatch follows not from a lack of syntactic parallelism per se, but from a failure to align contrastive arguments, which follows from the argument re-ordering effect of the voice manipulation' (Kertz 2008: 284). Here are some examples that illustrate her theory:

(147) #The material was skipped by the instructors and [the TA's]$_{top/foc}$ did too.
(148) #The problem was looked into by the committee, just like [the chair]$_{top/foc}$ did.
(149) A lot of this material can be skipped, and often I [do]$_{foc}$
(150) This problem was to have been looked into, but obviously nobody [did]$_{foc}$ [Kertz (2008: 285)]

According to Kertz (2008: 285), the data presented in Kehler (2000, 2002) 'confound information structure and coherence'. On the one hand, those examples of Resemblance coherence provided by Kehler exhibit contrastive topic structures with argument-focus, as in (151). On the other hand, the examples of Cause-Effect coherence focus the auxiliary, as in (152):

(151) #This problem was looked into by John, and [Bob]$_{top/foc}$ did too.
(152) This problem was to have been looked into, but obviously nobody [did]$_{foc}$.

In summary, therefore, Kertz (2008) argues that the auxiliary-focus cases of PAE allow active/passive mismatches whereas the subject-focus cases of PAE do not. It should be noted that her theory about information structure predicts the same as Kehler's coherence theory (2000, 2002), as evinced in this extract:

> To the extent that this confound between coherence and information structure persists, the predictions of the current analysis are identical to those of the coherence analysis: sensitivity to mismatch is predicted for *Resemblance* coherence relations with an argument focus structure; acceptable mismatch is predicted for *Cause-Effect* coherence relations with an auxiliary-focus structure. Predictions diverge where these features are in conflict [...], where *Cause-Effect* coherence relations exhibit argument-focus structures. [Kertz (2008: 286)]

As already pointed out in Section 1.2.4, another important claim in the literature about voice mismatches can be found in Merchant (2008a, 2013b), who defended that while VPE permits voice mismatches between the antecedent clause(s) and the ellipsis site, PG does not, as illustrated in examples (153) and (154):

(153) The system *can be used* by anyone who wants *to* ~~use it~~.
(154) * Klimt *is admired* by Abby more than anyone *does* ~~admire~~ Klee.
[Merchant (2008a: 169–70)]

Once we have revised the relevant literature concerning voice mismatches in ellipsis, we are in a position to analyse the examples of voice mismatches attested in our corpus study and check the validity of the predictions of the previous theories in Late Modern English. Table 47 presents the data regarding voice mismatches attested in PG in Late Modern English.

As can be gathered, strictly speaking, only one voice mismatch (passive-active) has been attested in PG in the period under study, which represents 1.16 per cent of the total and is reproduced in (155).

(155) and dip it in the spawn of Frogs, *beaten* as you *would* ~~beat~~ the whites of eggs, ALBIN-1736,4.75

The other example of mismatch would be a case where there is no voice in the antecedent because the verb *be* is implicit:

(156) In consequence of this, Dr. Franklin's principles bid fair to be handed down to posterity, as *equally expressive of the true principles of electricity*, as the Newtonian philosophy *is* ~~expressive~~ of the true system of nature in general. PRIESTLEY-1769,152.19

These findings are in line with Miller's study (2014: 87), as he found at least 10 occurrences of voice mismatches in PG (out of 1,415, yielding 0.70 per cent of the total) in a large corpus study on PG, some of which are quoted below:

(157) A whole poached wild striped bass *should be taken to the table* as you would ~~take to the table~~ a Thanksgiving turkey or a crown roast of pork, with a twinkle of extravagance.
(158) I mean for her to *be dressed – and addressed –* as we would ~~dress and address~~ Becky Sharp, or Ophelia, or Elizabeth Bennet, or Mrs. Ramsay, or Mrs. Wilcox, or even Hester Prynne.

Notice, however, that Miller (2014) only takes into account cases of Pseudogapping with NP remnants in his work, whereas this study takes into account a wider variety of remnants (see the previous subsection (*vii*)). In addition, Miller (2014) mentions that all of the examples of voice mismatches attested constituted cases

Table 47 Voice Mismatches between the Source and the Target of Ellipsis in PG

	VOICE TARGET	
	Active	
VOICE SOURCE	Abs. Freq.	%
Active	0	0.00
None	1	1.16
Passive	1	1.16
TOTAL	2	2.33

of comparative Pseudogapping. My data also support this claim, as my examples also occur in comparative constructions such as *as*-appositives.

Let us now check the validity of Kehler's (2000, 2002) and Kertz's (2008, 2013) theories in the light of the only example of voice mismatch found in PG. In (155) a Resemblance coherence relation is established, where the events of the two clauses are compared (*beaten as you would the whites of eggs*). Since Kehler (2000, 2002) predicts that cases that exhibit a Resemblance coherence relation do not license voice mismatches in ellipsis, it must be concluded that our data do not support this claim. In contrast, Kertz's (2008, 2013) predictions work: our example shares the same patient in both clauses (*the whites of eggs*) and the implicit agent is the same, as there is no *by*-phrase.

In conclusion, on the one hand, our data contradict Merchant's (2013b) claim about the impossibility of finding voice mismatches in PG as well as Kehler's (2000, 2002) theory about the unacceptability of voice mismatches in cases of PG that exhibit a Resemblance coherence relation. On the other hand, our data confirm Miller's (2014) findings about the possibility of finding examples of voice mismatch in PG and Kertz's (2008, 2013) theory about the interaction between information structure and voice mismatches.

Let us now have a look at the data concerning voice mismatches in cases of VPE in Late Modern English.

Table 48 shows that ten mismatches in voice have been attested in VPE (0.98 per cent), out of which seven of them are proper voice mismatches, yielding 0.68 per cent of the total. This means that the frequency of voice mismatches in PG (1.16 per cent) almost doubles that of VPE. There are, therefore, three cases in which the mismatch in voice would result from having no verbal material in the antecedent, as in (159):

(159) About three Fathom from the End, splice in a Snout or Snude of a smaller Line which the Fisher-men commonly make of Twine spun

by themselves of 3 or 4 Foot long, as the Tides are *of 3 or 4 Foot long*. DRUMMOND-1718,27.251

It should also be noted that the most frequent pattern for voice mismatches is one where the antecedent is active and the target of ellipsis passive (0.59 per cent), as illustrated below:

(160) Lucy. No, no, Madam! I have not that *to learn*. – Different, say you. – Ay, ay, 'tis proper it shou'd *be learnt*. STEVENS-1745,39.549.

(161) it was in my power *to entertain* your honour as you ought to be *entertained*. REEVE-1777,7.151.

(162) A. By Appearance we *engaged* as close as any Ship could be *engaged*, without being aboard of one another. HOLMES-TRIAL-1749,59.1054.

(163) A. They *could not have disabled* the Cornwal so much as she had been *disabled*, if the Lenox had kept her Station a-stern. HOLMES-TRIAL-1749,59.1054.

(164) it became impracticable *to manage* the Ship so readily as otherwise might be *managed*. HOLMES-LETTERS-1749,86.61.[4]

(165) How happy shall I be can I but *finish* the head this week – as it ought to be *finished*-. HAYDON-1808,1,34.886.

Neither Hardt and Rambow (2001) nor Bos and Spenader (2011) found any voice mismatches in their corpus-based studies on VPE in Present-Day English. On the one hand, Hardt and Rambow (2001) analysed Sections 5 and 6 from the Penn Treebank and created a balanced corpus containing a balanced number of positive and negative examples of VP ellipsis (that is, examples in which VPs were or were not elided respectively) by adding positive examples but no negative ones. They reported fifteen cases in which the antecedent and the target of ellipsis were both active in Sections 5 and 6 of the Penn Treebank, and ninety-seven cases where they were both active and four where they were both passive in the balanced corpus. On the other hand, Bos and Spenader reported that they found no voice mismatches in the 486 cases of VPE mentioned in their corpus study (a sample of the *Wall Street Journal*). A possible explanation for the fact that these voice mismatches in VP ellipsis were possible in Late Modern English and not in Present-Day English may have to do with the stylistics or register of the corpora under study. Certainly, textual variety constitutes an issue for further research as a factor that may have an impact on the occurrence of VP ellipsis voice mismatches. The results described in Bos and Spenader's (2011) work led Miller

(2014: 87) to conclude in his study of PG that 'it seems at first sight that voice mismatches are actually more frequent with PG than with VPE', admitting at the same time that 'this conclusion requires significant qualification'. Importantly, he observes that, 'contrary to VPE, mismatches are only found in comparative PG. With noncomparative PG they are systematically degraded'. We agree with Miller and Pullum (2014: 12) that Kertz (2008) makes the very significant point that the distinction mentioned above is relevant for the acceptability of voice mismatches in PAE: Auxiliary-focus PAE allows active/passive mismatches whereas subject-focus cases of PAE do not. Kertz (2008, 2013) predicts topic continuity between the antecedent and the ellipsis site in cases of voice mismatches, that is, with the same subject. For that reason, what matters is whether one is dealing with the same agent or not. According to her, then, in instances of acceptable[5] voice mismatches polarity, aspect, tense, mood or modality could be contrastive, as long as there are no contrastive topics. A close look at examples (160)-(165) reveals that they comply with the condition of topic continuity between the antecedent and the ellipsis site, as there is never a *by*-phrase which may contrast with the subject of the active clause. It should be noted, however, that in (162) the subject *we*, in order to refer to *our Ship*, would be a particular subcase of *any Ship* and therefore there is topic continuity too. What is more, in all of the examples there is a mismatch in modality between the antecedent and the ellipsis site and two contrasts in polarity (see (160) and (163)). But let us also check whether Kehler's (2000, 2002) theory about voice mismatches confirms the data attested in our corpus study. According to his hypotheses about discourse relations, there must exist an asymmetric kind of discourse relation between the antecedent and the ellipsis site (temporal succession, concessives, counter-expectation, causality, etc.) in order for voice mismatches to be judged acceptable in ellipsis (a Cause-Effect coherence relation). In our data there are only two cases where an asymmetric kind of coherence relation holds that may fit his theory, illustrated in (164) and (165). One should be cautious about example (165), however, as it may receive two interpretations: one where there is manner subordination and the reading would be 'like it should be finished', and another where a comparison is established and it would mean 'as it is true that it should be finished'. The ambiguity evinced in this example makes it difficult to discern the type of discourse relation established. But if it were interpreted as involving a comparison between the two clauses, it would be an instance of a symmetric relation and therefore it would not confirm his theory. The remaining examples (160)-(163), however, exhibit a symmetric kind of discourse relation (resemblance, parallelism or contrast) and therefore they serve as counterevidence to his theory.

Let us now comment on the last example of voice mismatch attested in VPE. As shown in Table 48, only one example of passive–active mismatch has been found, which is provided in (166):

(166) when once things *are got* into the state I fear they will *get*, nothing can save the country. GEORGE-1763,200.283.

As can be observed, in (166) the voice mismatch takes place within a relative clause. Once again, this example corroborates Kertz's (2008, 2013) theory because there is topic continuity, given that the subject argument of the antecedent and that of the ellipsis site coincide (*things* and *they*). In this case, there is tense (*are got* versus *will*) and modality (none versus *will*) contrast. However, as may be deduced, it does not confirm Kehler's (2000, 2002) theory, since there is no asymmetric discourse relationship established.

In summary, results show that voice mismatches were possible in PG and VPE in Modern English with low frequencies (1.16 per cent and 0.68 per cent of the examples of PAE, respectively). This fact serves as counterevidence for Merchant's (2008a, 2013b) claim about the impossibility of finding voice mismatches in cases of PG and confirms Miller's (2014) corpus-based findings for Present-Day English. As for VP ellipsis, neither Hardt and Rambow (2001) nor Bos and Spenader (2011) found any voice mismatches in their corpus-based study of VP ellipsis in Present-Day English. However, since they occur in Late Modern English with low frequencies, this contrast may be due to the stylistics or register of the corpora analysed. What is clear is that this aspect needs further research. Finally, it is also demonstrated that, whereas Kehler's (2000, 2002) theory regarding voice mismatches (there must exist an asymmetric kind of discourse relation between the antecedent and the ellipsis site – temporal succession, concessives, and so on – for voice mismatches to be judged acceptable in ellipsis) is not confirmed by our data, the validity of Kertz's (2008, 2013) theory (voice mismatches are acceptable as long as there is topic continuity) remains intact.

Table 48 Voice Mismatches between the Source and the Target of Ellipsis in VPE

VOICE SOURCE	VOICE TARGET					
	Active		Passive		TOTAL	
	Abs. Freq.	%	Abs. Freq.	%	Abs. Freq.	%
Active	0	0.00	6	0.59	6	0.59
None	3	0.29	0	0.00	3	0.29
Passive	1	0.10	0	0.00	1	0.10
TOTAL	4	0.39	6	0.59	10	0.98

- Aspect in PAE

We will now turn our attention to the types of aspect attested in PAE. We will start by describing aspect in PG. In the light of the data in Table 49, in the vast majority of the cases, the target VP has nonperfective-nonprogressive aspect (86.05 per cent), as in (167). Perfective-nonprogressive aspect is attested in the target VP in 12.79 per cent of the examples, as in (168). Importantly, only one case of nonperfective-progressive aspect (1.16 per cent) has been attested in the target VP of PG (see (169)). It should also be noted that no cases of perfective-progressive aspect have been found in either the source or the target of ellipsis.

(167) A skilled florist will produce a finer effect with a few inexpensive blossoms than an unskilled one *will with a cartload of choice material*. WEATHERS-1913,1,8.192

(168) Lou. Were I sure you would follow, as I *would have* you, DAVYS-1716,35.369

(169) Court. Do you remember before the Cornwal's Boat came on Board you, if you was going in a parallel Line with the Enemy, or whether you were more to Windward, or more from the Wind, than they *were*? HOLMES-TRIAL-1749,73.1372

If one pays attention to the aspect of the source and that of the target of ellipsis, it is clear that the most frequent pattern attested is one where both the source and the target have nonperfective-nonprogressive aspect (77.9 per cent) (see (167) above). To these examples of no mismatches, one can add those cases

Table 49 Aspect of the Source and Aspect of the Target of Ellipsis in PG

ASPECT SOURCE	ASPECT TARGET							
	Nonperfective-Nonprogressive		Nonperfective-Progressive		Perfective-Nonprogressive		TOTAL	
	Abs. Freq.	%	Abs. Freq.	%	Abs. Freq.	%	Abs. Freq.	%
None	3	4.05	0	0.00	0	0.00	3	3.49
Nonperfective-Nonprogressive	67	90.54	0	0.00	6	54.55	73	84.88
Nonperfective-Progressive	1	1.35	1	100.0	0	0.00	2	2.33
Perfective-Nonprogressive	3	4.05	0	0.00	5	45.4	8	9.30
TOTAL	74	86.05	1	1.16	11	12.79	86	100.00

of VPs with perfective-nonprogressive aspect (5.81 per cent, as in (170)) and nonperfective-progressive aspect (1.16 per cent, see (169) above) in both the source and the target of ellipsis.

(170) if this young man *has* only *profited* by the lessons of his maiden aunt, half as well as Lady Caroline *has* by those of her fox-hunting father, their society must be most desirable. COLLIER-1835,7.86

Therefore, in most cases of PG there are no mismatches in the type of aspect exhibited by the source and the target of ellipsis (84.88 per cent). Let us now check the types of mismatches attested, which amount to 15.12 per cent (see Table 50).

The most common type of mismatch attested in PG is one where the source VP has a nonperfective-nonprogressive aspect and the target VP a perfective-nonprogressive one, yielding 6.98 per cent of the total (see (171)). This type of mismatch is followed by examples where the VP source has a perfective-nonprogressive aspect (3.49 per cent, as in (172)), no aspect (3.49 per cent, as in (173)) or nonperfective-progressive aspect (1.16 per cent, as in (174)) and the target of ellipsis has a nonperfective-nonprogressive one.

(171) The Parliamentarian army of the South *was* as completely *wiped out* in September as the Royalist army of the North *had been* in July. OMAN-1895,392.263

(172) he judged himself *to have been* as broad awake during the whole Time, as he ever *was* in any Part of his Life; DODDRIDGE-1747,31.255

Table 50 Mismatches in Aspect between the Source and the Target of Ellipsis in PG

ASPECT SOURCE	ASPECT TARGET							
	Nonperfective-Nonprogressive		Nonperfective-Progressive		Perfective-Nonprogressive		TOTAL	
	Abs. Freq.	%	Abs. Freq.	%	Abs. Freq.	%	Abs. Freq.	%
None	3	3.49	0	0.00	0	0.00	3	3.49
Nonperfective-Nonprogressive	0	0.00	0	0.00	6	6.98	6	6.98
Nonperfective-Progressive	1	1.16	0	0.00	0	0.00	1	1.16
Perfective-Nonprogressive	3	3.49	0	0.00	0	0.00	3	3.49
TOTAL	7	8.14	0	0.00	6	6.98	13	15.12

(173) Dr. Franklin's principles bid fair to be handed down to posterity, as equally expressive of the true principles of electricity, as the Newtonian philosophy *is* of the true system of nature in general. PRIESTLEY-1769,152.19

(174) I heard the Men in the Top call out, that the Fore-Chain that slung the Foreyard was shot, and her Foretopsail Ties were shot, the Enemy *being* at that Time at a greater Distance from us than they *were* at any Time before that I saw them. HOLMES-TRIAL-1749,75.1408

Let us check whether the same tendency with respect to aspect is observed in VPE. As shown in Table 51, it is clear that the predominant aspect in the target of ellipsis is a nonperfective-nonprogressive one (93.46 per cent, see (175) below). Thus, perfective-nonprogressive aspect (5.66 per cent, illustrated in (176)) and nonperfective-progressive aspect (0.88, as in (177)) are much less common in the targets of ellipsis. Notice that no instances of perfective-progressive aspect have been attested in the target VP.

Once again, the most frequent pattern attested by far is one where the aspect of the antecedent and of the ellipsis site is nonperfective-nonprogressive (85.75 per cent, see (175)). To these examples of no mismatches between the aspect of the source and that of the target of ellipsis we can add cases of perfective-nonprogressive (3.31 per cent, as in (176)) and nonperfective-progressive VPs (0.78 per cent, as in (177)).

Table 51 Aspect of the Source and Aspect of the Target of Ellipsis in VPE

ASPECT SOURCE	ASPECT TARGET							
	Nonperfective-Nonprogressive		Nonperfective-Progressive		Perfective-Nonprogressive		TOTAL	
	Abs. Freq.	%	Abs. Freq.	%	Abs. Freq.	%	Abs. Freq.	%
None	12	1.25	0	0.00	1	1.72	13	1.2
Nonperfective-Nonprogressive	879	91.7	1	11.11	23	39.66	902	88
Nonperfective-Progressive	14	1.46	8	88.89	0	0.00	23	2.2
Perfective-Nonprogressive	53	5.53	0	0.00	34	58.62	87	8.4
TOTAL	958	93.4	9	0.88	58	5.66	1,025	100

(175) I can recollect nothing more to say. When my letter is gone, I suppose I *shall*. AUSTEN-180X,175.335
(176) Q. Have you seen the bill since you handed it over to the Grand Jury at Hicks's Hall? A. No, I *have not*. WATSON-1817,1,93.362
(177) was the person speaking when you got to the field? A. I believe he *was not*. WATSON-1817,1,182.2646

Altogether, there are no mismatches between the antecedent and the target of ellipsis in 89.85 per cent of the examples of VPE. Therefore, the percentage of mismatches is only slightly lower in the case of VPE if compared with PG (10.15 per cent versus 15.12 per cent, respectively). In Table 52 the mismatches in aspect found for VPE are provided.

In VPE the most frequent mismatch in aspect is one where the aspect of the antecedent VP is perfective-nonprogressive and that of the target of ellipsis nonperfective-nonprogressive (5.17 per cent, see (178)). This is followed by cases where the antecedent VP has nonperfective-nonprogressive aspect and the target VP perfective-nonprogressive aspect (2.24 per cent, as in (179)). Finally, the least frequent mismatches attested are those cases where either the aspect of the source VP is nonperfective-progressive (1.37 per cent, illustrated in (180)) or the source VP is not marked for aspect at all (1.17 per cent, as in (181)) and the aspect of the target of the ellipsis is nonperfective-nonprogressive. Two types of mismatches occur very rarely: in one of them the source VP has nonperfective-nonprogressive aspect while the aspect of the target VP is

Table 52 Mismatches in Aspect between the Source and the Target of Ellipsis in VPE

ASPECT SOURCE	ASPECT TARGET							
	Nonperfective-Nonprogressive		Nonperfective-Progressive		Perfective-Nonprogressive		TOTAL	
	Abs. Freq.	%	Abs. Freq.	%	Abs. Freq.	%	Abs. Freq.	%
None	12	1.17	0	0.00	1	0.10	13	1.27
Nonperfective-Nonprogressive	0	0.00	1	0.10	23	2.24	24	2.34
Nonperfective-Progressive	14	1.37	0	0.00	0	0.00	14	1.37
Perfective-Nonprogressive	53	5.17	0	0.00	0	0.00	53	5.17
TOTAL	79	7.71	1	0.10	24	2.34	104	10.15

nonperfective-progressive (0.10 per cent, see (182)) and in the other the source VP has no aspect and the target VP has perfective-nonprogressive aspect (0.10 per cent, as in (183)).

(178) Popery we see *has arisen* just as it was foretold it *would*; WOLLASTON-1793,12.78

(179) I *didn't dare to make* the smallest repartee, I need hardly tell you. If I *had*, it would have stopped the music at once. WILDE-1895,57.476

(180) you must let the Hive *be doing*, the best Way it *can*, till your first Hive swarm; MAXWELL-1747,30.365

(181) Mrs Cheveley: Wonderful woman, Lady Markby, *isn't she*? WILDE-1895,66.737

(182) and by *having* it, as all our christenings but two *were*, in the private chapel at Buckingham Palace, I think I shall be able to be present, and hold the dear baby myself, D. V., which, trying though it will be, I wish to do. VICTORIA-186X,1,151.389

(183) I do not desire to have you engaged in the least more glory than you *have been*. WALPOLE-174X,5,19.452

In sum, then, it has been found that the most frequent type of aspect attested in both PG and VPE in either the source or the target of ellipsis is nonperfective-nonprogressive. No mismatches in the aspect of the VP of the antecedent and that of the ellipsis site predominate in both constructions, but the percentage of mismatches is slightly higher in the case of PG.

- Modality in PAE

In this section we will have a look at the role of modality in instances of PAE. Table 53 shows the distribution of modals in PG.

Notice that modal auxiliaries *may/might, can/could, shall/should* and *will/would* have been grouped together because they only illustrate differences in tense. As can be gathered from Table 53, 82.6 per cent of the examples have no modal auxiliaries acting as licensors of ellipsis in PG. The most frequent modal auxiliaries that act as licensors of PG are *will/would*, since they trigger ellipsis in 11.63 per cent of the cases (see (184) below). The remaining modal auxiliaries license PG very rarely: *must* (3.49 per cent, as in (185)), *can/could* (1.16 per cent, as in (186)) and *shall/should* (1.16 per cent, as in (187)).

(184) and dip it in the spawn of Frogs, beaten as you *would* the whites of eggs, ALBIN-1736,4.75

Table 53 Modality of the Source and Modality of the Target of Ellipsis in PG

MODALITY SOURCE	MODALITY TARGET												
	can/could		Must		none		shall/should		will/would		TOTAL	
	Abs. Freq.	%	Abs. Freq.	%	Abs. Freq.	%	Abs. Freq.	%	Abs. Freq.	%	Abs. Freq.	%
may/might	0	0.00	0	0.00	2	2.82	0	0.00	0	0.00	2	2.33
can/could	0	0.00	1	33.3	1	1.41	1	100.00	0	0.00	3	3.49
none	0	0.00	2	66.6	60	84.5	0	0.00	7	70.00	69	80.2
ought to	0	0.00	0	0.00	1	1.41	0	0.00	0	0.00	1	1.16
shall/should	0	0.00	0	0.00	2	2.82	0	0.00	0	0.00	2	2.33
will/would	1	100.00	0	0.00	5	7.04	0	0.00	3	30.00	9	10.5
TOTAL	1	1.16	3	3.49	71	82.6	1	1.16	10	11.63	86	100.00

(185) Even the delicate associations with words can be expounded through our own language; just as they *must be* to the pupil who is studying the original. BAIN-1878,366.96

(186) this was a request I would have refused any other man; but *could not* one from whom I have gained so much. HAYDON-1808,1,33.839

(187) Lord Ellenborough. Do you read that paper which you put into his hand. Mr. Solicitor General. We cannot at present, my Lord, *we shall* after we have called the next witness. WATSON-1817,1,89.255

In the majority of cases of PG, there are no modal auxiliaries in either the source or the target of ellipsis (69.77 per cent), which amounts to saying that mismatches in modality are infrequent. No mismatches are attested when the modal auxiliary of the source and that of the target is *will/would* (3.49 per cent, as illustrated in (188) below).

(188) I know they will watch her as a Fox *would* a Poultry-Yard. DAVYS-1716,48.836

In the remaining 26.74 per cent of the examples there are mismatches in modality between the antecedent and the elliptical clause in PG, as shown in Table 54.

The most frequent mismatches in modality found in PG have to do with the presence or absence of *will/would* in either the source or the target of ellipsis, as they comprise 13.95 per cent of the total altogether. In 8.14 per cent of the cases of PG, there are no modals in the source of ellipsis but then modal auxiliaries *will/would* act as triggers for ellipsis, while the reverse pattern where *will/would* are present in the source and then there are no modals in the target represents 5.81 per cent of the total, as illustrated in (189) and (190), respectively:

(189) Mr. Serjeant Copley. How *did* you *read* it over? A. The same as I *would* any thing else. WATSON-1817,1,100.586

(190) and you *will* perceive that the gold leaf will fall as quickly in this vacuum as the coin *does* in the air. FARADAY-1859,30.295

The rest of the mismatches in my database are more infrequent: no modal auxiliaries in the antecedent and auxiliary *must* in the target of ellipsis (2.33 per cent, see (191)), modal auxiliaries *may/might* in the source and no modal auxiliaries in the target (2.33 per cent, see (192)), modal auxiliaries *shall/should* in the source and no modal auxiliaries in the target (2.33 per cent, illustrated in (193)), modal auxiliaries *will/would* in the antecedent and *can/*

Table 54 Mismatches in Modality between the Source and the Target of Ellipsis in PG

| MODALITY SOURCE | MODALITY TARGET ||||||||||||
| | can/could || must || none || shall/should || will/would || TOTAL ||
	Abs. Freq.	%	Abs. Freq.	%	Abs. Freq.	%	Abs. Freq.	%	Abs. Freq.	%	Abs. Freq.	%
may/might	0	0.00	0	0.00	2	2.33	0	0.00	0	0.00	2	2.33
can/could	0	0.00	1	1.16	1	1.16	1	1.16	0	0.00	3	3.49
none	0	0.00	2	2.33	0	0.00	0	0.00	7	8.14	9	10.47
ought to	0	0.00	0	0.00	1	1.16	0	0.00	0	0.00	1	1.16
shall/should	0	0.00	0	0.00	2	2.33	0	0.00	0	0.00	2	2.33
will/would	1	1.16	0	0.00	5	5.81	0	0.00	0	0.00	6	6.98
TOTAL	1	1.16	3	3.49	11	12.8	1	1.16	7	8.14	23	26.74

could in the target (1.16 per cent, shown in (194)), modal auxiliaries *can/ could* in the source and modal auxiliary *must* in the target (1.16 per cent, see (195)), modal auxiliaries *can/could* in the source and no modals in the target (1.16 per cent, illustrated in (196)), modal auxiliary *ought to* in the antecedent and no modals in the target (1.16 per cent, shown in (197)), and modal auxiliaries *can/could* in the source and modals *shall/should* in the target of ellipsis (1.16 per cent, illustrated in (198)). In sum, most mismatches are caused by the absence of modality in either the source or the target of ellipsis (10.47 per cent).

(191) if there is any thing to which they have a tendency and impulse, it *must be* to the supreme and all-sufficient good. BOETHRI-1785,124.260

(192) That all *might honour* the Son, as they *do* the Father. PURVER-NEW-1764,5,20J.338

(193) For *should* its defect for a short time *be supplied* by some more copious and increased evacuation, as it sometimes *is* by that of urine or stool. LIND-1753,275.219

(194) this was a request I *would have refused* any other man; but *could not* one from whom I have gained so much. HAYDON-1808,1,33.839

(195) Even the delicate associations with words *can be expounded* through our own language; just as they *must be* to the pupil who is studying the original. BAIN-1878,366.96

(196) he, who *can correct* Latin when it is writ as all School-masters *do* their Boy's Exercises can correct it when it is spoke. ANON-1711,16.163

(197) whereas pity is more justly due to the oppressors; who *ought* therefore *to be conducted* to judgment, as the sick *are* to the physicians. BOETHRI-1785,161.351

(198) Lord Ellenborough. Do you read that paper which you put into his hand. Mr. Solicitor General. We *cannot* at present, my Lord, we *shall* after we have called the next witness. WATSON-1817,1,89.255

Regarding VPE, Tables 55 and 56 show that the absence of modality in the target of ellipsis predominates (64.39 per cent), though the percentage is lower than in the case of PG. Following, the three most common types of modal auxiliaries that act as licensors of VPE are *can/could* (16.90 per cent), *will/would*

Table 55 Modality of the Source and Modality of the Target of Ellipsis in VPE

MODALITY SOURCE	MODALITY TARGET										
	may/might		can/could		dare to		must		Need		None	
	Abs. Freq.	%	Abs. Freq.	%	Abs. Freq.	%	Abs. Freq.	%	Abs. Freq.	%	Abs. Freq.	%
may/might	6	20.00	1	0.58	0	0.00	0	0.00	0	0.00	13	1.97
can/could	4	13.33	21	12.10	1	50.00	0	0.00	0	0.00	20	3.03
must	0	0.00	2	1.16	0	0.00	7	58.33	0	0.00	9	1.36
need	0	0.00	0	0.00	0	0.00	0	0.00	1	50.00	1	0.15
none	16	53.33	127	73.40	1	50.00	4	33.33	1	50.00	569	86.21
ought to	0	0.00	1	0.58	0	0.00	0	0.00	0	0.00	2	0.30
shall/should	1	3.33	3	1.73	0	0.00	1	8.33	0	0.00	19	2.88
will/would	3	10.00	18	10.40	0	0.00	0	0.00	0	0.00	27	4.09
TOTAL	30	2.93	173	16.90	2	0.20	12	1.17	2	0.20	660	64.39

Table 56 Modality of the Source and Modality of the Target of Ellipsis in VPE (continuation)

	MODALITY TARGET									
	ought to		shall/should		used to		will/would		TOTAL	
MODALITY SOURCE	Abs. Freq.	%	Abs. Freq.	%	Abs. Freq.	%	Abs. Freq.	%	Abs. Freq.	%
may/might	1	6.67	3	6.67	0	0.00	1	1.20	25	2.44
can/could	2	13.33	6	13.3	0	0.00	2	2.41	56	5.46
must	0	0.00	0	0.00	0	0.00	2	2.41	20	1.95
need	0	0.00	0	0.00	0	0.00	0	0.00	2	0.20
none	9	60.00	21	46.70	3	100.00	37	44.58	788	76.88
ought to	1	6.67	0	0.00	0	0.00	1	1.20	5	0.49
shall/should	1	6.67	9	20.00	0	0.00	3	3.61	37	3.61
will/would	1	6.67	6	13.30	0	0.00	37	44.58	92	8.98
TOTAL	15	1.46	45	4.39	3	0.29	83	8.10	1,025	100.00

(8.10 per cent) and *shall/should* (4.39 per cent), illustrated in (199)-(201), respectively (notice that their frequency decreases by half from one to the other):

- (199) Pray keep the English quiet, if you *can*. WELLESLEY-1815,855.362
- (200) but pray tell me how he died. – I *will* sir to the best of my knowledge. REEVE-1777,4.75
- (201) it is impossible for the person accused to make those enquiries which the Statute meant he *should*. WATSON-1817,1,106.686

The other modal auxiliaries that license VPE occur more rarely: *may/might* (2.93 per cent), *ought to* (1.46 per cent), *must* (1.17 per cent), *used to* (0.29 per cent), *dare to* (0.20 per cent) and *need* (0.20 per cent), as in (202)-(207):

- (202) if the second boy can not correct the first, the third or fourth *may*. LANCASTER-1806,60.377
- (203) It is also very gratifying to see how well all the different Members of the Cabinet have behaved – really behaving as they *ought* – by forgetting themselves. VICTORIA-186X,1,284.809
- (204) and may pity them for not discerning their error: more especially, if we consider Popery, as in truth we *must*, to be a corruption of Christianity; WOLLASTON-1793,31.241
- (205) is your love for your wife as strong as it *used to be*? BROUGHAM-1861,18.659
- (206) he stood as near the Shore as he *durst* with the Ship. DEFOE-1719,207.238
- (207) the objection was, that the contents of those letters were none of them stated; and the decision was, that they *need not be*. WATSON-1817,1,137.149

Therefore, when compared with PG, VPE shows a wider variety of modal auxiliaries that trigger ellipsis.

Let us now pay attention to the proportion of examples of VPE where there are no mismatches in modality. Once again, the most frequent pattern is the absence of modality in both the source and the target of ellipsis, yielding over 55 per cent of the total. This is followed by *will/would* (3.06 per cent), *can/could* (2.04 per cent), *shall/should* (0.87 per cent), *must* (0.68 per cent), *may/might* (0.58 per cent), *need* (0.09 per cent) and *ought to* (0.09 per cent) in both the source and the target of ellipsis, shown in (208)-(214), respectively:

- (208) my uncle says there *would* be no keeping the living without him and I do not believe there *would*, YONGE-1865,163.96

(209) *Can* I live anywhere else? I thought I *could not*.
DICKENS-1837,562.471

(210) And can we doubt that, when the time appointed arrives, both *shall* cease. The Jews we see dispersed over every country; a by-word and a proverb every where: Our Saviour declared they *should*. WOLLASTON-1793,12.82

(211) 'then I *must not* believe my own Eyes.' 'No, indeed, *must* you *not* always,' FIELDING-1749,3,13.435

(212) Q. *Might not* the Lenox, if she had directly obeyed the Signal for chasing to Leeward, when the Enemy was put to Flight, have got up to Action again as close and as soon as the Strafford did? A. Yes, I think she *might*. HOLMES-TRIAL-1749,25.417

(213) but I *need not* stay now, *need I*? YONGE-1865,160.36

(214) they should have assembled together, and taken into consideration the prayers of the dying multitude, and not have been deaf to our cries – They *ought* – they *ought*. WATSON-1817,1,145.1642

Consequently, in 63.51 per cent of the instances of VPE no mismatches are attested between the antecedent and the elliptical clause in terms of modality. The remaining 36.49 per cent of cases of VPE show mismatches in modality. Information about the type of mismatch is provided in Tables 57 and 58:

The most common mismatches attested in VPE correspond to cases where there are no modal auxiliaries in the source and modals *can/could* (12.39 per cent), *will/would* (3.61 per cent) and *shall/should* (2.05 per cent) license ellipsis (see (215)-(217) below). Also common are those cases where modal auxiliaries *will/would* (2.63 per cent), *can/could* (1.95 per cent) or *shall/should* (1.75 per cent) appear in the antecedent and there are no modal auxiliaries in the target (as illustrated in (218)-(220)). As shown in Tables 57 and 58, the remaining types of mismatches take place much more infrequently. What is clear is that most mismatches are also triggered by the absence of modality in either the source or the target of ellipsis (21.37 per cent).

(215) I lay down as soon as I *could*. WESLEY-174X,25.338

(216) Mr. Topping. A Mr. Castle came to you, on the 26th of November and asked you to print bills for the second of December. A. Yes, I told Mr. Castle I *would not*. WATSON-1817,1,98.509

(217) Can one ever hope you will make a figure, when you only fight because it was right you *should*, and not because you hated the French, or loved destroying mankind? WALPOLE-174X,5,20.473

Table 57 Mismatches in Modality between the Source and the Target of Ellipsis in VPE

MODALITY SOURCE	may/might		can/could		MODALITY TARGET dare to		Must		need		None	
	Abs. Freq.	%	Abs. Freq.	%	Abs. Freq.	%	Abs. Freq.	%	Abs. Freq.	%	Abs. Freq.	%
may/might	0	0.00	1	0.10	0	0.00	0	0.00	0	0.00	13	1.27
can/could	4	0.39	0	0.00	1	0.10	0	0.00	0	0.00	20	1.95
must	0	0.00	2	0.20	0	0.00	0	0.00	0	0.00	9	0.88
need	0	0.00	0	0.00	0	0.00	0	0.00	0	0.00	1	0.10
none	16	1.56	127	12.39	1	0.10	4	0.39	1	0.10	0	0.00
ought to	0	0.00	1	0.10	0	0.00	0	0.00	0	0.00	2	0.20
shall/should	1	0.10	3	0.29	0	0.00	1	0.10	0	0.00	19	1.85
will/would	3	0.29	18	1.76	0	0.00	0	0.00	0	0.00	27	2.63
TOTAL	24	2.34	152	14.82	2	0.20	5	0.49	1	0.10	91	8.88

Table 58 Mismatches in Modality between the Source and the Target of Ellipsis in VPE (continuation)

MODALITY SOURCE	MODALITY TARGET									
	ought to		shall/should		used to		will/would		TOTAL	
	Abs. Freq.	%	Abs. Freq.	%	Abs. Freq.	%	Abs. Freq.	%	Abs. Freq.	%
may/might	1	0.10	3	0.29	0	0.00	1	0.10	19	1.85
can/could	2	0.20	6	0.59	0	0.00	2	0.20	35	3.41
must	0	0.00	0	0.00	0	0.00	2	0.20	13	1.27
need	0	0.00	0	0.00	0	0.00	0	0.00	1	0.10
none	9	0.88	21	2.05	3	0.29	37	3.61	219	21.37
ought to	0	0.00	0	0.00	0	0.00	1	0.10	4	0.39
shall/should	1	0.10	0	0.00	0	0.00	3	0.29	28	2.73
will/would	1	0.10	6	0.59	0	0.00	0	0.00	55	5.37
TOTAL	14	1.37	36	3.51	3	0.29	46	4.49	374	36.49

(218) He *will* see it now; – and if he *does*,– Farewel all happy Day. STEVENS-1745,37.473

(219) Caecilius, who was a contemporary of Diodorus, *could not* know more of these rebellions than Diodorus *did*. LONG-1866,2,86.287

(220) My lord replied, 'If you *had not*, we *should* have done it ourselves.' WALPOLE-174X,5,5.67

To sum up, it has been found that the absence of explicit modality predominates in PAE: in PG around 70 per cent of the cases do not contain modal auxiliaries in either the source or the target of ellipsis, while in VPE this percentage goes down to 55 per cent of the cases. In PG, the most frequent modal licensors are *will/would* and *must*, whereas in VPE *can/could*, *will/would* and *shall/should* predominate. Finally, the most frequent mismatches attested in PG have to do with the presence or absence of *will/would* in either the source or the target of ellipsis, while mismatches in VPE are mainly triggered by the absence of modal auxiliaries in the source and modals *can/could*, *will/would* (3.61 per cent) and *shall/should* (2.05 per cent) licensing ellipsis.

- Tense in PAE

Lastly, let us pay attention to the types of tense attested in the sources and targets of PG and VPE. Table 59 reports the frequencies concerning PG.

The licensors of PG are either in the present or in the past and their distribution is very similar: present tense in 53.49 per cent of the cases and past tense in 46.51 per cent. In addition, the two most frequent patterns found between the source and the target of ellipsis have been the following: present tense in the source of

Table 59 Tense of the Source and Tense of the Target of Ellipsis in PG

TENSE SOURCE	TENSE TARGET					
	past		present		TOTAL	
	Abs. Freq.	%	Abs. Freq.	%	Abs. Freq.	%
bare infinitive	0	0.00	1	2.17	1	1.16
–en	1	2.50	0	0.00	1	1.16
–ing	2	5.00	3	6.52	5	5.81
none	1	2.50	1	2.17	2	2.33
past	29	72.50	6	13.04	35	40.70
present	5	12.50	33	71.74	38	44.19
to infinitive	2	5.00	2	4.35	4	4.65
TOTAL	40	46.51	46	53.49	86	100.00

ellipsis and present tense in the target (38.37 per cent of the total), and past tense in the source and past tense in the target (33.72 per cent), illustrated in (221) and (222), respectively:

> (221) Robert *is* as incapable of doing a foolish thing as he *is* of doing a wrong thing. WILDE-1895,54.391
>
> (222) but *did not admire* the strain of its poetry in general, though I *did* its morality. BOSWELL-1776,49.475

This amounts to saying that in 72.09 per cent of the examples of PG there are no mismatches in tense between the antecedent and the ellipsis site. In Table 60, I offer the percentages of the different types of mismatches in tense attested in PG.

The most frequent types of mismatches attested in PG correspond to those cases where the antecedent is in the past tense and the target of ellipsis in the present tense (6.98 per cent), followed by those where the reverse situation is observed: present tense in the source and past tense in the target of ellipsis (5.81 per cent):

> (223) he *was* more cruel and treacherous to his poor Hungarian subjects, than ever the Turk *has been* to the Christians. MONTAGU-1718,79.26
>
> (224) the hills *dip down* beneath them as they *would* beneath water. RUSKIN-1835,1,12.325

The remaining types of mismatches are marginally represented (in decreasing order): *-ing* in the source and present in the target (3.49 per cent), *-ing* in the

Table 60 Mismatches in Tense between the Source and the Target of Ellipsis in PG

TENSE SOURCE	TENSE TARGET					
	past		present		TOTAL	
	Abs. Freq.	%	Abs. Freq.	%	Abs. Freq.	%
bare infinitive	0	0.00	1	1.16	1	1.16
-en	1	1.16	0	0.00	1	1.16
-ing	2	2.33	3	3.49	5	5.81
none	1	1.16	1	1.16	2	2.33
past	0	0.00	6	6.98	6	6.98
present	5	5.81	0	0.00	5	5.81
to *infinitive*	2	2.33	2	2.33	4	4.65
TOTAL	11	12.79	13	15.12	24	27.91

source and past in the target (2.33 per cent), *to* infinitive in the antecedent and present in the elliptical sentence (2.33 per cent), *to* infinitive in the source and past in the target (2.33 per cent), no tense in the antecedent and past tense in the target (1.16 per cent), no tense in the antecedent and present tense in the target (1.16 per cent) and bare infinitive in the antecedent and present tense in the target (1.16 per cent), shown in (225)-(231), respectively:

(225) and says we shall see these locks *extending* themselves towards the table as the lower small clouds *do* towards the earth. PRIESTLEY-1769,174.237

(226) I have been always in the habit of *treating* my own Horses much after the same manner that I *would* myself; SKEAVINGTON-184X,27.C2.413

(227) One would think you wanted *to know* one's age, as they *do horses*, GOLDSMITH-1773,61.978

(228) the former seemed *to be* as much for Uniformity and Subscriptions in their own Way, as their Antagonists *were* in theirs. KIMBER-1742,260.C1.55

(229) I hope she returned to Godmersham as much pleased with Mrs. Knight's beauty and Miss Milles's judicious remarks as those ladies respectively *were* with hers. AUSTEN-180X,169.195

(230) Dr. Franklin's principles bid fair to be handed down to posterity, as equally expressive of the true principles of electricity, as the Newtonian philosophy *is* of the true system of nature in general. PRIESTLEY-1769,152.19

(231) Mary. Pray, now, let me *hear* your news. Dennis. That I *will*. COLMAN-1805,54.1126

Let us now check the tense combinations attested in VPE, provided in Table 61.

In more than half of the examples of VPE the licensor of ellipsis is in the past (50.93 per cent) and in the present in 48.10 per cent of them, as in (232) and (233):

(232) Did she make all the Sail she *could*? HOLMES-TRIAL-1749,56.998
(233) Dr. S. Cross over to the other. Mrs. H. Alas I *cannot*! BROUGHAM-1861,29.1066

This means that the other tense options in the target of ellipsis are marginally represented in VPE: only 0.68 per cent of the examples constitute cases of *to*

Table 61 Tense of the Source and Tense of the Target of Ellipsis in VPE

TENSE SOURCE	TENSE TARGET									
	bare infinitive		past		present		to infinitive		TOTAL	
	Abs. Freq.	%	Abs. Freq.	%	Abs. Freq.	%	Abs. Freq.	%	Abs. Freq.	%
bare infinitive	3	100	11	2.11	29	5.88	0	0.00	43	4.20
-en	0	0.00	0	0.00	2	0.41	0	0.00	2	0.20
-ing	0	0.00	17	3.26	21	4.26	0	0.00	38	3.71
none	0	0.00	3	0.57	4	0.81	0	0.00	7	0.68
past	0	0.00	356	68.20	43	8.72	2	28.57	401	39.12
present	0	0.00	80	15.33	363	73.63	3	42.86	446	43.51
to infinitive	0	0.00	55	10.54	31	6.29	2	28.57	88	8.59
TOTAL	3	0.29	522	50.93	493	48.10	7	0.68	1,025	100.00

infinitive, followed by bare infinitives (0.29 per cent), in (234) and (235), respectively:

> (234) and looking as if they never had been sat upon, nor were meant *to be*. READE-1863,222.536
>
> (235) on Wednesday in every Week, if it be not an Holy Day; and if it *be*, then on the next Day after that is not an Holy Day, answer and pay all the Monies arising by the said additional Impositions. STATUTES-1745,6,263.14

Table 61 also shows that the most frequent patterns as regards tense in VPE are present tense in the source and present tense in the target of ellipsis (35.41 per cent), followed by past tense in the source and past tense in the target (34.73 per cent), as instantiated in examples (236) and (237), respectively:

> (236) If the Church of Rome *approves of and countenances* monastic vows, or enjoins celibacy on certain orders in her communion; the Church of God *does not*. WOLLASTON-1793,40.317
>
> (237) Q. They *moved* from the waggon? A. They *did*. WATSON-1817,179.2543

Altogether, they account for 70.14 per cent of the cases where there are no mismatches in tense. If one adds the figures for bare infinitive source and bare infinitive target (0.29 per cent, as in (238)), and *to* infinitive source and *to* infinitive target (0.19 per cent, as in (239)), then the percentage of no mismatches in tense amounts to 70.63 per cent, in line with the aforementioned results for PG.

> (238) Does not every Affection necessarily imply, that the Object of it *be* itself loved? If it *be not*, 'tis not the Object of the Affection. BUTLER-1726,271.326
>
> (239) I do not perceive it *to be* more difficult in it self. But allowing it *to be*, yet all that can be fairly concluded from hence is, that it can not be so quickly learn'd as the Modern Tongues are. ANON-1711,12.126

In sum, in 29.37 per cent of the cases there are mismatches between the tense of the source and that of the target of ellipsis, as illustrated in Table 62.

The most common mismatches attested in VPE follow these patterns: present tense in the source of ellipsis and past tense in the target of ellipsis (7.80 per cent, as in (240)), *to* infinitive in the source and past tense in the target (5.37 per cent, as in (241)), past tense in the source and present tense in the target

Table 62 Mismatches in Tense between the Source and the Target of Ellipsis in VPE

TENSE SOURCE	bare infinitive		Past		TENSE TARGET present		to infinitive		TOTAL	
	Abs. Freq.	%	Abs. Freq.	%	Abs. Freq.	%	Abs. Freq.	%	Abs. Freq.	%
bare infinitive	0	0.00	11	1.07	29	2.83	0	0.00	40	3.90
-en	0	0.00	0	0.00	2	0.20	0	0.00	2	0.20
-ing	0	0.00	17	1.66	21	2.05	0	0.00	38	3.71
none	0	0.00	3	0.29	4	0.39	0	0.00	7	0.68
past	0	0.00	0	0.00	43	4.20	2	0.20	45	4.39
present	0	0.00	80	7.80	0	0.00	3	0.29	83	8.10
to infinitive	0	0.00	55	5.37	31	3.02	0	0.00	86	8.39
TOTAL	0	0.00	166	16.20	130	12.68	5	0.49	301	29.37

(4.20 per cent, as in (242)), and *to* infinitive in the source and present tense in the target (3.02 per cent, as in (243)).

(240) this matter *does not depend* on my brother's consent, and even if it *did*, Ermine's own true position is that which is most honourable to her. YONGE-1865,178.507

(241) But they now desired me, for God's Sake, *Not to go up*: for if I *did*, they said, there would surely be murder. WESLEY-174X,38.678

(242) he *could* have done even less than I *can*. VICTORIA-186X,1,154.439

(243) and *to have treated* Lady Caroline as I *have*. COLLIER-1835,29.1095

The other types of mismatches occur very rarely: bare infinitive in the source and present in the target of ellipsis (2.83 per cent), followed by –*ing* in the source and present in the target (2.05 per cent), –*ing* in the source and past in the target (1.66 per cent), bare infinitive source and past target (1.07 per cent), no tense in the source and present in the target (0.39 per cent), no tense in the source and past in the target (0.29 per cent), present tense in the source and *to* infinitive in the target (0.29 per cent) and past tense in the source and *to* infinitive in the target (0.20 per cent), shown in (244)-(251), respectively:

(244) Pray *be* as trivial as you *can*. WILDE-1895,55.416

(245) they most assuredly would be as much to blame for quitting it; as we, *thinking* as we *do*, should be if we were to go over to it. WOLLASTON-1793,31.243

(246) Islam, the religion of Mohammed, *fixing* its roots, as it *did*, on the faith of Israel, has kept the faith in a living God, TALBOT-1901,94.84

(247) *Run away* from a good father, as you *did*. COLMAN-1805,41.743

(248) Mrs Cheveley: Wonderful woman, Lady Markby, *isn't she*? WILDE-1895,66.737

(249) I never knew any paper so discussed as the Declaration *was*. WELLESLEY-1815,842.165

(250) An Egyptian donkey *is* a much more complying animal than I have ever understood an English one *to be*. MONTEFIORE-1836,158.395

(251) they, living in a profligate age, *were not* such patterns of righteousness, as Christian Bishops and Christian Preachers should endeavor *to be*.WOLLASTON-1793,33.251

In summary, it has been shown that the licensors of PG are almost equally distributed between past (46.51 per cent) and present tense (53.49 per cent).

The same is true of VPE, where past (50.93 per cent) and present licensors (48.10 per cent) predominate in the vast majority of the examples. It has also been found that lack of mismatch in tense between the source and the target of ellipsis is the tendency of both PG and VPE in around 70 per cent of the cases. The remaining 30 per cent of the examples illustrate mismatches between the source and the target, where the most frequent pattern is present tense in the source and past tense in the target of ellipsis and vice versa.

As a final remark on the type of mismatches attested in this study regarding polarity, voice, aspect, modality and tense, I would like to highlight that it would be interesting to carry out a regression analysis in order to detect factor groups and their weight in the explanation of cases of PAE. This issue has been left for further research.

3.1.2 Semantic, discursive variables

This section deals with the following semantic, discursive variables: (i) the type of clause of the source and the target of ellipsis (declarative, interrogative, imperative and tag question), (ii) the type of anaphora (anaphoric and cataphoric), (iii) the type of focus (subject choice, auxiliary choice and object choice), (iv) sloppy identity (pronoun and polarity mismatches) and (v) turn (potential change of speaker between the source and the target of ellipsis).

i. Type of clause of the source of ellipsis versus the type of clause of the target of ellipsis

The data presented in this section constitutes a novel contribution, as I am not aware of previous research on the type of clause of either the source or the target of ellipsis. The types of clauses have been classified according to their force: declarative, interrogative and imperative, as shown in Table 63.

PG is attested in declarative clauses in the vast majority of cases (95.35 per cent). This is not surprising if we take into account that in our data the percentage of comparative PG is 87.84 per cent. As a general rule, when one compares two entities or states of affairs, one normally makes use of a declarative sentence. Here are some examples, see (254) for an exception to this tendency:

(252) We cou'd not fail of learning the Latin Language, *as well as we do the Modern Languages*. ANON-1711,11.105

(253) He has no more notion, my dear Tom, of a modern 'good match', *than Eve had of pin-money*. COLMAN-1805,23.154

(254) Q. Did we not engage closer before Sun-set, and after it was Dark, *than we did when we were in a Line of Battle*? HOLMES-TRIAL-1749,78.1471

There are declarative clauses where there is no syntactic relation involved (12.19 per cent) due to the change of speaker in dialogues, as in (255), as well as declaratives where the syntactic relation is coordination (3.65 per cent), as in (256):

(255) Mr. Serjeant Copley. How did you read it over? A. The same *as I would any thing else*. WATSON-1817,1,100.586

(256) Crassus was the advocate of Orata, *and Antonius was for Marius*. LONG-1866,2,93.448

No cases of imperative clauses as targets of ellipsis have been attested in PG in my database.

As far as VPE is concerned, ellipsis also occurs mostly in declaratives (85.17 per cent). Not surprisingly, in around 50 per cent of these declaratives there is no syntactic linking between the antecedent and the ellipsis site. A careful analysis of these instances with no syntactic linking has revealed that in around 73 per cent of the cases they are the result of a change of speaker in dialogues (see (257)), while the remaining 27 per cent simply occur in a different sentence marked by punctuation (as in (258)):

(257) Do you remember whether the Cornwal made use of her Stern-Guns? A. *Yes, she did*. HOLMES-TRIAL-1749,28.489

(258) They call it being conceited. *Perhaps it is*. WILDE-1895,51.327

Following, around 35 per cent of the cases of declarative VPE are found in comparative constructions, which, as mentioned earlier for PG, is not surprising since comparatives normally occur in declaratives:

(259) He has got as far *as he can*. WILDE-1895,62.628

Table 63 Type of Clause of the Target of Ellipsis

TYPE OF CLAUSE	PG		VPE		TOTAL PAE	
	Abs. Freq.	%	Abs. Freq.	%	Abs. Freq.	%
Tag question	0	0.00	49	4.79	49	4.41
Declarative	82	95.35	873	85.17	955	85.96
Imperative	0	0.00	31	3.02	31	2.79
Interrogative	4	4.65	72	7.02	76	6.84
TOTAL	86		1,025		1,111	

The remaining 15 per cent of the examples of declarative VPE illustrate adverbial subordination (approximately 8.5 per cent) and coordination (around 6.5 per cent), as in (260) and (261), respectively:

(260) Since quite the beginning every man had built *because he wished to*. THRING-187X,225.271

(261) He continued praising God as often as he could speak, *and when he could not*, his Eyes were fixt upwards. WATSON-1817,1,157.1973

Interrogative clauses are the second most frequent type of clauses in VPE, though by far this type is less common than declaratives in our data (7.02 per cent of the examples). The interrogatives can be divided into two groups: those where the ellipsis and the antecedent are part of the same question (there are no different turns, comprising around 63 per cent of the examples), and those that are the result of a dialogue exchange and therefore the target of ellipsis and its antecedent appear in different turns (approximately 37 per cent), as shown in (262) and (263), respectively:

(262) Q. Did you hear any body, and if you *did*, who was it proposed any amendment to that? WATSON-1817,1,128.1312

(263) Phipps: I don't observe an alternation in your lordship's appearance. Lord Goring: You *don't*, Phipps? WILDE-1895,73.939

Tag questions are special constructions which also trigger ellipsis, as in (264):

(264) He won't take any interest in politics then, *will he*? WILDE-1895,63.650

Tag questions have been treated as constructions of their own because of the particular characteristics they exhibit, comprising 4.78 per cent of the cases of VPE. If tag questions are treated as a subtype of interrogative clauses and grouped with those cases of standard interrogatives, interrogative clauses will then be the targets of VPE in 11.8 per cent of the examples.

Unlike with PG, instances of imperatives in the target clause have been attested in VPE (3.02 per cent of the examples):

(265) Make haste after me, *do*, now! COLMAN-1805,36.601

(266) Bur. Don't take on so – *don't you*, now! COLMAN-1805,33.483

(267) Pray give me, as soon as you *can*, your opinion. VICTORIA-186X,1,65.45

(268) Take all the Ways you *can* to destroy them. MAXWELL-1747,23.239

(269) Let him deny it if he *can*. REEVE-1777,31.686
(270) But tell your story; and, if you *can*, intelligibly.
COLMAN-1805,28.296

Comparatives predominate as the most frequent type of syntactic relation established between the source and the target clause in imperatives (almost 42 per cent, see (267)), followed by the group of examples which do not exhibit any kind of syntactic relation (around 39 per cent, as in (265)-(266)), more marginally followed by relative subordination (9.6 per cent, as in (268)), adverbial subordination (6.45 per cent, as in (269)) and coordination (3.22 per cent, as in (270)).

In summary, it has been shown that PAE occurs mainly in declarative clauses (85.96 per cent), followed by interrogatives (6.84 per cent), tag questions (4.41 per cent) and imperatives (2.79 per cent) respectively. If the figures for standard interrogatives and tag questions are added, they comprise 11.25 per cent of the total. It is important to bear in mind, however, that neither tag questions nor imperatives have been attested in PG.

I will now comment on the mismatches observed between the type of clause of the antecedent and that of the target of the ellipsis. Table 64 provides the information for PG.

In 90.70 per cent of the cases there are no mismatches between the type of clause of the source and that of the target in PG. Declarative source – declarative target is by far the most prolific combination in PG, constituting over 88 per cent of the examples. The only mismatches found are composed of the following combinations: declarative source – interrogative target (2.56 per cent), imperative source – declarative target (2.33 per cent) and interrogative source – declarative target, as shown in (271)-(273), respectively:

(271) 'I did not think you would have held out against her.' '*Not when I had against you?*' YONGE-1865,168.266
(272) Lady Car. No; – don't fidget at my elbow, *as you do at the Opera*. COLMAN-1805,51.1035
(273) My question was, whether you had any conversation about the bills? A. No; *about Mr. Castle, I had*. WATSON-1817,1,99.550

Therefore, mismatches in the type of clauses represent only 9.30 per cent of the total cases of PG.

Let us now check the data regarding VPE, shown in Table 65.

Table 64 Type of Clause of the Source versus Type of Clause of Target of Ellipsis in PG

TYPE OF CLAUSE SOURCE	TYPE OF CLAUSE TARGET					
	Declarative		Interrogative		TOTAL	
	Abs. Freq.	%	Abs. Freq.	%	Abs. Freq.	%
Declarative	76	92.68	2	50.00	78	90.70
Imperative	2	2.44	0	0.00	2	2.33
Interrogative	4	4.88	2	50.00	6	6.98
TOTAL	82	95.35	4	4.65	86	100.00

In 70.73 per cent of the cases there are no mismatches between the type of clause of the source and that of the target in VPE. As was the case with PG, the combination declarative source – declarative target is the most common, yielding 58.73 per cent of the total. The second most frequent combination would be interrogative source – declarative target (24.58 per cent), followed by interrogative source – interrogative target (4.39 per cent) and imperative source – imperative target (2.82 per cent), exemplified in (274)-(277), respectively. The other combinations are much more marginal. Tag questions represent here 4.78 per cent of the examples.

(274) He relies very largely for his sales upon his catalogues which are often works of art, upon exhibitions in all parts of the kingdom, and upon judicious advertising, very much in the same way as the seedsman and bulb merchant *do*. WEATHERS-1913,1,4.82

(275) Q. Did you let him have any of the bills? A. No, I *did not*. WATSON-1817,1,85.146

(276) but is it not as natural for them to try to excel in knowledge and virtue as in wealth or power? Is it not prejudice, and a shameful perversion of their faculties, if they *do not*?

(277) Bur. Nay, consider what confusion! – pluck up a courage; *do*, now! COLMAN-1805,35.544

In summary, in VPE the mismatches affecting the type of clause of the source and that of the target of ellipsis represent around 29 per cent, over three times more than in PG. In addition, more possible combinations between the type of clause of the source and that of the target of ellipsis have been attested in VPE. Crucially, the most common combinations in both types of PAE have been declarative source – declarative target along with interrogative source – declarative target, representing over 60 per cent and 23 per cent of the total respectively.

Table 65 Type of Clause of the Source versus Type of Clause of Target of Ellipsis in VPE

TYPE OF CLAUSE SOURCE	TYPE OF CLAUSE TARGET									
	Tag question		Declarative		Imperative		Interrogative		TOTAL	
	Abs. Freq.	%	Abs. Freq.	%	Abs. Freq.	%	Abs. Freq.	%	Abs. Freq.	%
Tag question	49	100.00	0	0	0	0.00	0	0.00	49	4.78
Declarative	0	0.00	602	68.96	1	3.23	27	37.50	630	61.46
Imperative	0	0.00	19	2.18	29	93.55	0	0.00	48	4.68
Interrogative	0	0.00	252	28.87	1	3.23	45	62.50	298	29.07
TOTAL	50	4.78	873	85.17	31	3.02	72	7.02	1,025	100.00

ii. Type of anaphora

As mentioned in Section 2.2.4, there are three types of anaphora: anaphoric, cataphoric and exophoric. Anaphoric ellipses are those in which the ellipsis site (italics) appears after an earlier antecedent (underlined) (see (278)). Cataphoric ellipses are those in which the ellipsis site occurs before its antecedent, as in (279). Both anaphoric and cataphoric ellipses are known as endophoric anaphora, since they refer to a linguistic antecedent. Exophoric ellipses (280), in turn, have no linguistic antecedent available (Miller and Pullum 2014) and have been excluded from this piece of research, which focuses on cases of endophoric ellipsis exclusively.

(278) And yet no Man for many Years has Writ finer Latin than he *did*. ANON-1711,14.146

(279) My lord replied, 'If you *had not done it*, we should have done it ourselves.' WALPOLE-174X,5,5.67

(280) The aisles at the Lakewood Wal-Mart are surprisingly packed at 11 p.m. '*Can we? Can we?*' Vanessa tugs at her mother, pointing to a rack of 'Lady and the Tramp' DVDs. Diaz shrugs. OK. [Miller and Pullum (2014: 19)]

As pointed out in Section 2.2.1.3, the distribution of the types of anaphora is not identical in VPE and PG (Levin 1986; Hardt 1993; Bos and Spenader 2011; Miller 2014), since cataphoric examples are possible in VPE and not in PG (Hardt 1993: 18), as respectively shown in (281) and (282):

(281) Although I don't know if Tom *does write magazines*, I know Harry writes magazines.

(282) *Although I don't know if Tom *does write* books, I know Harry writes magazines.

The findings concerning the types of anaphora in the corpus study are sketched in Table 66.

Table 66 Types of Anaphora in Late Modern English

TYPE OF ANAPHORA	PG		VPE		PAE	
	Abs. Freq.	%	Abs. Freq.	%	Abs. Freq.	%
Anaphoric	86	100	1,014	98.93	1,100	99.01
Cataphoric	0	0	11	1.07	11	0.99
TOTAL	86		1,025		1,111	

Table 66 shows that PAE is anaphoric in the vast majority of cases (99.01 per cent). The frequencies also confirm that cataphoric PG is not possible in Late Modern English, in line with those examples of PG from Present-Day English described in Bos and Spenader's (2011) and Miller's (2014) studies. Miller (2014: 88), who admits that cataphoric uses of PG are hard to construct, reports one example from the COCA which, in his opinion, does not seem to be a speech error:

(283) Behind them, disguising her desire, one catches a poignant glimpse of the youthful, shaved-headed Cather. As it *did* me, work <u>rescued Willa Cather</u>.

I have found eleven cataphoric VPE examples in my data, which represent only 1.07 per cent of the total. The frequency of cataphoric VPE seems slightly higher in Late Modern English if compared with Bos and Spenader's (2011) results for Present-Day English, given that they found four examples of cataphoric VPE out of 486, yielding 0.82 per cent of cases, following the pattern '(*but*) (*just*) *as* [$_{target}$ NP AUX], [$_{source}$ NP VP]', which signifies that they all take place in comparative constructions. Below are the some of the instances attested in my corpus (the licensors of cataphoric ellipsis are in italics and the antecedents are underlined):

(284) I desired as many as *could*, <u>to meet me again at Eight in the Morning</u>. WESLEY-174X,12.44

(285) For if as many as *cou'd* conveniently <u>shou'd meet together every Night</u>. ANON-1711,16.161

(286) Q. Did we not as soon as we *could* after that <u>get into close Action with the enemy</u>? HOLMES-TRIAL-1749,56.988

(287) if dear Affie as, unberufen, we may confidently trust he *will* <u>should recover</u>, I think my own darling must return too! VICTORIA-186X,1,68.70

(288) 'If you *had not*, we <u>should have done it ourselves</u>.' WALPOLE-174X,5,5.67

(289) But would have been very glad, if I *could*, <u>to have overset every Canoe there, and drown'd every one of them</u>. DEFOE-1719,194.26

(290) he would go and help his Men, let what *would* <u>come</u>. DEFOE-1719,216.393

(291) *Do*, <u>let me go</u> now, COLMAN-1805,52.1042

(292) *Do*, <u>send the cloaths</u> if you send them in a wheelbarrow. JOHNSON-1775,2,33.645

In the light of the previous examples of cataphoric VPE, we observe that ellipsis occurs in contexts of subordination in the vast majority of cases, be they instances of comparative subordination (as in (284)-(287), comprising 36.36 per cent of the total), conditional subordination (as in (288)-(289), 36.36 per cent) or free relative clauses (as in (290), 9.09 per cent). Examples (291)-(292) are interesting cases of cataphoric VPE, which, seem to have never been mentioned in the literature. In these examples, emphatic *do* in the imperative mood is cataphoric to an antecedent which comes later in the form of a command (18.18 per cent). Examples (291)-(292), therefore, would be the only ones where a syntactic relation of subordination is not involved, as they are cases of parataxis. The results obtained with respect to both PG and VPE confirm Levin's (1986: 54) claims concerning the impossibility of cataphoric uses of PG because embedded uses of PG 'rapidly become awkward'. Since VPE may apply to contexts of subordination, it opens the possibility of cataphoric VPE. These data also confirm that cataphoric PG is not possible in Late Modern English, in line with those examples of PG from Present-Day English described in Bos and Spenader (2011) and Miller (2014).

Finally, it should be noted that there are some examples that could, at first glance, look like cataphoric VPE but are cases of Right-Node Raising (RNR):

(293) And every Person who shall enlist any Recruit shall first ask the person offering to enlist whether he *does or does not* belong to the Militia, and shall cause to be taken down, in Writing, the Name and Place of Abode of such Recruit; STATUTES-1835,75,8.75

(294) In regard the Duties of one Boiling of Sope so hid and concealed, *may and often do* amount to fifty Pounds or more, whereby some ill-disposed Persons have been encouraged and induced to hide and conceal several great Quantities of Sope STATUTES-171X,5,51.44

(295) Or they may be as others *are*, of much more variable value; TALBOT-1901,102.188

(296) And will, even he *will*, bring him whom he chooses near to himself. PURVER-OLD-1764,16,1N.518

(297) Lady Sophia is still, nay she *must be*, the beauty she was: WALPOLE-174X,5,10.221

In RNR, 'an elliptical phrase lacking a dependent or the head (in final position) precedes a complete phrase which determines its interpretation' (Bîlbîie 2013b). In (293)-(297) the elliptical phrases appear in italics and the part that completes the interpretation of the ellipsis is underlined. As mentioned earlier, except for cases like (291)-(292), where emphatic *do* was involved, cataphoric VPE must be embedded with respect to its antecedent. That is, examples (293)-(297) would be cases of cataphoric VPE if a subordinate clause came first. Let us take (295) and try to turn it into an instance of cataphoric VPE:

(298) *Or *as others are*, they may be of much more variable value.

As observed, the resulting construction is ungrammatical. What is more, the constraints that apply to cataphoric VPE are similar to the ones holding between cataphoric pronouns and their antecedents. A cataphoric pronoun must also be embedded with respect to its antecedent:

(299) When he$_i$'s at home, John$_i$ sleeps well.
(300) *He$_i$ thinks that John$_i$ is at home.

In (299) the cataphoric pronoun *he* and *John* can be coreferential, whereas in (300) this interpretation is ruled out, as the cataphoric pronoun should be embedded with respect to its antecedent. The same phenomenon holds for cases of coordination:

(301) John$_i$ is at home and he$_i$ sleeps well.
(302) *He$_i$ is at home and John$_i$ sleeps well.

Since in coordination both clauses are at the same level, the cataphoric interpretation of the pronoun also renders the example ungrammatical in (302). In conclusion, the antecedent should precede the pronoun unless the pronoun is embedded, that is, the pronoun cannot c-command its antecedent. This constraint on VPE and pronoun anaphora is known as the 'Backwards Anaphora Constraint' (see Sag 1976; Hardt 1993). Backwards Anaphora Constraint operates in the same way in cases of cataphoric VPE, as it needs to be embedded with respect to its antecedent VP.

Examples (293) and (294) illustrate RNR in coordination (*does or does not belong to the Militia* and *may and often do amount to fifty Pounds or more*, respectively). (295), in turn, would be an *as*-appositive construction, a type of comparative. Finally, (296) and (297) illustrate cases of parenthetical RNR, where a paractactic syntactic relation is involved. The elliptical parts seem to comment on the content of the complete clause (*even he will* and *nay she must be*). In the case of example (297), the parenthetical part acts as a self-repair, enhancing what has been previously said.

iii. Type of focus

The aim of this section is to determine certain discourse conditions on the use of PAE which have been already tackled by Kehler (2000, 2002); Kertz (2010, 2013); Miller (2011, 2014); Miller and Pullum (2014) and Miller and Hemforth (2014). Following Kertz (2008), Miller (2011, 2014) and Miller and Pullum (2014) distinguish two central uses of PAE (labelled VPE in this monograph), namely auxiliary choice and subject choice, and propose that the following conditions should be met (Miller and Pullum 2014: 12).

> Type 1: Auxiliary choice
>
> FORMAL CHARACTERISTICS: The subject of the antecedent is identical with the subject of the PAE construction and the auxiliary is (at least weakly) stressed, signalling a new choice of tense, aspect, modality, or (in the most overwhelmingly frequent case) polarity.
>
> DISCOURSE REQUIREMENT: A choice between the members of a jointly exhaustive set of alternative situations must be highly salient in the discourse context, and the point of the utterance containing the PAE is strictly limited to selecting one member of that set.
>
> Type 2: Subject choice
>
> FORMAL CHARACTERISTICS: The subject of the antecedent is distinct from the subject of the PAE construction, and stressed if it is a pronoun.
>
> DISCOURSE REQUIREMENT: A particular property must be highly salient in the discourse context, and the point of the utterance containing the PAE must be strictly limited to identifying something or someone possessing that property.

These two different types of focus are exemplified below in (303) and (304), respectively:

> (303) Q. Did you see the Boat come from the Cornwal? A. I *did not*. HOLMES-TRIAL-1749,48.824
>
> (304) Q. did *any body* in his presence address the mob. A. The younger *Mr. Watson* did. WATSON-1817,1,146.1679

In addition, there are cases where focus may involve both subject and auxiliary choice, as in (305):

(305) it cannot be so quickly learn'd as the *Modern Tongues are*. (ANON-1711,12.126)

In sum, these are the values for focus that have been assigned to cases of VPE: auxiliary choice, subject choice and subject-auxiliary choice.

With regard to cases of PG, Miller (2014: 78) argues that noncomparative PG constructions also seem to follow certain discourse conditions:

> Type 1: Object choice
>
> FORMAL CHARACTERISTICS: The subject of the antecedent is identical to that of the PG construction but the object is distinct, and stressed if it is a pronoun.
>
> DISCOURSE REQUIREMENT: Both the referent of the remnant and a particular open proposition $p(x)$ must be highly salient in the discourse context, and the point of the utterance containing the PG must be limited to identifying something or someone satisfying $p(x)$ and such that it forms a contrastive focus with the referent of the correspondent of the remnant in the antecedent.
>
> Type 2: Subject and object choice
>
> FORMAL CHARACTERISTICS: The subject and object of the antecedent are distinct from those of the PG construction, and both are stressed if they are pronouns.
>
> DISCOURSE REQUIREMENT: Both the referents of the remnant and subject and a particular doubly open proposition $p(x,y)$ must be highly salient in the discourse context, and the point of the utterance containing the PG must be limited to identifying a pair satisfying $p(x,y)$ and such that they form a pair of contrastive foci with the referents of the correspondent of the remnant and the subject of the antecedent.

Since PG always contains contrastive objects (see (306)), Miller (2014), following the terminology in Miller and Pullum (2014), calls these cases 'obj-choice' (object choice), which would be the counterpart of subject choice VPE, where two subjects are contrasted, as in (305). The constrastive objects appear in italics:

(306) You salt *them* with small Salt, just as you do *dry Cod*.
DRUMMOND-1718,37.416

As mentioned earlier, PG may involve both subject choice and object choice, that is, both the subject and object of the antecedent could be in contrast with those of the pseudogapped clause, as in (307):

(307) the *Prisoner* paid *the Men of his own Company* himself, as *all the Captains of Companies* did *theirs*. TOWNLEY-1746,21.71

Moreover, there could also be triple contrast on subjects, objects and auxiliaries, in which case the PG construction would involve secondary auxiliary choice (subject-object-auxiliary choice):

(308) I know *they will watch her* as *a Fox would a Poultry-Yard*. DAVYS-1716,48.836 (subject-object-auxiliary choice)

In sum, these will be the possible values for focus in cases of PG: object choice, subject-object choice, object-auxiliary choice and subject-object-auxiliary choice.

In Section 2.2.4 I mentioned that tag questions will not be considered for focus since these are constructions of their own in which the subject of the target of the ellipsis and that of the antecedent are always the same (as evinced in (309) and (310)). Therefore, focus distinctions cannot be applied to them in the same sense as they would be to standard cases of VPE, given that the latter would always involve auxiliary choice focus (because subjects are identical in the antecedent and in the ellipsis site):

(309) 'We$_i$ judge happiness to be good, *do we$_i$ not?*'
 BOETHJA-1897,106.146 [negative tag]
(310) Dr. S. You$_i$ wouldn't have her say it in earnest, *would you$_i$?*
 BROUGHAM-1861,11.361 [positive tag]

Miller (2011, 2014) studied the focus of the target of ellipsis in cases of PAE in Present-Day English. This section aims at extending these empirical studies and at casting new light in this research line. Table 67 provides the data corresponding to the types of focus attested in PG in Late Modern English.

As can be gathered from Table 67, the instances of PG in the period under study seem to favour object-auxiliary choice focus in most of the cases (37.21 per cent), illustrated in (311) and (312). The other types of focus attested in this construction are evenly distributed, as there are no big differences in their frequency. Hence, those cases where PG only focuses the contrastive object (object choice) represent 24.42 per cent of the total (exemplified in (313)-(314)),

Table 67 Type of Focus in PG

TYPE OF FOCUS	Abs. Freq.	%
Obj-aux choice	32	37.21
Obj choice	21	24.42
Subj-obj choice	18	20.93
Subj-obj-aux choice	15	17.44
TOTAL	86	100.00

followed by those where both the subject and the object are in focus (subject-object choice), which yield 20.93 per cent (see (315)-(316)). Finally, those instances of PG where there is a triple contrast between the source of ellipsis and the ellipsis site, thus exhibiting a subject-object-auxiliary choice, represent 17.44 per cent of the total, illustrated in (317)-(318).

(311) I did not think you *would have held out against her*. 'Not when I *had against you?*' YONGE-1865,168.266

(312) Mr. Serjeant Copley. How *did you read it over*? A. The same as I *would any thing else*. WATSON-1817,1,100.586

In the examples above the auxiliaries of the antecedents contrast with those in the ellipsis site (*would have* versus *had* and *did read* versus *would*) and so do the objects as well (*her* versus *you* and *it* versus *any thing else*). In (313) and (314), however, only the objects of both the source and the target of ellipsis contrast: *about the bills* versus *about Mr. Castle* and *the Light Day* versus *the Darkness Night*.

(313) My question was, whether you had any conversation *about the bills?* A. No; *about Mr. Castle*, I had. WATSON-1817,1,99.550

(314) God also called *the Light Day*, as he did *the Darkness Night*. PURVER-OLD-1764,1,1G.14

In (315) and (316), there is double contrast between the subjects and the objects of the antecedent and the ellipsis site: *A skilled florist* versus *an unskilled one* and *a finer effect with a few inexpensive blossoms* versus *with a cartload of choice material* and *we ourselves* versus *they* and *others* versus *us*.

(315) A skilled florist will produce a finer effect with a few inexpensive blossoms than an unskilled one will with a cartload of choice material. WEATHERS-1913,1,8.192

(316) we ourselves differ from others, just as much as they do from us. BUTLER-1726,245.137

Table 68 Focus Type in Comparative and Noncomparative PG with NP Remnants

TYPE OF FOCUS	Comparative PG		Noncomparative PG		TOTAL	
	Abs. Freq.	%	Abs. Freq.	%	Abs. Freq.	%
Obj-aux choice	9	30.00	9	30.00	18	60.00
Obj choice	6	20.00	0	0.00	6	20.00
Subj-obj-aux choice	3	10.00	0	0.00	3	10.00
Subj-obj choice	3	10.00	0	0.00	3	10.00
TOTAL	21	70.00	9	30.00	30	100.00

Finally, there were also examples where triple contrast was involved: subjects *your son* versus *you*, auxiliaries *will be* versus *are*, and remnants *by the two others* versus *by Albert Edward* (shown in (317)); and subjects *I* versus *your ladyship*, auxiliaries *will* (in contracted from) versus *does*, and objects *him* versus *your saddle*, as evinced in (318).

(317) your son will be known by the two others, as you are by Albert Edward. VICTORIA-186X,1,152.414

(318) Tho. I'll stick to him, as close as your ladyship does to your saddle. COLLIER-1835,17.550

Following, I will compare my results for focus in PG with those reported in Miller (2014). Since Miller's (2014) discourse conditions on comparative and noncomparative PG have been proposed in the light of cases of PG with NP remnants, below I provide the frequencies of PG with NP remnants:

Only thirty cases of PG with NP remnants have been attested and most of them appear in comparative constructions (70 per cent). In Miller's (2014) study the percentage of comparative PG examples goes up to over 96.7 per cent of the total. Therefore, it seems that PG in Present-Day English has an even stronger preference for comparative contexts than it used to in Late Modern English. As can be observed, object-auxiliary choice is the only type of focus that is attested in those examples of noncomparative PG (see (319) and (320)). As for the focus type in comparative PG with NP remnants, as in the case of noncomparative PG, most examples favour object-auxiliary choice (as in (321) and (322)), followed by object choice (see (323)), subject-object-auxiliary choice (see (324)) and subject-object choice (see (325)) – contrastive elements in italics:

(319) this was a request I *would have refused any other man*; but *could not one from whom I have gained so much*. HAYDON-1808,1,33.839

(320) but *did not admire the strain of its poetry in general*, though I *did its morality*. BOSWELL-1776,49.475

(321) *dip it* in the spawn of Frogs, beaten as you *would the whites of eggs*, ALBIN-1736,4.75

(322) If all the People in the Inn were not asleep, you *would have* awakened *them* as you *have me*. FIELDING-1749,3,10.382

(323) but could not eat them for want of Salt, because they occasioned a Looseness: except *Crawfish*, which he sometimes boil'd, and at other Times broil'd, as he did also *the Goats Flesh*, OFFICER-1744,241.600

(324) I know *they will* watch *her* as *a Fox would a Poultry-Yard*. DAVYS-1716,48.836

(325) *you* wanted to know *one's age*, as *they* do *horses*, by mark of mouth. GOLDSMITH-1773,61.978

Miller (2014) also notes that subjects of noncomparative PG are commonly pronominal and corefer with the subjects of the antecedent clauses. In his study, this was correct in thirty-eight out forty-seven cases in COCA. In my data, however, in all cases (nine examples), subjects in noncomparative PG corefer with the subject, as in (326) and (327):

(326) this was a request *I* would have refused any other man; but could not one from whom I have gained so much. HAYDON-1808,1,33.839

(327) *I* have been always in the habit of treating my own Horses much after the same manner that *I* would myself; SKEAVINGTON-184X,27.C2.413

In these examples, the subject of both the antecedent and that of the pseudogapped clause are identical (first person singular), that is, they corefer.

The frequencies of the types of pronominal subjects in noncomparative PG are provided in Table 69, which can be compared with Miller's (2014: 76) results in Table 70. Notice that, given that the number of noncomparative PG examples was low in Miller's corpus study, he decided to include also the results reported in Levin (1986) study.

Table 69 Subjects in Noncomparative PG with NP Remnants

SUBJECT	Abs. Freq.	%
I	6	66.66
You	2	22.22
NP	1	11.11
TOTAL	9	100.00

Table 70 Subjects in Noncomparative PG with NP Remnants in Miller's (2014) and Levin's (1986) Studies

SUBJECT	COCA		COCA+LEVIN	
	Abs. Freq.	%	Abs. Freq.	%
he	5	10.6	7	8.3
I	7	14.9	12	14.3
it	22	46.8	44	52.4
she	2	4.3	3	3.6
they	4	8.5	7	8.3
we	0	0.00	0	0.00
you	6	12.8	10	11.9
NP	1	2.1	1	1.2
TOTAL	47	100.00	84	100.00

Miller (2014) contends that of the cases where the subjects of the antecedent and the pseudogapped clause are not coreferent in noncomparative PG, the examples found in his corpus study fall into two different patterns: the mirror and the parallel patterns. On the one hand, in the mirror pattern, noticed first in Levin (1986), 'the referents of the subject and object of the antecedent clause appear in reverse order in the PG' (Miller 2014: 76), as exemplified in (328). On the other hand, the parallel pattern includes those cases 'where the subject and the dependent possessive in the object of the antecedent clause are coreferent, and the same is true of the PG, except that the object is reduced to an independent possessive' (Miller 2014: 76), illustrated in (329):

(328) I ain't scared of your gun. I got a gun, too. I can shoot you before you can me.

(329) Yes, you my [=might, PhM] love your baby and your toddler to death – I did mine – but that doesn't mean to say a child can fulfill all the needs of an adult. [Miller (2014: 77)]

In (328), the referents of the subject (*I* versus *you*) and the object (*you* versus *me*) appear in reverse order, while in (329) the subject (*you*) and the object (*your baby and your toddler*) are coreferent in the antecedent and the same can be stated about the pseudogapped clause (*I* and *mine*). Miller (2014: 76) found four cases of the mirror pattern and four of the parallel one. In my study, however, none of these patterns was attested. It should be noted, however, that one instance of each pattern was attested in comparative PG:

(330) [the Prisoner]$_i$ paid [the Men of his own Company]$_j$ himself, as [all the Captains of Companies]$_j$ did [theirs]$_j$. TOWNLEY-1746,21.71

(331) Lou. Were I sure you would follow, as I would have you, I should not care how soon I led up the Dance. DAVYS-1716,35.369

Example (330) would constitute an example of the parallel pattern, where the subjects (*the Prisoner* and *all the Captains of Companies*) and objects (*the Men of his own Company* and *theirs*) of both the antecedent and the pseudogapped clause are coreferring. Notice that in the example of the mirror pattern in (331) the object in the antecedent is not contrastive – it would be an implicit *me* which would contrast with the remnant *you*. Table 71 lists the types of subjects attested in comparative PG, which can be compared with those reported in Miller's (2014: 80) study in Table 72.

Due to the small number of examples of PG with NP remnants in my database, it is not possible to conclude whether one type of subject predominates over the other. What can be concluded here is that the types of subjects are varied, and that pronominal and nominal subjects have an even distribution, as pronouns occur in sixteen out thirty examples and NPs are found in fourteen out of thirty instances.

Table 71 Subjects in Comparative PG with NP Remnants

Subject	Abs. Freq.	%
I	3	14.29
you	3	14.29
he	4	19.05
we	2	9.52
they	3	14.29
one	1	4.76
NP.prop	1	4.76
NP.a	1	4.76
NP.the	2	9.52
Det.Poss NP	1	4.76
TOTAL	21	100.00

Table 72 Subjects in Comparative PG with NP Remnants in Miller's (2014) study

Subject	Abs. Freq.	%
I	124	9.1
you	310	22.7
it	269	19.7
they	219	16
other pronoun	321	23.5
full NP	125	9.1
TOTAL	1,368	100.00

Finally, I will pay attention to whether or not the type of linking in PG seems to exert any influence on the choice between having the same subject in the antecedent and the pseudogapped clause. Tables 73 and 74 present the data from my study and from Miller (2014).

PG prefers same subjects as antecedents regardless of whether the construction is comparative or not. These results are very much in line with Miller's (2014), as those cases where the PG has the same subject as its antecedent represent over 70 per cent of the total.

Let us now focus on the distribution of focus types in cases of VPE, shown in Table 75.

In the vast majority of cases (75 per cent, see (332) and (333)) VPE exhibits auxiliary choice focus. The second most frequent type of focus, namely subject-auxiliary choice, has a much more marginal representation in the corpus, rendering around 16 per cent of the examples of VPE (instantiated in (334) and

Table 73 Same Subject and Different Subject PGs with NP Remnants

TYPE OF LINKING	Same Subject		Different Subject	
	Abs. Freq.	%	Abs. Freq.	%
Noncomparative	8	88.89	1	11.11
Comparative	14	66.67	7	33.33
TOTAL	22	73.33	8	26.67

Table 74 Same Subject and Different Subject PGs with NP Remnants in Miller's (2014) Study

TYPE OF LINKING	Same Subject		Different Subject	
	Abs. Freq.	%	Abs. Freq.	%
Noncomparative	38	80.85	9	19.14
Comparative	1,192	87.13	176	12.86
TOTAL	1,230	86.92	185	13.07

Table 75 Type of Focus in VPE

TYPE OF FOCUS	Abs. Freq.	%
Auxiliary choice	774	75.51
Subject-auxiliary choice	166	16.20
Tag question	49	4.78
Subject choice	36	3.51
TOTAL	1,025	100.00

(335)). Tag questions, which, as mentioned earlier, have not been considered with respect to focus, comprise 4.78 per cent of the cases. Finally, the least frequent type of focus involves subject choice, yielding only 3.51 per cent of the examples (see (336) and (337) below).

(332) Q. Do you$_i$ know Coppice Row? A. No, I$_i$ do not.
WATSON-1817,179.2549

(333) My own work$_i$ here gets forward as well as it$_i$ can.
CARLYLE-1835,2,268.215

In these examples the focus is in the auxiliaries, that is, *do not* and *can*, respectively. In both examples there are no contrasting subjects, as the subjects of the antecedents corefer with those of the targets of ellipsis. However, in the following examples, both the subjects and the auxiliaries are contrastive with respect to their antecedent and thus they involve subject-auxiliary choice focus:

(334) he may use bell glasses or clothes to protect his early cauliflowers and marrows, much in the same way as *the French cultivators do*.
WEATHERS-1913,1,6.128

(335) The money he speaks of will be sent forward as *the last was*.
CARLYLE-1835,2,300.669

Examples (334) and (335) involve contrastive subjects (*he* versus *French cultivators* and *The money he speaks of* versus *the last*) and auxiliaries (*may* versus *do* and *will* versus *was*).

Subject choice, as mentioned above, was the least frequent type of focus attested. In these cases, the subject of the antecedent and that of the ellipsis site stand in opposition:

(336) You say it is likely that they could write. *The learned*, if any learned there were, could. JOHNSON-1775,2,11.210

(337) did she weep, Williams? Valet. No, sir; but *I* did afterwards.
COLMAN-1805,25.233

In (336) and (337) the contrastive subjects are *they* and *she* in the antecedent and *the learned* and *I* in the clause containing the ellipsis.

In conclusion, it has been shown that the instances of PG in the period under study seem to favour object-auxiliary choice focus in most of the cases, that is, contrastive objects and auxiliaries between the antecedent and the pseudogapped clause. The remaining types of focus attested in PG have a very similar distribution in their frequency (in decreasing order of frequency): object choice, subject-object choice and subject-object-auxiliary choice. When my results of PG with NP remnants were compared to those reported in Miller (2014), it was found that 70 per cent of the cases of PG with NP remnants attested were instances of comparative PG, while in Miller's (2014) study the percentage of comparative PG examples was significantly higher (96.7 per cent). These results may imply that PG in Present-Day English has an even stronger preference for comparative contexts than in Late Modern English, although this preliminary conclusion would require further research. In line with the results in Miller (2014), the subjects of the antecedents and the pseudogapped clauses were generally pronominal and coreferring. Also in line with Miller's results, PG prefers same subjects as antecedents regardless of whether the pseudogapped clauses occur within a comparative or a noncomparative construction. However, Miller (2014) mentions that those instances of noncomparative PG where the subjects of the antecedents and the pseudogapped clauses do not corefer usually involve mirror or parallel patterns. No instance of either pattern has been found in our examples of noncomparative examples, but I found one instance of each in comparative PG. Regarding the focus types attested in VPE, it was found that this construction exhibits a strong preference for auxiliary choice focus (three quarters of the examples). Subject-auxiliary choice is the second most frequent type of focus, followed by those instances that involve subject choice, though the representation of these two types of focus is rather marginal when compared with those that exhibit auxiliary choice focus.

iv. Sloppy identity

If you recall from Section 2.2.4, when ellipsis is resolved, lack of equivalence between the source clauses and their elliptical counterparts may emerge. This has been extensively studied in Fiengo and May (1994), who have coined the concept of 'vehicle change' (see Sag 1976; Williams 1977; Hardt 1993; Lasnik 1995; Murguia 2004). In this volume, the notion of sloppy identity is used in two ways (as in Murguia 2004): on the one hand, to refer to those cases where a pronoun (or other variable) in the source clause is interpreted differently in the elliptical clause (see example (338)a and (338)b below, where both the strict and the sloppy readings are possible). On the other hand, it is used in order to refer to cases of partial syntactic identity, where there are differences in the syntactic realization of certain elements, for instance, the alternation of *any/some* or *you/me, your/my* between the antecedent and the ellipsis site (see (339)-(341)):

> (338) Max saw his mother, and Oscar did too.
> a. Max saw Max's mother, and Oscar saw Oscar's mother. [sloppy]
> b. Max saw Max's mother, and Oscar saw Max's mother. [strict]
> [Murguia (2004: 24)]
> (339) Max didn't talk to *anyone*, but Oscar did ~~talk to someone~~. [Murguia (2004: 37)]
> (340) Mabel Chiltern: I wish I had brought *you* up!. Lord Goring: I am so sorry you didn't ~~bring me up~~. WILDE-1895,55.425
> (341) Mr. Wetherell. Did you give *your* note to Mr. Hone's publication? A. No, indeed, I did not ~~give my note to Mr. Hone's publication~~. WATSON-1817,1,163.2112

The proportions of sloppy identity in PAE are given in Table 76. Whereas no examples of sloppy identity have been attested in PG, in VPE they represent 9.37 per cent of the cases.

Importantly, only 2 per cent of the instances of sloppy identity belong to the type in which a pronoun in the antecedent is interpreted differently in the ellipsis site:

> (342) General Kruse$_i$, of the Nassau service, likewise conducted *himself*$_i$ much to my satisfaction; as did General Trip$_j$ ~~conduct himself$_j$ much to my satisfaction~~, WELLESLEY-1815,860.457
> (343) And they afforded opportunities to our cavalry to charge, in one of which Lord E. Somerset's brigade, consisting of [the Life Guards, the Royal Horse Guards, and 1st dragoon guards]$_i$, highly distinguished *themselves*$_i$, as did [that of Major General Sir W. Ponsonby]$_j$ ~~highly distinguish itself$_j$~~, having taken many prisoners and an eagle. WELLESLEY-1815,859.429

Table 76 Sloppy Identity in PAE in Late Modern English

SLOPPY IDENTITY	PG		VPE		TOTAL	
	Abs. Freq.	%	Abs. Freq.	%	Abs. Freq.	%
Absence	86	100	932	90.93	1,019	91.72
Presence	0	0	96	9.37	95	8.64
TOTAL	86		1,025		1,111	

In both examples, a third-person reflexive pronoun is interpreted sloppily with respect to the source clause, that is, these reflexive pronouns in the elliptical clause are not coreferential with the subject of the source clause. Another interesting fact is that a strict interpretation of the reflexive pronouns in both (342) and (343) is ruled out, as it would render the examples unacceptable. This type of sloppy identity represents 0.18 per cent of the total examples of PAE attested in the corpus. This finding is in line with Nielsen (2005), who encountered fifteen cases of sloppy readings in his corpus study (around 1 per cent). In addition, it is also in line with Bos and Spenader (2011), who found only nine examples of sloppy identity of this type (less than 2 per cent of all the instances of VPE found). Notice that the frequency of this type of sloppy identity is eleven times higher in Bos and Spenader (2011) than in my data. In any case, what is clear is that this phenomenon has a marginal representation in all the three studies.

Sloppy identity as understood in the second sense, that is, when there are differences in the syntactic realization of certain elements, represents 98 per cent of the examples of sloppy identity attested in my corpus. This type has been classified into cases of sloppy pronouns (57.29 per cent), sloppy possessives (27.08 per cent) and sloppy polarity (15.63 per cent). All of these types are illustrated in (344)-(345), (346)-(347), and (348)-(349), respectively:

(344) Q. Do you know, *yourself*, what has become of it? A. No. I do not know *myself* what has become of it. WATSON-1817,1,100.567.

(345) Q. Do you remember any thing more that he read to *you*? A. No, I do not remember any thing more than that he read to *me*. WATSON-1817,1,82.34

(346) Mr. Wetherell. Did you give *your* note to Mr. Hone's publication? A. No, indeed, I did not give *my* note to Mr. Hone's publication. WATSON-1817,1,163.2112

(347) Q. Were you examined there by the Jury, on the fact of *your* having been applied to print those bills? A. Yes, I was examined there by the Jury, on the fact of *my* having been applied to print those bills. WATSON-1817,1,91.311

(348) Q. Were there *any* police officers with the magistrates? A. There were *some* police officers with the magistrates. WATSON-1817,1,166.2202

(349) 'And there's *nothing* that I can send in my little box to the washerwoman's, is there *something* that I can send in my little box to the washerwoman's ?' DICKENS-1837,558.363

Regarding sloppy pronouns, all of the examples are cases of deictic first and second person pronouns which allude to the same referent in dialogue sequences. As mentioned in Hardt (1993), since deictics always designate the same individual, sloppy readings are banned. That is, the ellipsis of deictics can only have a strict reading because the pronoun in the ellipsis site cannot receive a sloppy interpretation. For instance, in (350) below, *you* in the source clause refers to the same subject as the one represented by the pronoun *I* in the ellipsis site. These are the possible combinations which have been found in our corpus: *you* in the antecedent clause and *I* in the ellipsis site (29.09 per cent), as well as *you-me* (29.09 per cent), *me-you* (18.18 per cent), *I-you* (10.91 per cent), reflexives *yourself-myself* (10.91 per cent) and reciprocal *each other-you* (1.82 per cent). All these combinations are illustrated in (350)-(355):

(350) Q. Do you see there either of the persons whom *you* saw at Greystoke Place? A. No, I do not ~~see there either of the persons whom *I* saw at Greystoke Place~~. WATSON-1817,1,114.919

(351) Q. They will say they did not send *you* perhaps? A. Not on that day, but subsequently they did ~~send *me*~~. WATSON-1817,1,157.1988

(352) Such occupations would never suit *me*. Sir G. I believe you – Nature never intended they should ~~suit *you*~~. COLLIER-1835,14.391

(353) Tell him not to neglect any Thing that he can turn to his Advantage; and that *I* have done *my* utmost Endeavours to serve him. Foot. Yes I shall ~~tell him not to neglect any Thing that he can turn to his Advantage; and that *you* have done *your* utmost Endeavours to serve him~~, fair Maid. STEVENS-1745,44.683

(354) Pray, explain *yourself*. Herb. I will ~~explain *myself*~~, if I can ~~explain *myself*~~. BROUGHAM-1861,6.167

(355) I hope you will understand *each other*, for confound me if I do ~~understand *you*~~. COLLIER-1835,18.614

As can be observed, in all of the examples there is a change of speaker between the source clause and the elliptical one, that is, they occur in different turns. Notice that in some examples, such as (353), there are two instances of sloppy identity in the ellipsis site: a sloppy pronoun and a sloppy possessive. Moreover, sloppy pronouns have only been attested in speech-related genres (see Section 3.2.2 for more details on the classification of genres) such as Trial proceedings (around 50 per cent), Drama comedy (approx. 34 per cent), Non-private letters (5.4 per cent), Fiction (5.4 per cent), Private letters (1.8 per cent) and Philosophy (1.8 per cent). This type of sloppy identity in pronouns has been studied in Nielsen (2005:

180–1), who found seventy-seven cases where the pronominals need to change to reflect the change in speaker (4.66 per cent of the total examples of VPE in his corpus, 5.36 per cent in ours). These are the examples he mentions (Nielsen 2005: 180–1):

(356) 'Take care of *yourself*$_i$ then.' 'I$_i$ will ~~take care of *myself*$_i$~~.'
(357) 'I ain't going to fight *you*$_i$ no more.' 'I know you ain't ~~going to fight *me*$_i$~~,' Dan affirmed, feeling ten feet tall.

It is not clear from his examples, however, whether he includes sloppy possessive determiners under this same label.

As far as sloppy possessives are concerned, the only possessives found have been first person *my* and second person *your*, which is not surprising since all of them have been attested in dialogues. These possessives act as deictics which allude to the same referent. As was the case with sloppy pronouns, all sloppy possessives take place in different turns. The most frequent combination is possessive *your* in the antecedent and possessive *my* in the ellipsis site (80 per cent), the opposite combination (i.e. *my-your*) representing 20 per cent of the cases. Here are some additional examples:

(358) Was he *your* Commander? M'Cormack. No, he was not ~~*my commander*~~; TOWNLEY-1746,36.333
(359) Lord Fitz. And I must go and walk *my* three miles, this morning. Sir Simon. Must you ~~go and walk *your* three miles~~, my lord? COLMAN-1805,46.878

Like sloppy pronouns, all the instances of possessives have been attested in speech-related genres such as Trial proceedings (61.5 per cent), Drama comedy (30.77 per cent) and the mixed genre of Fiction (7.69 per cent).

Finally, sloppy polarity, as mentioned earlier, represents 15.63 per cent of the cases of sloppy identity in our corpus (approximately 1.5 per cent of VPE). The combinations are: *nothing* in the source clause – *something* in the ellipsis site (40 per cent), followed by *any-some* (33.3 per cent), *no-some* (20 per cent) and *anything-something* (6.7 per cent):

(360) 'There's *nothing* you want to give out for the man to brush, my dear creature, is there ~~*something* you want to give out for the man to brush~~?' resumed Smangle. DICKENS-1837,558.360
(361) Q. Had you seen any advertisements or placards stuck up, advertising that second meeting? A. I had ~~seen *some* advertisements or placards stuck up, advertising that second meeting~~. WATSON-1817,1,128.1323

(362) Herb. Pshaw, that's of *no* consequence. Dr. S. Oh, I thought it was ~~of some consequence~~; BROUGHAM-1861,13.445

(363) 'Is *anything* the matter with the Girl?' 'I think there is ~~something~~', FIELDING-1749,2,8.126

What is clear from the patterns followed by sloppy polarity is that the direction of polarity is always the same: from a negative polarity item (*nothing, any, no* or *anything*) to a positive polarity one (*something* or *some*). Nielsen (2005) reported that this type of partial identity when determiners are involved amounted to 1.5 per cent of his corpus, which is in keeping with this study. A careful analysis of all the examples of sloppy polarity in my corpus reveals that in 60 per cent of the cases they are in a different turn (as in (361)-(363)) and in the remaining 40 per cent they are in tag questions (as in (360)). As was the case with sloppy pronouns and possessives, sloppy polarity is found in speech-related genres: Drama comedy (47 per cent), Trial proceedings (20 per cent), Fiction (20 per cent) and Private letters (13 per cent).

In summary, sloppy identity accounts for 9.37 per cent of the examples of VPE in my corpus (8.64 per cent of the total cases of PAE). As mentioned earlier, no instances of the two types of sloppy identity, as recognized in this study, have been found in PG. It has been shown that our results for sloppy identity when a pronoun in the antecedent clause is interpreted sloppily in the ellipsis site are very much in line with those in Nielsen (2005) and Bos and Spenader (2011). In all these studies this strategy has a marginal representation, ranging from 0.18 per cent in my study to 1 per cent in Nielsen's (2005) and less than 2 per cent in Bos and Spenader's (2011). Sloppy identity when there are differences in the syntactic realization of certain elements represents 98 per cent of the examples of sloppy identity in my corpus (9.07 per cent of the total cases of VPE). However, this finding could only be compared to Nielsen's (2005) empirical work on VPE, in which, as mentioned earlier, he reports a percentage of 4.66 of sloppy pronouns (5.36 per cent in this volume) and 1.5 per cent of cases of sloppy polarity, the same as in my study. Finally, it has been shown that all the cases of sloppy identity in general only occur in speech-related genres and, in the vast majority of cases, in a different turn. Third-person pronouns have been attested only in cases where the pronoun of the ellipsis site is understood sloppily with respect to the source clause. In the second type of sloppy identity, all pronouns belong to first and second person pronouns. Finally, within this type of sloppy identity, sloppy polarity has been shown to have a negative source and a positive ellipsis site.

v. Turn

By paying attention to turns in PAE, we will check whether the antecedent clause and the clause containing the ellipsis site have been uttered by the same speaker or not. As is well-known in the literature, VPE is an instance of PAE that can apply across sentence boundaries. However, the distribution of PG, in theory, appears to be more constrained in this sense, as it shows a preference for comparative contexts. This single fact could have an influence on the results for turn, as comparative constructions generally occur within the same turn. If you recall, when the variable of syntactic linking was dealt with, I mentioned that the antecedent and the ellipsis site could appear in different sentences, that is, in contexts where no syntactic relation is established between them. It is precisely in this type of syntactic context that changes of speaker apply. In other words, a change of turn is only applicable to contexts where the source and the target of ellipsis belong to different sentences. Figure 6 illustrates syntactic linking and its relevance for the type of turn exhibited by the examples of PAE.

It should be noted that although tag questions are constructions of their own which have specific characteristics, for the sake of classification they have been treated as constructions where the antecedent and the ellipsis site belong to different sentences and occur within the same turn, as illustrated in (364):

(364) That is a great comfort, *is it not?* WILDE-1895,66.726

In CP-questions, on the other hand, the antecedent and the ellipsis site also appear in different sentences but can occur either within the same turn or in another turn, as shown in (365) and (366), respectively:

(365) and felt it was my duty to counteract it. *Did I?*
BROUGHAM-1861,20.734

(366) Phipps: I don't observe an alternation in your lordship's appearance.
Lord Goring: *You don't*, Phipps? WILDE-1895,73.939

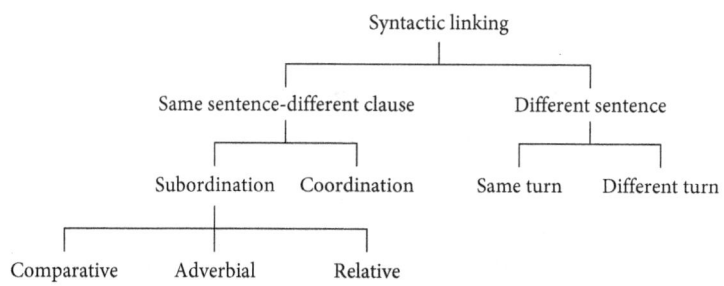

Figure 6 Syntactic linking and type of turn.

Table 77 Turn in PAE in Late Modern English

TURN	PG Abs. Freq.	%	VPE Abs. Freq.	%	PAE Abs. Freq.	%
Same turn	4	33.33	174	33.79	178	33.78
Different turn	8	66.67	341	66.21	349	66.22
TOTAL	12		515		527	

Let us now have a look at the frequency with which examples of PAE appear in a different turn with respect to their antecedents, shown in Table 77.

Interestingly enough, the data show that the categories of turn are evenly distributed in both types of PAE: over 33 per cent of the cases of PG and VPE occur within the same turn, while in the remaining 66 per cent the source and the target of ellipsis are uttered by different speakers. This amounts to saying that whenever there is a syntactic context that would allow the presence of different turns, there is a change of speaker 6.6 times out of 10 in PAE in the period under study. Therefore, it is clear that the frequency of different turns is not only high in VPE, as could be expected *a priori*, since it remains alike in PG too. Below, there are some examples that illustrate PG ((367) and (368)) and VPE ((369) and (370)) with a change of turn:

(367) Q. My question was, whether you had any conversation about the bills? A. No; *about Mr. Castle, I had*. WATSON-1817,1,99.550

(368) Mr. Serjeant Copley. How did you read it over? A. The same as I *would any thing else*. WATSON-1817,1,100.586

(369) Q. Do you know Coppice Row? A. No, I *do not*. WATSON-1817,179.2549

(370) Q. Were you examined there by the Jury, on the fact of your having been applied to to print those bills? A. Yes, I *was*. WATSON-1817,1,91.311

Example (367) is interesting because the remnant of PG (*about Mr. Castle*) has been topicalized and the auxiliary left in final position. In addition, illustrative examples of PG ((371)) and VPE ((372)) without a turn are also provided below:

(371) Lord Ellenborough. Do you read that paper which you put into his hand. Mr. Solicitor General. We cannot at present, my Lord, we *shall after we have called the next witness*. WATSON-1817,1,89.255

(372) it is a great Self-denial, to rise out of a warm Bed. But if I *do not*, I am immediately condemned as a slothful Servant. If I *do*, I find a great inward Blessing. WESLEY-174X,34.546

Notice that in example (371) there is a case of VPE in the antecedent of PG, whose antecedent appears in the previous sentence (and also in a different turn), yielding the interpretation 'We cannot ~~read that paper which I put into his hand~~ at present, my Lord, we *shall* ~~*read that paper which I put into his hand*~~ *after we have called the next witness*.'

Although it would be interesting to compare these results with other corpus-based studies, I am not aware of other empirical works on either VPE or PG that have addressed this variable.

3.2 Usage variables

In this section I will focus on the analysis and description of the diachronic evolution and the distribution of PAE per genres. First, I will concentrate on the comparison of the frequency of PAE in the two centuries under study, that is, eighteenth and nineteenth centuries, in order to check whether the variation is statistically significant within the Late Modern English period. Then, I will provide a detailed account of the distribution of PAE per text types, which will pave the way for the description of its productivity in speech-related and writing-related genres, thus allowing an analysis of the properties that PAE exhibits in each of the two varieties.

3.2.1 Diachronic evolution of PAE

As mentioned repeatedly throughout this volume, the empirical works on ellipsis have focused on Present-Day English, with the exception of those by Warner (1993, 1997), Gergel (2009) and Nykiel (2006, 2015). This study provides new empirical data on PAE in Late Modern English, in an attempt to widen the diachrony in the investigation of ellipsis. In order to check whether there is variation in PAE in Late Modern English or not, I have grouped them into two main periods: 1700–1800 (eighteenth century) and 1801–1914 (roughly nineteenth century). Table 78 shows the distribution of PAE in both centuries.

As observed in Table 78, VPE predominates in both centuries, comprising 92.26 per cent of the total examples of PAE. PG, on its part, has a more marginal

Table 78 Distribution of PAE in Late Modern English

TYPE OF PAE	Eighteenth century		Nineteenth century		TOTAL	
	Abs. Freq.	%	Abs. Freq.	%	Abs. Freq.	%
PG	50	11.49	36	5.33	86	7.74
VPE	385	88.51	640	94.67	1,025	92.26
TOTAL	435		676		1,111	

representation in the corpus, yielding 7.74 per cent of the cases of PAE. Interestingly, whereas VPE increases its frequency from the eighteenth to the nineteenth century (it goes from 88.51 per cent to 94.67 per cent), the reverse is true of PG, whose frequency decreases to almost half of the total examples attested in the previous century (from 11.49 per cent to 5.33 per cent). Graph 2 shows the distribution of these two types of PAE in both centuries.

The proportions of VPE and PG in Late Modern English are highly significant ($\chi^2(1)=13.25$, p=0.0003).

Let us have a look at the distribution of both types of PAE with respect to the normalized frequencies per IPs in the period under investigation.

Table 79 reveals that while the normalized frequency of PG per 1,000 IPs in the eighteenth century is 0.78, it goes down to 0.49 in the following century. Once again, the opposite is true of VPE, since it increases from 6.02 occurrences per 1,000 IPs in the eighteenth century to 8.74 in the nineteenth century. Therefore, PAE takes place 6.80 times per 1,000 IPs in the eighteenth century and 9.23 in the following century. As can be inferred, these normalized frequencies confirm the previous tendency already observed when I discussed the proportion of both

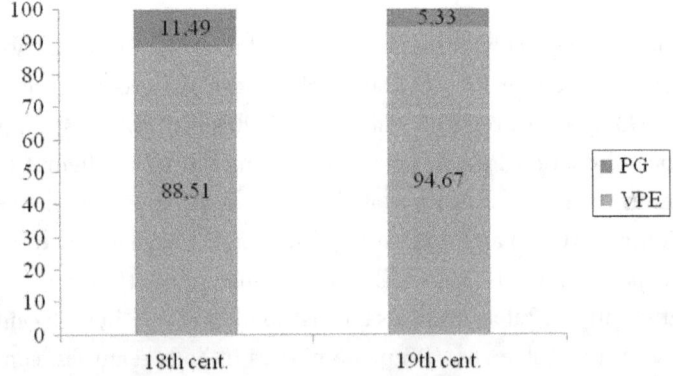

Graph 2 Distribution of PAE in Late Modern English.

Table 79 Normalized Frequency of PAE in Late Modern English

TYPE OF PAE	Eighteenth century	N.f. 1,000 IPs	Nineteenth century	N.f. 1,000 IPs	TOTAL
PG	50	0.78	36	0.49	86
VPE	385	6.02	640	8.74	1,025
TOTAL	435	6.80	676	9.23	1,111

types of PAE. Crucially, it has also been found that the distribution of PAE in both centuries with respect to the total number of IPs in each of these periods is highly significant too ($\chi^2(1)=24.47$, $p<.0001$) (see Table 80).

In summary, the distribution of PAE undergoes a statistically significant increase from the eighteenth century to the nineteenth century thanks to the rise of VPE, supported by the fact that the presence of PG undergoes a decrease in its frequency. This conclusion is confirmed in the light of both the proportions and the normalized frequencies of PAE in both centuries. These data also reveal that PG was a more marginal construction than VPE in Late Modern English, a tendency which is evinced in Present-Day English on the basis of studies like Bos and Spenader (2011). They report 487 cases of VPE within the 53,561 IPs present in the 25 sections of the *Wall Street Journal* that they analysed, which amounts to saying that VPE occurs once every 109 IPs, that is, 9.09 times every 1,000 IPs. This result is very much in line with ours: 9.23 occurrences every 1,000 IPs. However, one word of caution is in order here, as they included PG as a subtype of VPE in their classification. In their study they found only one instance of PG in the whole corpus, which implies that the normalized frequency of PG per 1,000 IPs was 0.02 and that of VPE 9.07. This may mean that the frequency of PG in Present-Day English seems to have continued the tendency already highlighted by the Late Modern English data towards lower frequency. In their empirical study, Bos and Spenader (2011) also revised the findings reported by Nielsen (2005) with respect to the frequency of VPE. Nielsen had reported one instance of VPE in every 77 sentences – 118 examples of VPE in seven sections of the *Wall Street Journal*. Bos and Spenader (2011: 481) registered 14,811 sentences

Table 80 Distribution of PAE in Late Modern English with respect to the Total Number of IPs

	Eighteenth century	Nineteenth century
PAE	435	676
Nr. IPs	63,969	73,210

altogether in these seven sections, rendering thus a VPE rate of one in every 125 sentences (7.97 per 1,000 IPs). Finally, it would be interesting to be in a position to compare my results for PG with those of Miller (2014), who found 1,415 examples in his large-scale corpus study of PG with NP remnants in the COCA. Since the latter corpus is not parsed, it remains to be known with what frequency PG occurs with respect to a certain number of IPs. But certainly, the fact that he found 1,415 examples when he only concentrated on those examples of PG with NP remnants already tells us something: it may be even more marginal nowadays than it used to be in Late Modern English.

3.2.2 Genre distribution of PAE

This section will be devoted to the analysis and description of genre distribution of PAE. The aim will be to try to elucidate whether there is statistically significant variation in its frequency by text types in Late Modern English. As will be shown, a detailed account of the distribution of PAE per text types will be provided first. This will pave the way for a dichotomous distinction between speech-related and writing-related genres, thus allowing an analysis of the features that PAE exhibits in each of the two varieties. If you recall from Section 2.2.2, there are eighteen genres represented in the PPCMBE: Diary, Drama comedy, Non-private letters, Private letters, Trial proceedings, Sermon, Philosophy, Bible, Biography autobiography, Biography other, Educational treatise, Handbook other, History, Law, Science medicine, Fiction, Science other and Travelogue. In Tables 81, 82 and 83, you will find the data concerning the distribution of PG, VPE and PAE per type of genre.

As shown in Table 81, PG occurs most frequently in Drama comedy (15.12 per cent), followed closely by Trial proceedings (13.95 per cent). The third position is shared by three types of genres: Private letters, Educational treatise and Fiction, where each of them represents 9.30 per cent of the total. These are followed by Diary (8.14 per cent), Sermon (6.98 per cent), Bible (5.81 per cent) and Science other (5.81 per cent). Much more marginally, PG occurs in genres such as Handbook other (4.65 per cent), History (3.49 per cent), Philosophy (3.49 per cent), Biography other (2.33 per cent), Non-private letters (1.16 per cent) and Science medicine (1.16 per cent). Interestingly, no instances of PG have been attested in genres such as Biography autobiography, Travelogue and Law.

Let us compare these data with those concerning VPE.

At first sight, what is clear is that the first seven genres where VPE occurs the most are the same as in PG (namely Trial proceedings, Drama comedy, Private

Table 81 Genre Distribution of PG in Late Modern English

	PG	
TYPE OF GENRE	**Abs. Freq.**	**%**
Drama comedy	13	15.12
Trial proceedings	12	13.95
Private letters	8	9.30
Educational treatise	8	9.30
Fiction	8	9.30
Diary	7	8.14
Sermon	6	6.98
Bible	5	5.81
Science other	5	5.81
Handbook other	4	4.65
History	3	3.49
Philosophy	3	3.49
Biography other	2	2.33
Non-private letters	1	1.16
Science medicine	1	1.16
Biography autobiography	0	0
Travelogue	0	0
Law	0	0
TOTAL	86	

Table 82 Genre Distribution of VPE in Late Modern English

	VPE	
TYPE OF GENRE	**Abs. Freq.**	**%**
Trial proceedings	297	28.98
Drama comedy	196	19.12
Private letters	97	9.46
Fiction	91	8.88
Diary	61	5.95
Sermon	48	4.68
Educational treatise	36	3.51
Handbook other	35	3.41
Non-private letters	32	3.12
Philosophy	28	2.73
Travelogue	24	2.34
Biography other	19	1.85
Science other	18	1.76
History	17	1.66
Bible	14	1.37
Biography autobiography	6	0.59
Law	4	0.39
Science medicine	2	0.20
TOTAL	1,025	

letters, Fiction, Diary, Sermon and Educational treatise). The only differences are found in the positions and percentages of these genres. For instance, the first and second positions in PG (Drama comedy and Trials proceedings, respectively) are switched in the case of VPE, since it occurs most in Trial proceedings (28.98 per cent), followed by Drama comedy (19.12 per cent). The presence of VPE in these two genres represents over 48 per cent of the cases. It should also be noted that the percentage of VPE in the genre Trial proceedings almost doubles that of the most frequent genre in PG (Drama comedy 15.12 per cent). The third most common genre where VPE occurs is Private letters (9.46 per cent), followed by Fiction (8.88 per cent) and Diary (5.95 per cent), respectively. The other genres have a much more marginal representation: Educational treatise (3.51 per cent), Handbook other (3.41 per cent), Non-private letters (3.12 per cent), Philosophy (2.73 per cent), Travelogue (2.34 per cent), Biography other (1.85 per cent), Science other (1.76 per cent), History (1.66 per cent), Bible (1.37 per cent), Biography autobiography (0.59 per cent), Law (0.39 per cent) and Science medicine (0.20 per cent). In contrast with PG, VPE has been attested in all of the genres, even if its presence is minimally represented.

The eighteen genres from the PPCMBE have been classified following Culpeper and Kytö's (2010: 16ff) distinctions among the different text types as either speech or writing related. Below, those genres that they consider speech related are quoted:

> Genres that might relate to spoken interaction are variously labeled in the literature, including the labels 'oral', 'spoken' and 'colloquial'. These labels are applied to genres such as: Autobiography, Plays (especially Comedy), Diaries, Fiction, Correspondence (especially personal), Trial proceedings, Witness depositions and Handbooks. As one can see, there is huge variation in the kind of genre; for example, Diaries and Trial proceedings are obviously unlike each other in many respects. A further problem is that the particular genres that research labels 'oral', 'spoken' or 'colloquial' are usually taken as homogenous. In fact, there is huge variation *within* particular genres. For example, Prose fiction and Witness depositions contain both narrative and speech report – they are a kind of mixed genre. [Culpeper and Kytö (2010: 16); italics in the original]

These are the genres that are considered speech related: Diary, Drama comedy, Non-private letters, Private letters, Trial proceedings, Sermon, Biography autobiography and Biography other. Fiction, as in Culpeper and Kytö (2010: 16), will be treated as a mixed genre because it contains both narrative and speech report. The remaining half of the genres, that is, Educational treatise, Handbook other, History, Law, Philosophy, Science medicine, Science other, Travelogue and Bible will be taken as writing related. As we proceed with the analysis of the data concerning the genre distribution of PAE, it will be clear why this preliminary distinction among genres will need to be slightly modified. In Table 83 the data for the distribution of PAE per type of genre have been gathered.

The six genres where PAE is more frequent belong in the speech-related group, comprising around 77 per cent of the total. Notice, however, that Fiction, as mentioned earlier, is a mixed genre that may contain both narrative and speech report and occupies the fourth position. The remaining genres represent 23 per cent of the total and they are composed of writing-related genres mainly, with the exception of Non-private letters, Biography other and Biography autobiography (5.56 per cent altogether), where PAE has a marginal representation.

In addition to this broad distinction among the different text types, Culpeper and Kytö (2010: 17–18) propose a more fine-grained classification of speech-related genres by distinguishing three subtypes: 'speech-like', 'speech-based' and 'speech-purposed'. Culpeper and Kytö (2010: 17) 'conceive the term "speech-like" as scalar and consisting of the features of "communicative immediacy". [...] This scale may overlap to varying degrees with the other categories.' In their

Table 83 Genre Distribution of PAE in Late Modern English

TYPE OF GENRE	PAE	
	Abs. Freq.	%
Trial proceedings	309	27.81
Drama comedy	209	18.81
Private letters	105	9.45
Fiction	99	8.91
Diary	68	6.12
Sermon	54	4.86
Educational treatise	44	3.96
Handbook other	39	3.51
Non-private Letters	33	2.97
Philosophy	31	2.79
Travelogue	24	2.16
Science other	23	2.07
Biography other	21	1.89
History	20	1.80
Bible	19	1.71
Biography autobiography	6	0.54
Law	4	0.36
Science medicine	3	0.27
TOTAL	1,111	

view, Personal correspondence (Private letters or Non-private letters in our case) does not overlap with the other categories, namely 'speech-based' and 'speech-purposed'. This is so because neither is it based on speech nor is it designed to be like speech, but it exhibits features that are speech like. In the present study, I have considered the following five genres as speech like: Biography autobiography, Biography other, Diary, Non-private letters and Private letters. The second category mentioned, namely 'speech-based', refers to 'those that are based on an actual "real-life" speech event. There is no claim here that such genres involve the accurate recording of a speech event. In the absence of audio or video recording equipment or even full systems of shorthand, most speech-based texts are reconstructions assisted by notes' (Culpeper and Kytö 2010: 17). Within this category, I only include the genre Trial proceedings, in line with Culpeper and Kytö (2010: 17). Those genres that belong in the third category, that is, 'speech-purposed', 'are designed to be articulated orally. Some genres, Sermons and Proclamations for example, are designed to produce monologue (they are "read out"), but others, most notably Plays, are designed to produce real-time spoken interaction ("they are performed")' (Culpeper and Kytö 2010: 17). Within this category, then, I have included the genres Sermon and Drama comedy. Finally, Culpeper and Kytö (2010: 18) categorize the writing-related genres distinguished earlier (Educational treatise, Handbook other, History, Law, Philosophy, Science medicine, Science other and Travelogue) as 'writing-based and purposed'. As mentioned before, Fiction will be treated separately, given that it is a mixed genre. In the case of the genre of Bible, it will also be treated separately due to the fact that it contains archaic language which is not illustrative of the period under study.

In the light of Table 84, PAE predominates in speech-based genres (27.81 per cent), especially due to the high frequency of VPE in this type of texts (28.98 per cent). Speech-based genres are closely followed by speech-purposed ones, yielding a total of 23.67 per cent of the total cases of PAE. Notice that in this case almost the same proportion is found in both PG (22.09 per cent) and VPE (23.80 per cent). The third position is occupied by speech-like genres, which represent 20.97 per cent of the total. Once again, there is an even distribution of PG (20.93 per cent) and VPE (20.98 per cent) within this category. Writing-based and purposed genres comprise 16.92 per cent of the cases of PAE, but this time we observe that they are slightly predominant in PG (27.91 per cent) than in VPE (16 per cent). Finally, the genre of Fiction represents 8.91 per cent of the total and that of Bible 1.71 per cent. In sum, it has been shown that PAE occurs in speech-related genres in over 72 per cent of the cases, while the remaining 28 per cent is composed of writing-related ones (including Bible and Fiction).

Table 84 PAE Genre Distribution according to Culpeper and Kytö's (2010) Fine-Grained Classification of Genres

GENRE	PG Abs. Freq.	%	VPE Abs. Freq.	%	TOTAL PAE Abs. Freq.	%
Biography other	2	2.33	19	1.85	21	1.89
Biography autobiography	0	0	6	0.59	6	0.54
Diary	7	8.14	61	5.95	68	6.12
Non-private Letters	1	1.16	32	3.12	33	2.97
Private letters	8	9.30	97	9.46	105	9.45
Total Speech-like	18	20.93	215	20.98	233	20.97
Travelogue	0	0	24	2.34	24	2.16
Educational treatise	8	9.30	36	3.51	44	3.96
Handbook other	4	4.65	35	3.41	39	3.51
History	3	3.49	17	1.66	20	1.80
Law	0	0	4	0.39	4	0.36
Science medicine	1	1.16	2	0.20	3	0.27
Science other	5	5.81	18	1.76	23	2.07
Philosophy	3	3.49	28	2.73	31	2.79
Total Writing-based and purposed	24	27.91	164	16.00	188	16.92
Total Speech-based (Trial proceedings)	12	13.95	297	28.98	309	27.81
Sermon	6	6.98	48	4.68	54	4.86
Drama comedy	13	15.12	196	19.12	209	18.81
Total Speech-purposed	19	22.09	244	23.80	263	23.67
Total Fiction	8	9.30	91	8.88	99	8.91
Total Bible	5	5.81	14	1.37	19	1.71
TOTAL	86		1,025		1,111	

As announced earlier, there will be slight modifications concerning the genres that will be labelled as either speech or writing related from now on. For instance, examining the texts from the genre of Philosophy, it was found that they were composed by translations from Latin of Boethius's sixteenth-century work named *De consolatione philosophiae* (*The Consolation of Philosophy*). These translations were carried out by Philip Ripath in 1785 and by Henry Rosher James in 1897. Since this piece of work was written as if Boethius himself were having a conversation with Lady Philosophy, it has been excluded from the group of writing-related genres and included within that of speech-related ones. In the case of Fiction, since it contains both narrative and speech report, I provide the figures for the examples of PG and VPE that form part of either Fiction narrative

Table 85 Preliminary Normalized Frequency of PAE by Genre in Late Modern English

TYPE OF GENRE	PG	VPE	Nr. IPs	N.f. 1,000 IPs
Speech-related	49	756	59,872	13.45
Writing-related	21	136	54,246	2.89
Fiction speech report	2	54	10,355	5.41
Fiction narrative	6	37	10,355	4.15
Total Fiction	8	91	10,355	9.56
Philosophy	3	28	2,881	10.76

or Fiction speech report (see Table 85). The genre of Bible will be excluded from this classification for the reasons already mentioned: it contains archaic language which is not illustrative of the period under study. In summary, these are the genres that will be considered speech related from now on: Biography autobiography, Biography other, Drama comedy, Trial proceedings, Diary, Private letters, Non-private letters, Sermon and Philosophy. On the other hand, the writing-related genres taken into account will be Educational treatise, Handbook other, Science medicine, Science other, Law, History and Travelogue. Let us now have a look at the preliminary normalized frequencies of PAE by genre, shown in Table 85.

In the face of the data from Table 85, PAE occurs 13.45 times per 1,000 IPs in speech-related genres, over four times more than in writing-related ones, whose normalized frequency is 2.89 per 1,000 IPs. In the case of Fiction, the normalized frequency of the subtype that contains examples of PAE in speech report is slightly higher than that of Fiction narrative (5.41 versus 4.15 per 1,000 IPs respectively). However, these figures for both subtypes of Fiction are not accurate, since the normalized frequencies would need to be calculated with respect to the number of times PAE occurs in IPs which contain either speech report or narrative, respectively. What is clear is that the normalized frequency of PAE in the genre of Fiction is fairly high (9.56) when compared to that of speech-related and writing-related genres. In the case of the genre of Philosophy, it has been found that the normalized frequency of PAE is 10.76 per 1,000 IPs, a very high ratio if this were considered a writing-related genre. However, the actual frequency is reasonable if one takes into account that the texts in this genre are translations from Boethius's work written as a conversation between the author himself and Lady Philosophy. In Table 86, I offer the final results concerning the normalized frequency of PAE by genre, where Philosophy has been included within the group of speech-related genres.

Table 86 Final Normalized Frequency of PAE by Genre in Late Modern English

TYPE OF GENRE	PG	VPE	Nr. IPs	N.f. 1,000 IPs
Speech-related	52	784	62,753	13.32
Writing-related	21	136	54,246	2.89
TOTAL	73	920	116,999	8.49

The final normalized frequency of PAE in speech-related genres is practically identical to the one in Table 85, that is, 13.32 occurrences per 1,000 IPs versus 13.45, respectively. The normalized frequency of writing-related genres remains alike: 2.89 hits per 1,000 IPs. In conclusion, then, PAE takes place in speech-related genres over four times more than in writing-related ones. Finally, if both types of genres are taken into account, PAE occurs 8.49 times per 1,000 IPs.

Let us now have a look at the normalized frequencies of PG and VPE by genre separately. In Table 87, you will find the data regarding PG and in Table 88 those concerning VPE.

The normalized frequency of PG by genre evinces that its presence is rather marginal in the PPCMBE, since it occurs on 0.83 occasions per 1,000 IPs in speech-related genres and in 0.39 in writing-related ones. The overall normalized frequency of PG in the corpus has been found to be 0.62 per 1,000 IPs. As far as the normalized frequency of VPE by genre, the data reveal that it is almost five times more frequent in speech-related genres than in writing-related ones (12.49 versus 2.51) per 1,000 IPs. The overall frequency of VPE in the corpus per 1,000 IPs is 7.86. This means that VPE is twelve times more frequent than PG. Graph 3

Table 87 Normalized Frequency of PG by Genre in Late Modern English

TYPE OF GENRE	Abs. Freq.	Nr. IPs	N.f. 1,000 IPs
Speech-related	52	62,753	0.83
Writing-related	21	54,246	0.39
TOTAL	73	116,999	0.62

Table 88 Normalized Frequency of VPE by Genre in Late Modern English

TYPE OF GENRE	Abs. Freq.	Nr. IPs	N.f. 1,000 IPs
Speech-related	784	62,753	12.49
Writing-related	136	54,246	2.51
TOTAL	920	116,999	7.86

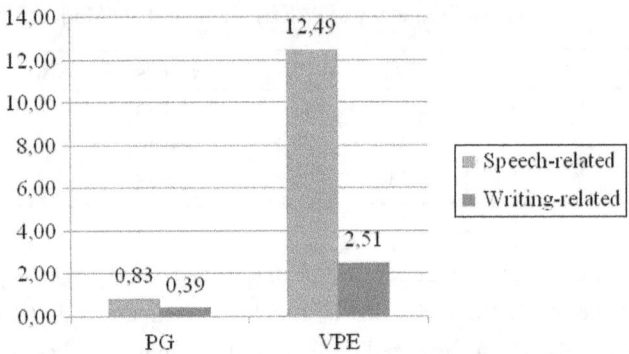

Graph 3 Graphical representation of the normalized frequencies of PG and VPE by genre.

offers a graphical representation of the normalized frequencies of PG and VPE by type of genre.

A chi-squared test reveals that the distribution of PG per genre category (speech versus writing related) is statistically significant ($\chi^2(1)=8.39$, p=0.0038), while in VPE it is highly statistically significant ($\chi^2(1)=365.12$, p<.0001). In addition, it has also been tested whether textual categorization plays a role in ellipsis (see Table 89).

The result of the chi-squared test shows that textual categorization plays a role in ellipsis and that it is highly statistically significant ($\chi^2(1)=368.69$, p<.0001).

Let us now have a look at whether textual categorization and diachrony play a role in ellipsis (see Table 90).

Table 89 Absolute Frequency of PAE per Type of Genre

TYPE OF GENRE	Abs. Freq.	Nr. IPs
Speech-related	836	62,753
Writing-related	157	54,246
TOTAL	993	116,999

Table 90 Absolute Frequency of PAE per Type Genre and Period

GENRE/ PERIOD	Abs. Freq.	Nr. IPs
Speech-related/Eighteenth century.	309	27,830
Speech-related/Nineteenth century	527	34,923
Writing-related/Eighteenth century	68	24,246
Writing-related/Nineteenth century	89	30,000

Whereas the distribution of speech-related genres in the periods under study has been found highly statistically significant ($\chi^2(1)=17.94$, p<.0001), this is not true of the distribution of the examples in the writing-related genres in the same periods, since the chi-squared test reveals that it is not significant ($\chi^2(1)=0.07$, p=0.7913).

Lastly, it has been checked whether textual categorization, diachrony and ellipsis type play a role in ellipsis (see Tables 91 and 92).

The chi-squared tests show that in PG neither the speech-related genres ($\chi^2(1)=0.92$, p=0.3375) nor the writing-related genres ($\chi^2(1)=0.86$, p=0.3537) play a statistically significant role in ellipsis in the periods under study. This is also true of the writing-related genres in VPE ($\chi^2(1)=0.55$, p=0.4583), but not of the speech-related ones, which have been proved to be highly significant ($\chi^2(1)=21.7$, p<0.0001).

In the light of the data just presented, one can draw three main conclusions. First, ellipsis occurs more frequently in speech-related genres and this frequency is highly significant. Second, from a diachronic point of view, the only statistically significant rise of ellipsis between the eighteenth and nineteenth centuries takes place in speech-related genres. Finally, this statistically significant rise of ellipsis in the periods under study is only due to the rise of VPE.

Table 91 Absolute Frequency of PG per Type Genre and Period

GENRE/ PERIOD	Abs. Freq.	Nr. IPs
Speech-related/Eighteenth century	27	27,830
Speech-related/Nineteenth century	25	34,923
Writing-related/Eighteenth century	12	24,246
Writing-related/Nineteenth century	9	30,000

Table 92 Absolute Frequency of VPE per Type Genre and Period

GENRE/ PERIOD	Abs. Freq.	Nr. IPs
Speech-related/Eighteenth century	282	27,830
Speech-related/Nineteenth century	502	34,923
Writing-related/Eighteenth century	56	24,246
Writing-related/Nineteenth century	80	30,000

3.3 Processing variables

The processing variables taken into account in this study have to do with distance: lexical distance (measured in number of words) and syntactic distance (measured in number of IPs) existing between the source clause and the target of ellipsis in PAE. Distance has also been studied empirically in Hardt (1990), Hardt and Rambow (2001), Nielsen (2005) and Martin and McElree (2008). I will first describe the findings concerning lexical distance and will then focus on the results obtained for syntactic distance and the interaction between these two types of distance.

3.3.1 Lexical distance

As mentioned earlier, lexical distance refers to that between the antecedent clause(s) and the ellipsis site, in number of words (in the same vein as in Hardt and Rambow 2001 and Nielsen 2005). This measure will be later compared with syntactic distance (distance in number of IPs) since, as previously mentioned in Section 2.2.4, there can be cases where clauses are very long (and therefore the antecedent clause(s) and the ellipsis site are far away in number of words) but there are no intervening IPs (as in (373)) – the opposite situation is also true since there are cases where the antecedent clause(s) and the target of ellipsis are very close in number of words but separated by several IPs (see (374)):

(373) *it cannot be very material*, as far as regards mental discipline, whether *it is by inflexion or by auxiliaries*. (BAIN-1878,371.189)

Here there are no intervening IPs between the antecedent clause (*it cannot be very material*) and the ellipsis site (*it is by inflexion or by auxiliaries*), but there are nine words of distance between the two. Compare this example with the following one, where the same amount of words intervenes between the antecedent clause and the elliptical sentence but in this case there are two IPs in between (italics):

(374) I can recollect nothing more to say. When *my letter is gone, I suppose I shall*. (AUSTEN-180X,175.335)

The lexical distance in the examples of PG and VPE in my database is provided in Table 93.

Table 93 Lexical Distance between the Source and the Target of Ellipsis in PAE

DISTANCE NR. WORDS	PG		VPE		TOTAL PAE	
	Abs. Freq.	%	Abs. Freq.	%	Abs. Freq.	%
0–5	35	40.70	800	78.05	835	75.16
6–10	36	41.86	166	16.20	202	18.18
11–15	15	17.44	42	4.10	57	5.13
>15	0	0.00	17	1.66	17	1.53
TOTAL	86		1,025		1,111	

While in PG the lexical distance existing between the source and the target of ellipsis ranges from zero to ten words in 82.56 per cent of the cases (see (375)), in VPE it goes up to 94.24 per cent (see (376)).

(375) If all the People in the Inn were not asleep, you would have awakened *them as you have* me. FIELDING-1749,3,10.382

(376) Q. Did you hear any body, *and if you did*, who was it proposed any amendment to that? WATSON-1817,1,128.1312

In terms of distance in number of words, VPE is more local than PG, given that only in 5.76 per cent of the cases the existing lexical distance between the antecedent and the target of ellipsis is composed of eleven or more words (versus 17.44 per cent in PG), illustrated in examples (377) and (378), respectively:

(377) is it not as natural for them to try to excel in knowledge and virtue, as in wealth or power? Is it not prejudice, and a shameful perversion of their faculties, if they do not? CHAPMAN-1774,33.70

(378) the Prisoner paid the Men of his own Company himself, as all the Captains of Companies did theirs. TOWNLEY-1746,21.71

Whereas in PG the lexical distance of eleven to fifteen words represents 17.44 per cent of the total, no instances of fifteen words or more have been attested. In contrast, in VPE this latter group represents 1.66 per cent of the cases:

(379) That is the one thing the modern woman never understands. Lady Markby: And a very good thing too, dear, I dare say. It might break up many a happy home if they did. WILDE-1895,63.641

(380) Probably there is none of us here to whom the thought has not at some time come, 'I should like to be really good.' If we knew what had happened to that thought and what had followed it, we should

> know the secret history, the true beauty, or the deep tragedy, or the provoking emptiness of many lives. But this is certain, that it has been quickly followed by this second thought, 'I never shall.'
> TALBOT-1901,190.345

Let us have a look at the distribution of lexical distance of both PG and VPE in writing-related and speech-related genres by calculating the average number of words existing between antecedent and ellipsis site (see Table 94).

In order to check whether these results constitute a significant tendency given the differences in lexical length between these two textual macro-categories, I calculated the average number of words per IP in both types of genres (see Table 95).

The average number of words per IP in writing-related genres is 6.43, slightly lower than that found in speech-related genres, which is 7.87. These two figures will act as baselines for the ideal number of words per IP in these two kinds of genres. In fact, the average number of words between the antecedent and ellipsis site in both PG and VPE, along with the baselines for the average number of words per IP, has allowed us to calculate the normalized average number of

Table 94 Average Number of Words between Antecedent and Ellipsis Site in Writing and Speech-Related Genres

LEXICAL DISTANCE	PG	VPE
Writing-related genres	8.04	5.37
Speech-related genres	6.5	4.57

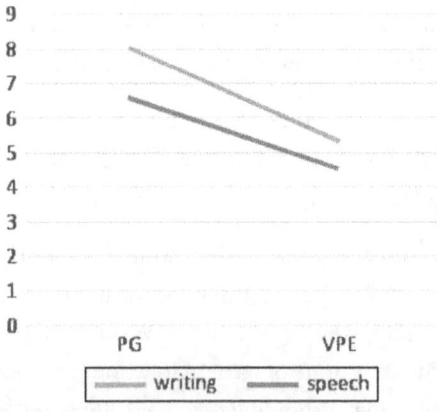

Graph 4 Graphical representation of the average number of words between antecedent and ellipsis site in writing and speech-related genres.

Table 95 Average Number of Words per IP in Writing and Speech-Related Genres

TYPE OF GENRE	Raw Nr. of Words	Raw Nr. of IPs	Average Nr. of Words per IP
Writing-related	403,506	62,753	6.43
Speech-related	426,854	54,246	7.87

words between antecedent and ellipsis site in PG and VPE per type of genre. The data are provided in Tables 96 and 97.

In the light of the data presented in Tables 96 and 97, one can conclude that if the average number of words in an IP in a writing-related genre is 6.43, then the distance in 'lexically ideal IPs', that is, in IPs whose length is the average length in number of words in the textual category, between the antecedent and the ellipsis site will be 1.25 in PG and 0.84 in VPE. On the other hand, if the average number of words in an IP in a speech-related genre is 7.87, then the distance in 'lexically ideal IPs' between the antecedent and the ellipsis site will be 0.83 in PG and 0.58 in VPE (see Table 98).

This means that, according to this normalized metric, VPE is more local than PG both in writing and in speech-related texts. What is more, PAE (both PG

Table 96 Normalized Average Number of Words between Antecedent and Ellipsis Site per Type of Genre in PG

TYPE OF GENRE	Average Nr. of Words between Antecedent and Ellipsis site	Baseline Nr. of Words/IP/Type of Genre	Normalized Average Nr. of Words between Antecedent and Ellipsis Site
Writing-related	8.04	6.43	1.25
Speech-related	6.5	7.87	0.83

Table 97 Normalized Average Number of Words between Antecedent and Ellipsis Site per Type of Genre in VPE

TYPE OF GENRE	Average Nr. of Words between Antecedent and Ellipsis Site	Baseline Nr. of Words/IP/Type of Genre	Normalized Average Nr. of Words between Antecedent and Ellipsis Site
Writing-related	5.37	6.43	0.84
Speech-related	4.57	7.87	0.58

Table 98 Normalized Average Number of Words between Antecedent and Ellipsis Site per Type of Genre in PG and VPE

TYPE OF GENRE	PG	VPE
Writing-related genres	1.25	0.84
Speech-related genres	0.83	0.58

and VPE), according to this metric, involves lower lexical distance in speech-related genres than in writing-related ones. These conclusions are represented in Graph 5, which, if compared with Graph 4, shows that these findings are also corroborated by the non-regularized absolute word counts (see Table 93).

Finally, it has also been checked whether the type of boundedness existing between the source and the target of ellipsis may have an impact on the length of lexical distance observed in ellipsis. In other words, I will try to answer the question of whether lexical distance is higher across different sentences or within the same sentence. According to Hardt (1993: 32), 'it is generally believed that memory for syntactic structure is relatively short-lived, while semantic information is retained over longer stretches of discourse.' Here we will try to check whether this statement is true. As claimed by Hardt (1993: 33), 'most of the literature on VP ellipsis focuses on examples in which the antecedent and VP ellipsis are in the same sentence, or in two adjacent, conjoined sentences. However, it is clear that VP ellipsis is not restricted to such configurations.' The fact that there are cases in which the antecedent

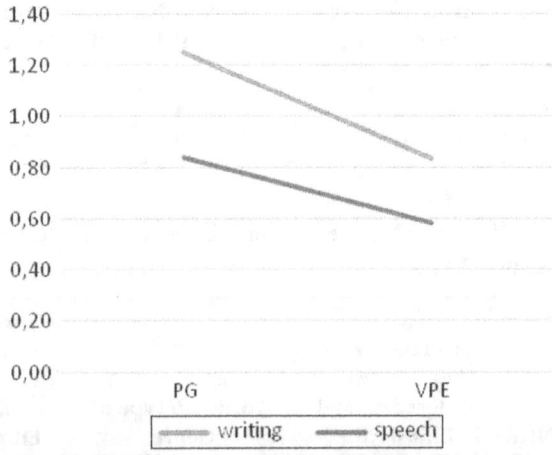

Graph 5 Representation of the normalized average number of words between antecedent and ellipsis site per type of genre in PG and VPE.

clause(s) and the ellipsis site are not contained within the same syntactic tree would imply that the relation that is established would be beyond the scope of syntactic rules. Moreover, Hardt (1993: 33) points out that it 'appears that the distance between antecedent and VP ellipsis can exceed the normal memory for syntactic structure'. What is more, as pointed out in Section 2.2.1, Levin (1986: 53) claims that while VPE is possible in contexts of subordination, embedded PGs 'rapidly become awkward'. We repeat the example she provides here for convenience:

(381)   Since tornadoes petrify Harold, I can't for the life of me figure out *why he's so surprised about the fact that* *they do ø me too/ hurricanes do ø too.

Therefore, this measure will provide us with an insight into how much syntactic complexity may be present between the antecedent clause(s) and the elliptical clause in both PG and VPE. Table 99 presents the data concerning PG.

According to Hardt's (1993) hypothesis, the expectation would be that lexical distance should be higher in cases where the antecedent and the ellipsis site appear in different sentences. However, in light of the data shown in Table 99, this hypothesis is not confirmed in PG: the more lexical distance increases, the fewer instances of PG are found where the antecedent and the ellipsis site occur in different sentences. In other words, the antecedent and the ellipsis site are attested in different sentences only in cases where the lexical distance ranges from zero to ten words (13.95 per cent of the cases of PG), but not from ten to fifteen words. Most instances of PG occur in contexts where the antecedent is within the same sentence, the target of ellipsis in a different clause, there are no intervening clauses and the lexical distance goes from zero to five words (42.65 per cent, yielding 33.72 per cent of the total occurrences of PG). The second most common pattern would be illustrated by examples where the same type of boundedness as the one just mentioned holds, but the lexical distance ranges from six to ten words (39.71 per cent, representing 31.39 per cent of the total). Altogether, these two patterns account for over 65 per cent of the instances of PG. The third most frequent pattern exhibits the same type of boundedness but the lexical distance goes up to eleven to fifteen words (17.65 per cent, rendering 13.95 per cent of the total). Finally, the least frequent patterns attested in PG are those where the type of boundedness exhibited contains the antecedent in the same sentence, the target of ellipsis in a different clause, there is an intervening IP and the lexical distance ranges from six to fifteen words (6.98 per cent). Consequently, these last results would be in line with Levin's findings, as PG

Table 99 Lexical Distance and Boundedness in PG

BOUNDEDNESS	LEXICAL DISTANCE									TOTAL	
	0–5		6–10			11–15					
	Abs. Freq.	% (of boundedness type)	Abs. Freq.	% (of boundedness type)		Abs. Freq.	% (of boundedness type)		Abs. Freq.	% (of all types)	
Different sentence	6	50.00	6	50.00		0	0.00		12	13.95	
Same sentence-different clause-intervening clause	0	0.00	3	50.00		3	50.00		6	6.98	
Same sentence-different clause-no intervening clause	29	42.65	27	39.71		12	17.65		68	79.07	
TOTAL	35		36			15			86		

does not seem to favour those syntactic contexts where the pseudogapped clause is embedded, as in (382):

(382) Q. Had you no preventer Braces? A. I believe *we had at the lower Yards, but don't know [whether we had at Topsail-Yards or not]*~IP-SUB~ HOLMES-TRIAL-1749,67.1248

In conclusion, then, almost 80 per cent of the examples of PG occur in cases where the antecedent is within the same sentence and the target of ellipsis appears in a different clause, with no intervening clauses. These are followed by cases where the antecedent and the ellipsis site occur in different sentences (13.95 per cent) and by cases where the antecedent is within the same sentence, the target of ellipsis in a different clause and there is an intervening clause (6.98 per cent), respectively. Moreover, most examples of PG occur within a lexical distance of six to ten words (41.86 per cent), followed by zero to five words (40.70 per cent) and eleven to fifteen words (17.44 per cent), respectively. Notice that there are no examples of PG where the lexical distance existing between the antecedent and the ellipsis site is composed of over fifteen words.

Now let us check whether the same situation is found in cases of VPE. The data are shown in Table 100.

As can be gathered from Table 100, the situation in VPE contrasts with that in PG: as lexical distance increases, most examples of VPE contain the source and the target of ellipsis in different sentences. In other words, in those instances of VPE where the lexical distance between the source and the target of ellipsis ranges from eleven to fifteen (4.85 per cent) or over fifteen words (3.11 per cent), the most frequent type of boundedness attested by far is one where both the source and the target are in different sentences, representing 4 per cent of the total cases of VPE. As a result, the remaining two types of boundedness represent only 0.19 per cent of the total altogether where the same lexical distance holds. These facts confirm Hardt's (1993) hypothesis for VPE: as lexical distance increases, the source and the target of ellipsis occur in different sentences. Notice, also, that in the majority of the examples of VPE the antecedent and the ellipsis site occur in different sentences (38.82 per cent of the total) and the number of words existing between the two goes from zero to five. These examples are followed very closely by those cases with the same lexical distance, but a different type of boundedness: the antecedent would be contained within the same sentence, the target of ellipsis would appear in a different clause and, in addition, there would be no intervening clauses in between (38.14 per cent). Altogether, these two patterns account for almost 77 per cent of the cases of VPE. In the third most

Table 100 Lexical Distance and Boundedness in VPE

	LEXICAL DISTANCE										
	0–5		6–10		11–15		>15		TOTAL	
BOUNDEDNESS	Abs. Freq.	% (of boundedness type)	Abs. Freq.	% (of boundedness type)	Abs. Freq.	% (of boundedness type)	Abs. Freq.	%	Abs. Freq.	% (of all types)
Different sentence	398	77.28	76	14.76	25	4.85	16	3.11	515	50.24
Same sentence-different clause-intervening clause	11	16.18	46	67.65	10	14.71	1	1.47	68	6.63
Same sentence-different clause-no intervening clause	391	88.46	43	9.73	7	1.58	1	0.23	442	43.12
TOTAL	800		165		42		18		1,025	

frequent pattern, the antecedent and the ellipsis site are in different sentences, and the lexical distance between them rises up to six to ten words (7.41 per cent). The rest of the cases have a much more marginal representation in VPE and altogether they represent around 15 per cent of the data. It should be noted that in over half of the cases of VPE (50.24 per cent), the antecedent and the ellipsis site appear in different sentences. These are closely followed by those cases where the source of the ellipsis is contained within the same sentence while the target of ellipsis appears in a different clause and there are no intervening clauses (43.12 per cent). Those cases where the source of the ellipsis is within the same sentence and the ellipsis site in a different clause and, at the same time, there are intervening clauses, only yield 6.63 per cent of the total. Moreover, the vast majority of cases of VPE appear within a range of zero to five words between the source and the target of ellipsis (78.05 per cent), followed by those where the lexical distance goes from six to ten words (16.10 per cent), ten to fifteen words (4.10 per cent) and over fifteen words (1.76 per cent) respectively. Therefore, even if its representation is marginal in our corpus, in contrast with PG, in VPE we find cases where the lexical distance may be composed of over fifteen words.

In sum, it has been shown that most instances of PG occur in contexts where the antecedent is contained within the same sentence, the target of ellipsis appears in a different clause, there are no intervening clauses and, in addition, the lexical distance is zero to ten words (around 65 per cent). Regarding VPE, in almost 80 per cent of the examples the lexical distance is smaller, that is, zero to five words. Notice, however, that our data show that lexical distance in VPE can be higher than fifteen words, contrary to PG. Moreover, the most frequent type of boundedness established is also different with respect to PG: the antecedent and the ellipsis site may either appear in different sentences or within the same sentence and in a different clause (with no intervening clauses) respectively. These data confirm that VPE tends to be more local than PG in our corpus. Finally, it has been shown that the results for PG would be in line with Levin's findings, as PG does not seem to favour those syntactic contexts where the pseudogapped clause is embedded. In addition, it has been found that Hardt's (1993) hypothesis stating that lexical distance is higher in cases where the antecedent and the ellipsis site appear in different sentences is not confirmed in PG. The higher the lexical distance, the fewer instances of PG are found where the antecedent and the ellipsis site occur in different sentences. In contrast, Hardt's (1993) hypothesis for VPE is confirmed: if lexical distance increases, the antecedent and the ellipsis site occur in different sentences in the vast majority of cases.

3.3.2 Syntactic distance

Syntactic distance determines sentential distance; in other words, it measures the distance existing between the antecedent clause(s) and the target of ellipsis, in number of clauses (coded with the label 'IP' in the corpus). For that purpose, the parsing of the PPCMBE has been used. As in Hardt and Rambow's (2001) and Nielsen's (2005) studies, a value of zero means that the VPs are in the same sentence. Table 101 presents the data concerning syntactic distance between the source and the target of ellipsis in cases of PAE in Late Modern English.

At first glance, Table 101 shows that in most instances of PAE there are no intervening clauses between the antecedent and the target of ellipsis (78.03 per cent). In fact, the more the syntactic distance existing between the source and the target of ellipsis is enlarged, the fewer the examples: one intervening clause represents 16.74 per cent of the cases of PAE, followed by two intervening clauses (3.51 per cent). Three intervening clauses (0.81 per cent) or more (0.90 per cent) are much more marginally represented in my data. Regarding PG, in over 90 per cent of the examples there are no intervening clauses between the source and the ellipsis site (see (383)). Then, in the rest of the examples there is either one clause intervening (5.81 per cent, as in (384)) or two (2.33 per cent, as in (385)). Therefore, no examples of PG have been found where the syntactic distance is composed of over two clauses in between the antecedent and the target of ellipsis.

(383) we cou'd not fail of learning the Latin Language, as well as we do the Modern Languages. ANON-1711,11.105

(384) I answer, That I take it to be undoubtedly certain, that he, who can correct Latin *when it is writ as* all School-masters do their Boy's Exercises can correct it when it is spoke. ANON-1711,16.163

Table 101 Syntactic Distance between the Source and the Target of Ellipsis in PAE

SYNTACTIC DISTANCE	PG		VPE		TOTAL PAE	
	Abs. Freq.	%	Abs. Freq.	%	Abs. Freq.	%
0	79	91.86	788	76.87	867	78.03
1	5	5.81	181	17.65	186	16.74
2	2	2.33	37	3.61	39	3.51
3	0	0	9	0.88	9	0.81
4	0	0	5	0.49	5	0.45
>5	0	0	5	0.49	5	0.45
TOTAL	86		1,025		1,111	

(385) If therefore we did but hear others talk Latin, and endeavour'd to *understand them, and talk with them,* as much as we do to understand and talk with those who speak in the Modern Tongues. ANON-1711,11.105

In turn, in VPE there are no intervening clauses between the source and the target of ellipsis in 76.87 per cent of the examples (see (386)), followed by those cases where there is one intervening clause (17.65 per cent, as in (387)). A syntactic distance of two clauses in between the source and the target of ellipsis is less frequent (3.61 per cent, illustrated in (388)), and the cases where there are three (0.81 per cent, as in (389)), four (0.45 per cent, as in (390)) or even five or more (0.45 per cent, as in (391)) intervening clauses are statistically more marginal. Hardt (1990), in his study of VPE in Present-Day English in the Brown Corpus, found that in around 5 per cent of the examples of VPE there were one or more clauses intervening between the antecedent and the ellipsis site. In this piece of research, the percentage goes up to 23.12 per cent in Late Modern English. This implies that long-distance antecedents were over 4.6 times more frequent in this previous stage of the language. However, if only those instances of VPE where the syntactic distance is materialized in two or more clauses were taken into account, the percentage would be in the same line as that reported in Hardt (1990), viz 5.47 per cent. This is due to the fact that in 17.65 per cent of the cases of VPE, there is one IP intervening between the source and the ellipsis site.

(386) this matter does not depend on my brother's consent, and even if it did, Ermine's own true position is that which is most honourable to her. YONGE-1865,178.507

(387) Q. Can you see him in court? A. *I cannot say* that I do. WATSON-1817,1,94.398

(388) If he can not answer correctly, *the monitor puts the question to another boy, till he finds* one who can. LANCASTER-1806,68.514

(389) Q. Can you take upon yourself to swear that Watson heard you? A. *I think I can take upon myself to swear* that he did. WATSON-1817,1,101.591

(390) Cha. But first of all tell me, if you can lie with a good grace, and stick to it. Frank. *What do you take me for? I haven't been your servant for three years without making some progress. I flatter myself* I can. COLLIER-1835,9.197

(391) Probably there is none of us here to whom the thought has not at some time come, 'I should like to be really good.' If we knew what

> had happened to that thought and what had followed it, we should know the secret history, the true beauty, or the deep tragedy, or the provoking emptiness of many lives. But this is certain, that it has been quickly followed by this second thought, 'I never shall.'
> TALBOT-1901,190.345

Regarding the interaction between syntactic and lexical distance, I will check whether the number of intervening clauses correlates with the number of words between the antecedent and the ellipsis site in PAE. First, the data for PG are given in Table 102.

Over 90 per cent of the examples of PG have no clauses intervening between the source and the target of ellipsis. Out of these, those examples of PG whose lexical distance ranges from zero to five (44.30 per cent) and from six to ten (40.51 per cent) words comprise over 77 per cent of the total. In addition, the third most frequent pattern attested is one whose lexical distance ranges from eleven to fifteen words and there are no clauses intervening between the antecedent and the target of ellipsis (15.19 per cent, yielding 13.95 per cent of the total). Those cases where there is one intervening clause represent 5.81 per cent of the total: in 80 per cent (4.65 per cent of the total) of the cases the lexical distance ranges from six to ten words, while in 20 per cent of them the lexical distance goes up to eleven to fifteen words (1.16 per cent of the total). Finally, there are also cases where the syntactic distance is measured by two clauses in between the antecedent and the ellipsis site, amounting to 2.33 per cent of the instances of PG. In these cases, the lexical distance exhibited ranges from eleven to fifteen words. In conclusion, then, it has been found that, unsurprisingly, the higher the lexical distance, the higher the syntactic distance in PG. Let us now compare these data with the situation found in VPE, shown in Table 103.

In the vast majority of the examples of VPE there are no clauses intervening between the source and the target of ellipsis (76.88 per cent). Out of these, those whose lexical length is zero to five words are the most frequent (92.64 per cent, representing 71.21 per cent of the total). The second most frequent pattern that arises from the interaction between lexical and syntactic distance is one where there is one clause intervening between the source and the target of ellipsis and its lexical length is six to ten words (53.04 per cent, representing 9.36 per cent of the total cases of VPE). It should be highlighted that, as expected, as the number of intervening clauses increases, so does the number of words, as was the case with PG. For instance, all those examples of VPE whose syntactic distance is made up four, five or more clauses exhibit a lexical length of over fifteen words between the source and the target of ellipsis, yielding 0.96 per cent of the total.

Table 102 Lexical and Syntactic Distance in PG

SYNTACTIC DISTANCE	LEXICAL DISTANCE								
	0–5		6–10		11–15		TOTAL	
	Abs. Freq.	%	Abs. Freq.	%	Abs. Freq.	%	Abs. Freq.	%
0	35	44.30	32	40.51	12	15.19	79	91.86
1	0	0.00	4	80.00	1	20.00	5	5.81
2	0	0.00	0	0.00	2	100.00	2	2.33
TOTAL	35		36		15		86	

Table 103 Lexical and Syntactic Distance in VPE

SYNTACTIC DISTANCE	LEXICAL DISTANCE									
	0–5		6–10		11–15		>15		TOTAL	
	Abs. Freq.	%	Abs. Freq.	%	Abs. Freq.	%	Abs. Freq.	%	Abs. Freq.	%
0	730	92.64	50	6.35	7	0.89	1	0.13	788	76.88
1	69	38.12	96	53.04	15	8.29	1	0.55	181	17.66
2	1	2.70	17	45.95	15	40.54	4	10.81	37	3.61
3	0	0.00	2	22.22	5	55.56	2	22.22	9	0.88
4	0	0.00	0	0.00	0	0.00	5	100.00	5	0.49
>5	0	0.00	0	0.00	0	0.00	5	100.00	5	0.49
TOTAL	800		165		42		18		1,025	

As a conclusion on processing, it has been shown that most instances of PG occur in contexts where the antecedent is contained within the same sentence, the target of ellipsis appears in a different clause, there are no intervening clauses and, in addition, the lexical distance goes from zero to ten words. Regarding VPE, in the vast majority of the examples the lexical distance is lower, that is, zero to five words. VPE differs from PG also with respect to the most frequent type of boundedness established: the antecedent and the ellipsis site may appear either in different sentences or within the same sentence and in a different clause (with no intervening clauses), respectively, and this highlights the more local status of VPE. In addition, it has been shown that the results for PG corroborate Levin's (1986) findings, as PG disfavours those syntactic contexts where the pseudogapped clause is embedded. It has also been found that Hardt's (1993) hypothesis that lexical distance is higher in cases where the antecedent and the ellipsis site appear in different sentences is not confirmed in PG. The higher the lexical distance, the fewer instances of PG are found where the antecedent and the ellipsis site occur in different sentences. In contrast, Hardt's (1993) hypothesis for VPE is confirmed: if lexical distance increases, the antecedent and the ellipsis site occur in different sentences in the vast majority of cases. Finally, after checking the interaction of lexical and syntactic distance, it has been found that the higher the lexical distance, the higher the syntactic distance in both PAE constructions.

3.4 Concluding remarks on the characteristics of PG and VPE in Late Modern English

In order to conclude this chapter, I will address the debate concerning the possibility of treating PG as a subcase of VPE. As already pointed out, Miller (2014), Levin (1986) and Hoeksema (2006) argued that PG and VPE have too many different characteristics and this discourages their unitary treatment. Miller (2014: 86), however, is more cautious in tackling this debate and claims that since VPE and PG exhibit many similarities too: 'The question arises of the extent to which it might be possible to consider them as subconstructions of a more general VPE construction, explaining away the differences on the basis of a better understanding of their discourse uses.' In other words, Miller (2014) tried to explain the differences between PG and VPE as a direct consequence of the different uses that these constructions serve in discourse. Below, I will review the main differences between PG and VPE reported in the literature and the explanation of these alleged differences provided by Miller (2014), to then analyse them in light of my data.

First, PG is said to occur mainly in comparative environments in Present-Day English. In fact, comparative PG comprises 87 per cent of the total in Hoeksema (2006), 90 per cent in Sharifzadeh, and almost 97 per cent in Miller (2014). In the light of my data from Late Modern English, this is clearly true: PG also takes place in comparative environments in the vast majority of cases: 74 per cent of the total. But it should be noted that the percentage of comparative constructions in cases of VPE, though much lower than that of PG, is also high: over 31 per cent of the total (the second most frequent type of syntactic linking attested), very much in line with the findings reported in Bos and Spenader (2011) for VPE in Present-Day English. Miller (2014: 87) also mentions that, unlike VPE, noncomparative PG occurs almost exclusively in spoken registers. Our data do not confirm this claim since noncomparative PG has occurred in speech-related genres on 90 per cent of the occasions, and noncomparative VPE on almost 92 per cent, which means that their distribution is practically alike.

As mentioned in studies like Levin (1986) and Hoeksema (2006), PG prefers subject identity in the antecedent, contrary to VPE. However, our data from Late Modern English suggest the opposite direction: while in PG the percentage of same subjects comprises almost 62 per cent of the examples, in VPE it goes up to over 80 per cent. Therefore, it seems that both constructions favour subject identity and that this preference is stronger in the case of VPE. This would be in line with Miller's (2011, 2014) findings. In his (2011) corpus study, Miller reports that 83 per cent of his examples of VPE from COCA have the same subjects as their antecedents. Moreover, Miller (2014) found that almost 80 per cent of his examples of PG with NP remnants favoured the same subjects as their antecedents. Therefore, the results of his studies show that both constructions have a preference for subject identity and that the proportions of same versus different subjects in both constructions are quite alike at present.

In addition, as already mentioned in this volume, the literature has supported that PG does not allow voice mismatches while VPE does (Merchant 2008a, 2013b). In this investigation I found one instance of a voice mismatch in PG in Late Modern English (1.16 per cent) and seven in VPE (0.68 per cent). If compared with Bos and Spenader's (2011) findings on VPE and Miller's (2014) on PG in Present-Day English, the tendency is very similar: Bos and Spenader found no voice mismatches in cases of VPE, and Miller (2014) found 10 occurrences out of 1,415 in cases of PG, that is, 0.70 per cent of the examples.

Therefore, in the light of their corpus studies and the findings presented in this monograph, voice mismatches are more frequent in PG than in VPE, although this conclusion would require further research. What is clear is that both constructions, and not only VPE, allow voice mismatches.

Another difference between PG and VPE that has been mentioned in the literature has to do with the fact that PG does not occur cataphorically, contrary to VPE (Levin 1986; Hardt 1993; Bos and Spenader 2011; Miller 2014). This is confirmed in my data from Late Modern English, as no instances of cataphoric PG have been attested. It is worth mentioning, however, that Miller (2014) found one example of cataphoric PG (out of 1,415) which, in his opinion, was not a speech error. The cataphoric uses of VPE represent only 1.07 per cent of the total in this investigation. This result is very much in line with that in Bos and Spenader's (2011) study on VPE Present-Day English, who reported a frequency of 0.82 per cent for cataphoric uses of VPE. PG and VPE clearly differ in this respect. Miller (2014) points out that this difference may be due to the fact that cataphoric VPE generally shows auxiliary choice and PG can never be only auxiliary choice. This observation is indeed confirmed in this volume and may therefore explain the difference attested between the two constructions.

Another difference between PG and VPE reported in the literature affects the number of auxiliaries: PG involves a single auxiliary, while the latter may contain more than one (Levin 1986; Hoeksema 2006; Miller 2014). Levin (1986) reported only one example of PG where there was an auxiliary before the licensor. However, the opposite tendency has been attested in Late Modern English: while the percentage of auxiliaries before the licensor in PG was 8.14 per cent, it decreased to 4.39 per cent in the case of VPE. Miller (2014) explains this difference between the two constructions by alluding, once again, to the impossibility of finding auxiliary choice PG. He illustrates this by pointing out that 'a simple search on the COCA suggests that VPE with multiple auxiliaries is almost never Subj-choice' (Miller 2014: 88). This fact is indeed corroborated in my study: most examples of VPE with auxiliaries before the licensor involve auxiliary choice focus. What is not clear is why PG allowed the existence of an auxiliary before the licensor in Late Modern English and does not seem to do so in Present-Day English.

Lastly, it is well-known that PG is not licensed by infinitival marker *to*, contrary to VPE (Levin 1986; Miller 2014). This has been corroborated in my Late Modern English data since not a single example of PG has been licensed by *to*. Miller (2014: 88) suggests that this may be due the fact that VPE allows auxiliary choice focus, and PG cannot.[6] This hypothesis is confirmed by my data: all of the examples of VPE licensed by *to* attested in Late Modern English illustrate auxiliary choice.

To conclude, I will also summarize other differences between PG and VPE in Late Modern English. To start with, even though the distribution of both PG and VPE in the different syntactic domains is fairly similar (subordination and matrix clauses), there are three syntactic domains where only VPE has been attested: CP-questions, tag questions and IP-imperatives. Also, with respect to the categories of the target of ellipsis, it has been found that while PG and VPE license the ellipsis of the same types of elements (namely, NPs, APs, PPs), AdPs have not been attested in PG. Moreover, split antecedents have only been found in VPE, although their representation is rather marginal. Furthermore, no examples of sloppy identity of either kind have been attested in cases of PG, even though they represent almost 10 per cent of the total of the VPE constructions. Finally, since both constructions differ in their discourse uses, they involve different types of focus. PG can never involve auxiliary choice, and the types of focus attested in PG are object choice, subject-object choice and subject-object-auxiliary choice. In the case of VPE, these were the types of focus: subject choice, auxiliary choice and subject-auxiliary choice.

4

Conclusions and issues for further research

This volume reports the results of an in-depth analysis of Post-Auxiliary Ellipsis (PAE) in Modern English based on data extracted from the Penn Parsed Corpus of Modern British English (1700–1914). Two main goals have been pursued in this study: an analytical one and a methodological one. On the one hand, I have tried to provide an answer to the null hypothesis stating that 'ellipsis does not undergo significant changes in the Modern and Contemporary periods in the history of English'. To that end, I have extended previous empirical studies on PAE in Present-Day English by providing new data from an earlier period of the language, namely, Modern English (1700–1914), and by comparing the findings obtained for those periods of the recent history of the English language. In an attempt to offer a multifaceted view and explanation of PAE constructions, the variables explored in this study have tackled this kind of ellipsis from four different perspectives: grammatical, semantic/discursive, usage and processing. On the other hand, I have also presented a new algorithm in order to detect and retrieve examples of PAE in Modern English automatically via CorpusSearch 2, which obtained successful recall ratios. In what follows, the current chapter provides the summary and concluding remarks of this investigation and suggests some possible new lines of research.

As mentioned above, the variables under study were divided into four different blocks: grammatical, semantic/discursive, usage and processing variables. First, within the group of grammatical variables, I have analysed the type of licensor of PAE (modal auxiliaries, auxiliaries *be*, *have* and *do* and infinitival marker *to*); the existence of auxiliary(ies) before the licensor; the type of syntactic linking established between the antecedent and the ellipsis site (coordination, subordination, etc.); the syntactic domain where ellipsis takes place (matrix, subordinate clause, etc.); the category of the antecedent and that of the elided material (NP, VP, AP, etc.); the existence of split antecedents (also known as *combined antecedents*, as in *I can walk, and I can chew gum. Gerry can walk and*

~~chew gum~~ *too, but not at the same time*; Webber 1978); the types of remnants attested in PG (classified by category (NP, PP, etc.)) and syntactic function (object, adverbial, etc.); and, finally, auxiliary-related variables such as polarity, voice, aspect, modality and tense. Second, the semantic/discursive variables analysed include the type of clause attested in the antecedents and in the ellipsis sites (declarative, interrogative and imperative); the type of anaphora (anaphoric, cataphoric and exophoric); the type of focus (subject choice, auxiliary choice, object choice, etc.); the existence of sloppy identity (that is, non-equivalences between the source clauses and their elliptical counterparts, as in *Have you bought anything? I have* ~~bought something~~, or *I know how to crane my neck, but you don't know how to* ~~crane your neck~~, for example), and the type of turn (i.e. whether there is a change of speaker or not). Third, I also paid attention to usage variables such as the distribution of PAE constructions by period (eighteenth and roughly nineteenth century) and genre (speech-related vs. writing-related genres). Finally, I analysed processing variables such as the lexical distance (in number of words) and the syntactic distance (in number of clauses) between the antecedent and the ellipsis site in PAE constructions.

Below, I will summarize the main findings concerning all the grammatical variables taken into account and will then comment on the results gathered from the study of the semantic/discursive, usage and processing variables, respectively. To begin with, the study of the distribution of licensors of PAE has shown that modal auxiliaries are the most common triggers of PAE in Modern English, followed by auxiliaries *be* and *have*, and (much more marginally) infinitival marker *to*. As predicted by the literature, no instances of infinitival marker *to* as a licensor of PG have been attested, in line with empirical works like Miller (2014) on PG in Present-Day English. On the one hand, the genre distribution of the licensors of VPE has revealed that modal auxiliaries are the most frequent triggers of ellipsis in both speech and writing-related genres, followed by *be*, *have* and infinitival marker *to*, respectively. In fact, the comparison with the results described in Bos and Spenader (2011) on VPE in writing-related genres in Present-Day English has revealed that the relative frequency of the licensors of VPE in writing-related genres in Modern English is much alike. On the other hand, the frequencies of the licensors of PG in writing-related genres were the following (in decreasing order): auxiliary *be*, modal auxiliaries and auxiliary *have*. Interestingly, the trend is reversed in speech-related genres, in which the order is (from most to least common): auxiliary *have*, modal auxiliaries and auxiliary *be*. Lastly, it must be noted that there were some examples whose licensors are no longer attested in Present-Day English, namely, *shouldest*, *shalt*, *dost, durst* and *ought*. A careful analysis of these licensors has revealed that, except for *durst* (the past tense of *dare to*) and *ought*, the other licensors are attested in the Bible samples and thus constitute archaic uses of auxiliary *do* and modal auxiliaries *shall* and *should*. Hence, it goes without saying that these licensors were not triggers of PAE in Modern English. However, it remains to be known whether licensor *ought*, which was only attested in speech-related genres, was only possible in this kind of genres.

Besides, the hypothesis that claims that VPE can be licensed by more than one auxiliary, whereas PG as a general rule cannot has also been verified. In fact, the opposite tendency has been attested in my data: the percentage of auxiliaries before a licensor in PG almost doubles that of VPE in Modern English. It must be noted, however, that this difference in percentage is not statistically significant. In any case, these results were not expected, as in Present-Day English it is VPE that normally licenses the presence of one or more auxiliaries before the licensor, and not PG (see Levin 1986 and Miller 2014). More specifically, it has been observed that PG only permits the presence of a single auxiliary before the licensor, and that it is mainly restricted to comparative contexts. As for VPE, it allows the presence of one or two auxiliaries before the licensor of ellipsis. Those examples that exhibit two auxiliaries before the licensor have only been attested in comparative constructions. Those where there is a single auxiliary before the licensor of VPE also tend to occur in comparative contexts almost exclusively, followed by coordination, by contexts in which no syntactic relation between the source and the target of ellipsis can be detected and, much more marginally, in relative subordination.

In addition, the kind of syntactic linking established between the antecedent and the ellipsis site in cases of PAE has also been object of my analysis. As has been shown, PG occurs in comparative contexts in almost three quarters of the total, followed by those examples with lack of syntactic linking, and much more marginally, coordination, adverbial subordination and relative subordination. The comparison of the results obtained for PG in Modern English with those from studies on PG in Present-Day English (Hoeksema 2006; Sharifzadeh 2012; Miller 2014) has revealed that instances of PG with NP remnants have a stronger preference for comparative constructions in Present-Day English (around 90 per cent) than in Modern English (70 per cent). Regarding VPE, in over half of the examples no syntactic linking holds between the source and the target of ellipsis. Following, comparative subordination represents almost a third of the examples of VPE found. It should be noted, however, that the percentage of comparative subordination in cases of PG is over two times higher than in VPE. The least common types of syntactic linking in instances of VPE are, in decreasing order, relative subordination, coordination and adverbial subordination. With the exception of relative subordination, whose frequency is higher in VPE than in PG, that of coordination and adverbial subordination in VPE is in line with the percentages attested in PG. Moreover, within those instances exhibiting relative subordination, almost three quarters of the examples are bound relative clauses, while the others constitute cases of free relatives. Out of these instances of bound relative clauses, over a third was formed by cases of antecedent-contained deletion. When these results were compared with those reported in Bos and Spenader (2011) on VPE in Present-Day English, it was found that the three most frequent types of linking coincide in both works, namely *as*-appositives, comparatives and lack of syntactic linking. Then, slight differences have been found: while relative subordination, coordination and adverbial subordination occupy the last positions (in decreasing order of frequency) in this investigation, the order is slightly altered in Bos and Spenader (2011) (coordination, adverbial subordination and relative subordination). In addition, it should be mentioned that Hardt and Rambow (2001) reported that the different forms of subordination seem to favour VPE in Present-Day English, whereas the lack of syntactic linking disfavours its presence. However, my results do not confirm this result since the lack of syntactic linking constitutes the third most frequent type of linking in both Bos and Spenader (2011) and in the present volume.

With respect to the syntactic domains where the ellipsis sites take place in examples of PAE, the data reveal that in most cases they occur in domains of subordination, a tendency which is clearly more marked in the case of PG. Following, about a third of the examples of PAE takes place in syntactic domains of coordination. Lastly, those examples attested in tag questions, CP-questions and imperatives have a marginal representation and have only been found in cases of VPE. Also, an analysis of the interaction between the type of syntactic linking and the type of syntactic domain evinced in instances of PAE has revealed that in most cases there exists a one-to-one correspondence between the type of syntactic linking established between the antecedent and the ellipsis site and the domain where the ellipsis site takes place. That is, in contexts where the type of syntactic linking established is subordination, the ellipsis site generally occurs within the domain of a subordinate clause, whereas in cases of coordination or of absence of syntactic linking, the ellipsis site often appears within the domain of a matrix clause. Yet, it has been found that in both subtypes of PAE there may be cases where this correspondence is not observable. To give an example, there are instances where the antecedent and the ellipsis site are attested in different sentences (there is no syntactic linking) and, at the same time, the ellipsis site appears embedded in a subordinate clause. Also, there are also cases where the antecedent and the ellipsis site are coordinated, but the ellipsis site appears further embedded. Lastly, there are cases where the antecedent and the ellipsis site are linked via adverbial subordination but the ellipsis site appears within a matrix clause.

As far as the category of the target of ellipsis in instances of PAE is concerned, it has been shown that PG licenses the omission of verbal material in almost three quarters of the examples. In the remaining examples, PG licenses the omission of non-verbal material, thanks to auxiliaries *be* and *have*. Within these cases of ellipsis of non-verbal material, auxiliary *be* acts as a licensor in almost two thirds. The omission of APs has been the most common option (around half of the examples of non-verbal material), followed by NPs and PPs, respectively. Hence, the ellipsis of verbal material after licensor *be* represents around a third of the total. Regarding licensor *have*, ellipsis of verbal material predominates in PG (around two thirds of the total), whereas ellipsis of NPs represents over a third of the total. In the case of VPE almost the same tendencies have been corroborated by the data: the ellipsis of verbal material comprises over three quarters of the examples and the rest correspond to instances of ellipsis of non-verbal elements. Within those instances of ellipsis of non-verbal material, licensor *be* prevails, yielding over two thirds of the cases. Therefore, the ellipsis of verbal material after *be* is the rule in almost a third of the examples. As was the case with PG, APs are the most common non-verbal material omitted (almost a third), followed closely by NPs and, more marginally, by PPs (around a tenth of the total) and AdPs (around 1 per cent). However, it should be noted that no instances of ellipsis of AdPs have been attested in PG. As for licensor *have* in examples of VPE, it licenses the ellipsis of verbal material in most cases (over three quarters of the total), whereas the ellipsis of NPs comprises a third of the total, as in PG. The comparison of my results with those provided in Bos and Spenader (2011) has shown that practically the same tendencies and proportions have been attested by the latter with respect to the category of the sources of ellipsis in Modern English and in Present-Day English. This means that verbal antecedents triggered by licensors other than *be* and *have* predominate, followed by cases of VPE licensed by auxiliary *be* and VPE licensed by auxiliary *have*. The only significant difference concerns the licensor *have*, since it appears to license ellipsis three times more frequently in Present-Day English than in the previous period of the English language. What is more, Bos and Spenader (2011) report that auxiliary *have* possesses only verbal antecedents, whereas in this study NP sources are more frequent – though both verbal and non-verbal antecedents are marginally represented in the writing-related genres of our study. Broadly speaking, therefore, no significant changes concerning the category of the source of VPE have been attested in the transition from Modern English to Present-Day English. Furthermore, it has been found that there is categorial identity between the source and the target of ellipsis in cases of PG in Modern English. Besides, one case of categorial identity mismatch has been attested in cases of VPE due to the existence of split antecedents. Therefore, in the light of the examples of PAE, syntactic identity between the source and the target of ellipsis is required in Modern English (except for the examples of split antecedents just mentioned). These results are in line with those reported in Bos and Spenader (2011).

Regarding split antecedents, their representation is rather marginal since it does not even amount to 1 per cent of the examples and, as predicted by the literature, it has only been attested in cases of VPE. Interestingly, all the examples of split antecedents take place in contexts of dialogues in speech-related genres, where there is a change of turn. Only Nielsen (2005) and Bos and Spenader (2011) have studied split antecedents empirically. The latter found no examples of split antecedents in their study of the twenty-five sections of the *Wall Street Journal* corpus of the Penn Treebank. However, Nielsen (2005) found some examples split antecedents and their frequency was exactly the same as the one reported in this volume. Therefore, split antecedents were as uncommon in Modern English as they seem to be in the present (around 1 per cent of the total).

With respect to the types of remnants found in cases of PG, I have offered a classification according to their category and function in the clause/phrase where they take place. On the one hand, apart from the types of remnants usually mentioned in the literature such as NPs, PPs and ProNPs, four new categories have been attested: infinitival VPs, AdPs, double NPs and CPs. My results show that prepositional-based remnants represent around two thirds of the examples, noun-based remnants around a third, and the additional types, which had never been considered before in the literature, less than a tenth. In addition, some cases where the remnant does not appear to be contrastive with any element in the antecedent have been attested, together with examples of PG where there are no overt objects in the antecedents corresponding to the remnant, though their representation is rather marginal. Also, no examples of deprepositionalized remnants have been attested. This contrasts with Miller's (2014) results, who found around 8 per cent in his database. Further research seems in order here so as to check whether or not deprepositionalized remnants were an innovation of the Present-Day English period. As for the syntactic function of the remnants of PG, they involve clausal functions in around three quarters of the examples: adverbials (around half of the instances) or objects of the clause (over a third of the data). As a result, in around a quarter of the cases, the remnants of PG involve phrasal functions, either as complements of nouns or as complements of adjectives.

Finally, I will summarize the main findings concerning auxiliary-related variables, that is, polarity, voice, aspect, modality and tense. First, it has been shown that, in most cases, there are no mismatches in polarity between the antecedent and the ellipsis site in examples of PAE, positive polarity in both PG and VPE being the statistically unmarked option. Besides, it must be noted that positive polarity has been the only alternative attested in cases of PG with lack of mismatches. As for VPE, in around two thirds of the examples the polarity of the source and of the target of ellipsis is positive, whereas those examples where both the antecedent and the ellipsis site exhibit negative polarity have a very marginal representation. As a consequence, mismatches represent only around a tenth of the examples in PG and almost a third in VPE.

As far as voice in PAE is concerned, voice mismatches were licensed in both PG and VPE in Modern English. This finding offers evidence against Merchant's (2008a, 2013b) hypothesis on the impossibility of finding voice mismatches in cases of PG, while it corroborates Miller's (2014) results for Present-Day English. Actually, the only example of PG attested in this piece of research involved a comparative construction, just like all of the examples reported in Miller's (2014) study. Regarding VPE, no voice mismatches have been attested in Bos and Spenader's (2011) study of VPE in Present-Day English. However, since they occur in Late Modern English with low frequencies, this contrast may be due to the stylistics or register of the corpora analysed. In any case, this preliminary conclusion requires further research. Furthermore, it has also been shown that while Kehler's (2000, 2002) theory regarding voice mismatches is not corroborated by the data reported in this volume, the validity of Kertz's theory accounts for almost all of the examples.

With respect to aspect in examples of PAE, the most common aspectual option in either the source or the target of ellipsis has been nonperfective-nonprogressive (over three quarters of the examples), followed by perfective-progressive and nonperfective-progressive. The vast majority of cases of PG and VPE do not exhibit aspect mismatches.

Modality in PAE constructions has also been the object of my study. Its analysis has revealed that there is lack of modality explicitness in the vast majority of the examples: whereas in PG around three quarters of the total do not exhibit any modal auxiliaries in either the source or the target of ellipsis, in VPE this amounts to around half of the cases. In addition, it has been found that in PG the most frequent modal licensors are *will/would* and *must*. In turn, *can/could*, *will/would* and *shall/should* are the most common in VPE. Lastly, the most common mismatches observed in PG are triggered by the presence or absence of *will/would* in either the source or the target of ellipsis. In contrast, mismatches in VPE are mainly caused by the absence of modal auxiliaries in the source, with the modals *can/could*, *will/would* and *shall/should* acting as licensors of ellipsis.

Finally, I will concentrate on the findings with respect to tense in PAE. My analysis has revealed that the licensors of PG are present-tensed in around half of the examples, and the other half are in the past. The same is true in VPE: past and present tense comprise almost half of the examples each, although very few examples are cases of bare and *to* infinitives. In addition, it has been found that in around three quarters of the examples of PG and VPE tense matches between the source and the target of ellipsis are favoured. The remaining quarter of the examples of PAE exhibits tense mismatches between the source and the target of ellipsis. The most common tense mismatches are those in which the source appears in the present tense and the ellipsis site in the past tense, and vice versa.

In what follows, I will offer a general overview of the main findings concerning the semantic and discursive variables that have been studied in this monograph: the types of clauses where the antecedents and the ellipsis sites occur (and whether there are any mismatches), the types of anaphora, focus and turn evinced by the examples of PAE, and sloppy identity between the antecedent and the ellipsis site. With regard to the types of clauses where the antecedents and the ellipsis sites take place, the data have shown that the most frequent combinations in PAE are declarative source – declarative target, together with interrogative source – declarative target, which represent over half of the examples and around a fifth of the instances, respectively. Besides, the mismatches in VPE concerning the type of clause of the source and that of the target of ellipsis render almost a third of the examples, a proportion which is over three times higher than in PG. Indeed, more possible combinations between the type of clause of the source and that of the target of ellipsis have been attested in examples of VPE than of PG.

As for the types of anaphora attested, our data show that PAE is overwhelmingly anaphoric, since cataphoric examples only represent around 1 per cent of the database. Also, these data have confirmed that cataphoric PG is not possible in Modern English, a result which is in line with the findings from Present-Day English reported in Bos and Spenader's (2011) and Miller's (2014) contributions.

As far as the focus types in PAE are concerned, it has been found that in the period under study PG seems to favour object-auxiliary choice focus in the vast majority of the cases, which implies that there are contrastive objects and auxiliaries in the antecedent and the pseudogapped clause. The frequency of the other types of focus in PG is evenly distributed (in decreasing order of frequency): object choice, subject-object choice and subject-object-auxiliary choice. In addition, it was also found that the subjects of the antecedent and those of the pseudogapped clause were commonly pronominal and coreferring, a result which is in line with the results reported in Miller (2014). Again, as in Miller (2014), PG tends to favour the presence of the same subject in both the antecedent and the pseudogapped clause, regardless of whether the pseudogapped clause takes place within a comparative or a noncomparative construction. According to Miller (2014), the examples of noncomparative PG where the subjects of the antecedent and the pseudogapped clauses are not coreferring often involve mirror or parallel patterns. However, whereas no instances of either pattern have been attested in my examples of noncomparative PG, I attested one instance of each in comparative PG. In the case of the focus types attested in instances of VPE, the data have shown that this construction favours auxiliary choice focus in the vast majority of examples (three quarters), hence placing the focus on the auxiliary that licenses ellipsis. Then, subject-auxiliary choice is the second most frequent type of focus, followed by those instances that involve subject choice. However, the representation of these two types of focus is rather marginal when compared with those that exhibit auxiliary choice focus.

In addition, sloppy identity, as understood in the two senses used in this monograph (when a pronoun in the antecedent clause is interpreted sloppily in the ellipsis site or when there are differences in the syntactic realization of certain elements), represents almost a tenth of the total examples of VPE attested. Notice that no instances of either kind of sloppy identity have been found in cases of PG. On the one hand, the results for sloppy identity as understood in the first sense are very much in line with those of Nielsen (2005) and Bos and Spenader (2011). More specifically, this strategy has a marginal representation in all these studies, ranging from less than 1 per cent in my investigation to 1 per cent in Nielsen (2005) and less than 2 per cent in Bos and Spenader (2011). On the other hand, sloppy identity as understood in the second sense (differences in the syntactic realization of certain elements) accounts for practically all the examples of sloppy identity in my corpus (almost a tenth of the cases of VPE). When compared to Nielsen's (2005) empirical study on VPE, my results are much alike: he reports a percentage of almost 5 per cent of sloppy pronouns (over 5 per cent in my account) and over 1 per cent of cases of sloppy polarity, the same as in this volume. Our results show that, broadly speaking, all cases of sloppy identity have been attested in speech-related genres and the antecedent and the ellipsis site usually appear in a different turn. Furthermore, third-person pronouns have only been found in examples where the pronoun of the ellipsis site needs to be interpreted sloppily in relation to the source clause. Within those cases of sloppy identity as understood in the second sense, all pronouns are first and second person pronouns. Finally, in those instances of this second type of sloppy identity which evince sloppy polarity, the antecedent is always negative and the ellipsis site positive.

With regard to the semantic and discursive variables under study, I will summarize the main findings related to the types of turn attested in cases of PAE. In light of the data, the distribution of the two possible types of turn options, that is, same turn or different turn, coincides in PG and VPE. More specifically, it has been shown that over a third of the cases of PG and VPE occur within the same turn, whereas in the remaining examples the source and the target of ellipsis are pronounced by different speakers. This means that every time there is a context that permits that the antecedent and the ellipsis appear in different turns, there is a change of speaker over six times out of ten in both subtypes of PAE.

Usage variables related to PAE have also been explored in this monograph, namely, genre and period distribution. On the one hand, the analysis of PAE across time (eighteenth century and roughly nineteenth century) has revealed that VPE predominates in both centuries in the vast majority of cases, since PG has a rather marginal representation. Furthermore, whereas VPE increases its frequency from the eighteenth to the nineteenth century, the reverse is true of PG, whose frequency decreases to almost half of the total examples in the previous century. The normalized frequencies of PAE per number of clauses in Modern English have also revealed that PG was already a much more marginal construction than VPE in Modern English, a tendency which is evinced in Present-Day English if compared with studies such as Bos and Spenader (2011). On the other hand, the analysis of the distribution of PAE per genre categories of the sort speech versus writing related has shown that PAE is four times more frequent in speech-related genres than in writing-related ones. In the case of PG, its normalized frequency by genre shows that the frequency of PG in speech-related genres doubles that of writing-related texts. As far as the normalized frequency of VPE by genre is concerned, the data suggest that VPE is twelve times more frequent than PG and that the former is almost five times more frequent in speech-related genres than in writing-related ones. Lastly, the application of statistical tests has supported three main concluding remarks with respect to usage variables in instances of PAE in Modern English. First, ellipsis has a much higher frequency in speech-related genres than in writing-related ones and the difference is highly significant. Second, from a diachronic point of view, the only statistically significant rise of ellipsis between the eighteenth and nineteenth centuries is attested in speech-related genres. Third, this statistically significant rise of ellipsis in the periods under analysis can only be attributed to the increase of VPE and not to PG.

Finally, I will provide a summary on the main conclusions with respect to processing in ellipsis. On the one hand, most of the examples of PG appear in contexts where the antecedent is contained within the same sentence, the target of ellipsis occurs in a different clause, there are no intervening clauses and, in addition, the lexical distance ranges from zero to ten words. On the other hand, in the vast majority of the instances of VPE the lexical distance is smaller, that is, zero to five words. Therefore, these results confirm that VPE tends to be more local than PG. Notice, however, that a lexical distance of over fifteen words has only been attested in VPE. Moreover, VPE differs from PG as regards the most frequent type of boundedness established between the antecedent and the ellipsis site: either in different sentences or within the same sentence and in a different clause (with no intervening clauses). In addition, the data on PG corroborate Levin's (1986) findings, as PG disfavours those syntactic contexts where the pseudogapped clause appears embedded. What is more, it has also been found that Hardt's (1993) hypothesis that lexical distance is higher in cases where the antecedent and the ellipsis site appear in different sentences has not been confirmed in cases of PG. The higher the lexical distance, the fewer instances of PG have been found where the antecedent and the ellipsis site are in different sentences. By contrast, Hardt's (1993) hypothesis for VPE is confirmed: if the lexical distance increases, the antecedent and the ellipsis site occur in different sentences in the vast majority of cases. Finally, after checking the interaction of lexical and syntactic distance, it has been found that the higher the lexical distance, the higher the syntactic distance in both PAE constructions.

Last of all, in Chapter 3 I addressed the debate concerning the possibility of treating PG as a subcase of VPE in light of my empirical findings and the relevant literature. Levin (1986) and Hoeksema (2006) had argued that PG and VPE possess too many different properties for them to be regarded as the same kind of construction. However, I followed Miller (2014) in being more cautious when tackling this debate, as the analysis of VPE and PG has revealed that they exhibit many similarities too. As Miller (2014) pointed out, their differences may be a direct consequence of the different uses in discourse that these constructions serve. Since Miller's (2014) arguments in favour of this possibility can also explain the results for VPE and PG in Modern English in this study, he may be in the right path. Yet, it remains to determine whether all the differences between PG and VPE observed in this piece of research can lead one to conclude that PG is a subcase of VPE and not a distinct type of ellipsis which simply shares some characteristics with VPE.

To conclude this chapter, I will list some issues that had to be left for further research. My main concern about the investigation presented here has to do with the comparison between the results obtained for PAE constructions in Modern English with those reported for Present-Day English in previous empirical works. Due to the limited number of empirical studies on PAE and the consequent scarcity of the data, the conclusions resulting from this comparison must be taken with caution. With respect to the types of mismatches attested regarding polarity, voice, aspect, modality and tense, I am aware that it would be of high importance to undertake a regression analysis so as to detect factor groups and their weight in the explanation of cases of PAE. It would also be of interest to study the length (in number of words) and syntactic complexity (in number of IPs) of the antecedent of ellipsis itself, since in Chapter 3 I have focused on the study of the lexical and syntactic distance existing between the antecedent and the target of ellipsis. This possibility was considered because there were some examples of PAE whose antecedents were fairly long and syntactically complex, while the distance holding between the source and the target of ellipsis was not that large. The analysis of the length and complexity of the antecedent would complement the results reached when I investigated the lexical and the syntactic distance between the source and the target of ellipsis and would provide a more exact measure of the facts that may exert an influence on ellipsis. Furthermore, this investigation could be taken as a starting point for the empirical study of instances of PAE both quantitatively and qualitatively in earlier or later periods of the English language, such as Middle English (1150–1500), Early Modern English (1500–1700) and Present-Day English, since there are three parsed corpora that would enable its analysis in a very similar vein: the Penn-Helsinki Parsed Corpus of Middle English (PPCME2), the Penn-Helsinki Parsed Corpus of Early Modern English (PPCEME) and the Penn Treebank-3, respectively. Elliptical constructions other than PAE (Gapping, Stripping, Sluicing, etc.) could also be subject of analysis in such corpora by following the steps taken in this study: a preliminary manual analysis that will detect the patterns in the different elliptical constructions and the design of an algorithm for their automatic detection and retrieval. For sure, every scholar working on ellipsis, regardless of the approach adopted for its analysis, would be interested in the conclusions reached in a diachronic study of the qualitative and quantitative evolution of ellipsis in the English language.

Appendix 1

Corpus search 2 and its query language

i. AND

AND, OR and NOT are used as in basic formal logic. The same applies to the use of parentheses. In the case of AND, it looks for instances where the conditions of both conjuncts are met in a single boundary node. Here is an example:

((MD* iPrecedes HV*) AND (HV* iPrecedes [.,]))

This query returns examples where any modal auxiliary (MD*) immediately precedes HV* (that is, auxiliary *have*) and this same auxiliary, in turn, immediately precedes any punctuation mark ([.,]) (comma, dot, etc.). Here is an example:

(1) but in a little time I hope to do all you *would have*.
JOHNSON-1775,2,9.177

    (IP-INF (TO to)
        (DO do)
        (NP-OB1 (Q all)
            (CP-REL (WNP-1 0)
                (C 0)
                (IP-SUB (NP-OB1 *T*-1)
                    (NP-SBJ (PRO you))
                    (MD would)
                    (HV have)))))
    (. .))
(ID JOHNSON-1775,2,9.177))

ii. OR

OR represents a logical disjunction. It will retrieve all the trees within the query's selected boundary node in which either the property *x* or *y* or both hold.

As mentioned in CorpusSearch Home (2005), these 'properties may consist of single search functions or be built up out of conjunctions, disjunctions and negations of simple search functions'. This can be illustrated with the following query:

(BE* iPrecedes [.,]) OR (BE* iPrecedes NEG)

This query will detect trees where the first condition (auxiliary *be* immediately precedes a punctuation mark), the second one (auxiliary BE immediately precedes a negator) or both are met. Below, you will find two examples that this condition would retrieve:

(2) it cannot be so quickly learn'd as the Modern Tongues *are*. ANON-1711,12.126

```
(IP-SUB (NP-SBJ (PRO it))
        (MD $can)
        (NEG $not)
        (CODE {TEXT:cannot})
        (BE be)
        (ADVP (ADVR so)
              (ADV quickly)
              (PP *ICH*-2))
        (VAN learn'd)
        (PP-2 (P as)
              (CP-CMP (WADVP-3 0)
                      (C 0)
                      (IP-SUB (ADVP *T*-3)
                              (NP-SBJ (D the) (ADJ Modern) (NS Tongues))
                              (BEP are))))))
   (. .))
(ID ANON-1711,12.126))
```

(3) is the agent I am in search of? Mrs. I'm quite certain he *is not*. BROUGHAM-1861,21.774

```
           (IP-SUB (NP-SBJ (PRO he))
                   (BEP is)
                   (NEG not))))
      (. .))
(ID BROUGHAM-1861,21.774))
```

iii. NOT

NOT retrieves trees rooted in the node boundary that do not possess the structure described in the query. Here are is one example:

NOT(NP* precedes VB*)

This query would retrieve trees that do not possess the structure (NP* precedes VB*), that is, any NP that precedes a verb, along with those structures that do not include neither NP* nor VP*.

iv. ! (not)

! is used in order to negate an argument to a search function. For instance, let us imagine that we are interested in analysing instances where any modal auxiliary does not have a verb as its sister (either preceding or following the modal auxiliary), as in (4) and (5) below, but avoiding the retrieval of examples such as (6):

(4) He will go.

(5) Will he go?

(6) I told the governor [of the prison] that I wasn't sure how I was going to manage it – but manage it I would. [*Guardian*, G2, 15. 5. 2003, p. 7, col. 4; in Haegeman (2006: 81)]

Then, we could make use of the following query:

(MD* hasSister !VB*)

HasSister will look for instances whose mother is the same. This query would return examples like the following:

(7) Well, one must go on and *do the best one can* with one's powers. BENSON-190X,124.589

```
          (IP-MAT=1 (DO do)
              (NP-OB1 (D the)
                  (ADJS best)
                  (CP-REL (WNP-2 0)
                      (C 0)
                      (IP-SUB (NP-OB1 *T*-2)
```

```
                              (NP-SBJ (ONE one))
                              (MD can))))
              (PP (P with)
                    (NP (ONE$ one's) (NS powers)))))
        (. .))
    (ID BENSON-190X,124.589))
```

v. HasSister

As can be gathered from the previous example illustrating the use of *!* (not), HasSister looks for strings of elements that have the same mother, that is, the element searched for can either precede or follow another element. '*X* hasSister *y*' will return examples in which *x* either precedes or follows *y* as long as they have the same mother.

vi. Doms or iDoms

'*X* Doms (or IDoms) *y*' will look for an element *y* that is contained within any subtree dominated by *x*, therefore 'Doms means "dominates to any generation"' (CorpusSearch Home 2005). IDoms will look for *y* contained in the same tree or subtree as *x*. It should be noted that iDoms 'describes the relationship between a label and its associated text.' For instance, this query

    (VB* iDoms *)

will retrieve trees where a VB immediately dominates an asterisk *, which in this corpus indicates that a verb has been elided. As will be shown below, asterisks are normally used as wild cards that substitute for any string of symbols, as is the case with the string *VB** used above, which can mean VBD, VBI, VBN and so on. In order to escape this use of the asterisk and look for the literal *, this is the way to do it: *. Therefore, the string *(VB* iDoms *)* would look for any verb (wild card use) that immediately dominates the asterisk (escape use).

vii. Precedes and IPrecedes

This function searches for a string that either precedes *x* (Precedes) or immediately precedes *x* (IPrecedes) in '*x* Precedes (or IPrecedes) *y*'. See examples (2) and (3) above for an illustration.

viii. HasLabel

X hasLabel *y* if the label of node *x* is the string *y*. This function is useful when carrying out coding queries. For instance, the query (CP* hasLabel CP-QUE-TAG*) could be used to look for cases of CPs whose label is 'CP-QUE-TAG,' that is, cases of tag questions. Here is one example of tag question found by part of the algorithm presented in this study:

(8) We shall not be at Worthing so soon as we have been used to talk of, *shall we?* AUSTEN-180X,169.204

(CP-QUE-TAG (IP-SUB (MD shall)
                          (NP-SBJ (PRO we))))
(.?))
(ID AUSTEN-180X,169.204))

ix. The | operator

The pipe | stands for 'or' at the level of arguments to a search function. The query (MD* hasSister !VB*|BE*|DO*|HV*) will retrieve cases of modal auxiliaries that are neither preceded nor followed by a verb or the auxiliaries *be, have* and *do,* that is, cases of VPE whose licensor is a modal auxiliary, like in the following example:

(9) They will. (BOETHJA-1897,110.189)

((IP-MAT-SPE (' ')
       (NP-SBJ (PRO They))
       (MD will)
       (..)
       (' '))
(ID BOETHJA-1897,110.189))

x. Wild card *

The character * is a wild card which stands for any string of symbols. If you would like to look for any kind of (IP) (e.g. IP-MAT and IP-IMP), then you can just write *IP** and the programme will retrieve all the different types of IP present in the corpus. It can also be used in order to retrieve structures which are contained in all possible nodes of a particular corpus, that is, IPs, CPs, NPs and so on. As was shown in Section 2.2.3.2, in the algorithm used to obtain examples of PAE, the query file used indicated that examples of PAE should be retrieved from all the nodes contained in the corpus in the following way: 'node: *'. However, as mentioned earlier, this character may also be used to indicate that ellipsis has occurred, as happens with some cases of VPE, where the elided VP is marked as follows: (VB *).

xi. Ignore_words

Here is the list of the characters that CorpusSearch ignores by default:

COMMENT|CODE|ID|LB| '|\"|,|E_S|.|/|RMV:*|0|**

If one wished to ignore any more words or characters, those elements would just need to be added to this list and the query file. The reverse also works, so if one removes some of these elements from the ignore list, the programme will retrieve examples that contain them.

Appendix 2

List of the basic POS (part of speech) labels used in the Penn Treebank:

Tag	Meaning
.	sentence-final punctuation
,	sentence-internal punctuation
ADJ	adjective
ADV	adverb
BAG	BE, present participle
BE	BE, infinitive
BED	BE, past (including past subjunctive)
BEI	BE, imperative
BEN	BE, perfect participle
BEP	BE, present (including present subjunctive)
C	complementizer
CONJ	coordinating conjunction
D	determiner
DAG	DO, present participle
DAN	DO, passive participle (verbal or adjectival)
DO	DO, infinitive
DOD	DO, past (including past subjunctive)
DOI	DO, imperative
DON	DO, perfect participle
DOP	DO, present (including present subjunctive)
HAG	HAVE, present participle
HAN	HAVE, passive participle (verbal or adjectival)
HV	HAVE, infinitive
HVD	HAVE, past (including past subjunctive)
HVI	HAVE, imperative
HVN	HAVE, perfect participle
HVP	HAVE, present (including present subjunctive)
MD	modal verb
MD0	modal verb, untensed
N	common noun, singular
NEG	negation
NPR	proper noun, singular
NPRS	proper noun, plural
P	preposition or subordinating conjunction
PRO	personal pronoun
PRO$	possessive pronoun

Q	quantifier
TO	infinitival TO
VAG	present participle
VAN	passive participle (verbal or adjectival)
VB	infinitive, verbs other than BE, DO, HV
VBD	past (including past subjunctive)
VBI	imperative
VBN	perfect participle
VBP	present (including present subjunctive)
WPRO	wh-pronoun

Generally, phrase labels are formed by combining the core tag for a particular category and an additional 'P' standing for 'Phrase', for example, N (Noun) plus P yields NP (Noun Phrase). Here are some of the basic phrases:

Tag	Meaning
ADJP	adjective phrase
ADVP	adverb phrase
CP	complementizer phrase
CONJP	conjunction phrase
IP	inflectional phrase (clause)
NP	noun phrase
PP	prepositional phrase
QP	quantifier phrase

These phrase labels, in turn, can be extended by 'dash' tags which can be added thanks to hyphens. These tags provide information about the phrases' particular function in the sentences. These are some of the most common function tags.[1]

Tag	Meaning
-SBJ	subject
-OB1	direct object
-OB2	indirect object
-ATR	attributive
-COM	complement
-PRD	predicate
-MAT	matrix
-SUB	subordinate

Finally, there are some extended tags that determine the type of clause in question and are therefore more specific to CPs and IPs. Here are the most frequent ones:[2]

Tag	Meaning
IP-MAT	matrix (main) clause
IP-SUB	subordinate clause
IP-INF	infinitival clause
IP-PPL	participial clause
CP-THT	THAT clause
CP-CMP	comparative clause
CP-ADV	adverbial clause
CP-REL	relative clause
CP-QUE	question (direct or indirect)
CP-QUE-TAG	tag question

Notes

Chapter 1

1. Struck-out words represent elided material. Strikethrough is merely used as an expository device in this volume, as no syntactic or semantic analysis is intended.
2. See Chapters 2 and 3 for a detailed account of this elliptical phenomenon.
3. See Section 1.2 for more information on these two restrictions on ellipsis.
4. Ungrammatical examples are marked with an asterisk.
5. Bearing these criteria in mind, it must be noted that greetings (*hi, good morning*, etc.) fall out of the definition of ellipsis (because their descriptive content is not resolved contextually), so do expressions without an antecedent which belong to specific registers like telegrams, titles or labels (Bîlbîie 2011: 129).
6. Gapping refers to an elliptical structure which occurs only in coordinate structures and omits identical elements from the second of two conjoined clauses.
7. Sluicing implies the ellipsis of the whole clause (IP) except for a *wh*-phrase, which corresponds to either an argument or an adjunct.
8. For more details on the exact taxonomies proposed, I refer the reader to Quirk et al. (1985) and Huddleston and Pullum (2002).
9. For reasons of space, this section only provides a general account of the phenomenon of ellipsis as defined in these three influential grammars of English, which is the scope of analysis of this volume. For more information about pro-forms, I refer the reader to Quirk et al. (1985) and Huddleston and Pullum (2002).
10. The elements in between parentheses indicate ellipsis in Quirk et al (1985).
11. The salient linguistic antecedent is present, that is, it does not need to be inferred from the context of the situation, as in *I'll buy the red* wine *if you'll buy the white*, where the antecedent *wine* is present in the linguistic context and can be easily retrieved in the ellipsis site.
12. Δ indicates deletion, that is, ellipsis.
13. < > indicate ellipsis in Biber et al.'s (1999) grammar.
14. Underlined material indicates the antecedent of the ellipsis site in Huddleston and Pullum (2002).
15. This NP is an instance of a complex NP, that is, a syntactic island from which nothing can be extracted (known as the Complex NP Constraint in Transformational Generative Grammar).

16 Also known as 'ellipsis from the right', where the main lexical verb has been omitted (*laughing*).
17 See Section 2.2.4 for Miller and Pullum's (2014) distinction between auxiliary choice focus and subject choice focus in Post-Auxiliary Ellipsis.
18 I cannot do any justice here to the large amount of literature on ellipsis within this framework. Therefore, as examples of seminal overviews on this topic, I refer the reader to Johnson (2001, 2008), Winkler (2005), Dalrymple (2005), Aelbrecht (2009, 2010), van Craenenbroeck (2010a), Bîlbîie (2011), Gallego (2011), van Craenenbroeck and Merchant (2013), Merchant (2013a), van Craenenbroeck and Temmerman (2019).
19 *e* stands for 'ellipsis site' in van Craenenbroeck and Merchant (2013).
20 For reasons of space, this section concentrates on the findings regarding VPE and PG, the types of Post-Auxiliary Ellipsis studied in this volume.
21 Bare Argument Ellipsis (also known as Stripping) is an elliptical construction with only a non-verbal element as the remnant in the elided sentence, often accompanied by a negator or an intensifier (a polarity element); as in *Marta cooked an omelette, and Julia too*.
22 The definition of light verb (*v*) in Radford (2004: 339) is 'null verb with much the same causative interpretation as the verb MAKE [in] *They will make the ball roll down the hill*'. This abstract light verb is affixal in nature, that is, it has a strong V-feature which demands attachment, adjoins to another verb and conveys a causative interpretation.

Chapter 2

1 See also Pérez-Lorido (2011) for a corpus study on Gapping in English from the tenth and eleventh centuries and Bîlbîie (2012, 2013a,b) for Gapping and Right-Node Raising in Present-Day English.
2 See Hardt (1992b) for more details about the algorithm.
3 See Hardt (1995) for the exact details on the steps taken in order to identify cases of VPE, which are very similar to those used in the present volume.
4 See Hardt (1995) for a definition of all these preference factors.
5 The exact details of his experiments with machine learning techniques fall beyond the scope of this monograph, and therefore I refer the reader to Nielsen (2005).
6 Recall is calculated by dividing the number of relevant examples retrieved automatically by the gold standard (the number of examples found manually). That is, it provides us with the measure of how much coverage the algorithm has, namely, the number of correct examples obtained automatically with respect to the ones found manually. See Section 2.2.3.2 for more details.

7. Precision is calculated by dividing the number of relevant examples of ellipsis found by the number of attempts (correct and incorrect), providing a measure of the accuracy of the algorithm. See Section 2.2.3.2 for more details.
8. 'TV' stands for 'transitive verb'.
9. The Corpus of Contemporary American English contains 'more than 560 million words of text (20 million words each year from 1990–2017' (COCA website http://corpus.byu.edu/coca/, November 2018). According to its official website, the COCA 'is equally divided among spoken, fiction, popular magazines, newspapers, and academic texts'. For more information, please visit http://corpus.byu.edu/coca/.
10. The # symbol is used to indicate that something is pragmatically or semantically weird, but not necessarily ungrammatical.
11. Infinitival marker *to* is believed to be a defective nonfinite auxiliary verb in this study (see Gazdar et al. 1985; Levine 2012; Miller and Pullum 2014).
12. PAE is also known as 'Predicate Ellipsis' in van Craenenbroeck and Merchant (2013), where they distinguish five different types: VPE, PG, British English *do*, Modal Complement Ellipsis and Predicate Phrase Ellipsis.
13. The % sign is used to indicate that this is grammatical for a percentage of the population, but it is not widespread.
14. In this example there are two instances of this construction (*has done* and *will do*) and only the second one has been coded as an example of British English *do* in the corpus.
15. Section 2.2.4 describes the different variables that have an effect on the occurrence and distribution of both VPE and PG.
16. For more information on the corpora, please visit http://www.ling.upenn.edu/hist-corpora/.
17. http://www.ling.upenn.edu/histcorpora/annotation/index.html
18. A complete list of the POS tags employed in the Penn Treebank is available at http://www.ling.upenn.edu/histcorpora/annotation/index.html
19. The label *plain form* is used for cases of VP antecedents which are composed of a bare infinitive or an imperative.

Chapter 3

1. In order to check the distribution of the licensors of PAE per genres, I have left out the genres Bible and Fiction for the reasons stated in Section 3.2.2.
2. Known as as-*appositives* in Hardt and Rambow (2001) and Nielsen (2005).
3. Note that only writing-related genres have been taken into account, as Bos and Spenader's (2011) study is based on twenty-five sections of the *Wall Street Journal*.

4. Based on the antecedent, the target of ellipsis of this example could be interpreted as *impracticable to manage* and not *managed*. In that case, this would not constitute a case of voice mismatch between the antecedent and the ellipsis site. However, since both interpretations are available, I have decided not to exclude this example from the classification of voice mismatches.
5. Kertz's (2008, 2013) explanation of voice mismatches is based on the preservation of the discourse topic both in the ellipsis site and in the antecedent. Since my analysis of the PAE examples relies mostly on the contextual information provided by the passage ranging from the antecedent to the ellipsis site, topic continuity has been checked here by the identification of sentence rather than discourse topics. Since sentence topics unmarkedly instantiate (fully or partially) discourse topics, my findings can be claimed to corroborate Kertz's postulates.
6. Merchant (personal communication) has pointed out that PG does not tolerate object-auxiliary choice focus in examples involving auxiliaries co-occurring with the infinitival marker *to*, as in (i) and (ii), versus (iii) without *to*:

   (i) *Abby is able to eat more strawberries now than she was able to blueberries when she was a child.
   (ii) *Abby has to grade more papers now than she had to exams when she was in grad school.
   (iii) Abby can eat more strawberries now than she could blueberries when she was a child.

Appendix 2

1. Please, visit the following webpage for a full list of common phrase and function tag combinations: https://www.ling.upenn.edu/ppche/ppche-release-2016/annotation/index.htm
2. A detailed list of the syntactic annotation of the PPCMBE can be found on this website: https://www.ling.upenn.edu/ppche/ppche-release-2016/annotation/index.htm

References

Aelbrecht, L. (2009), 'You Have the Right to Remain Silent. The Syntactic Licensing of Ellipsis', PhD diss., Catholic University of Brussels, Brussels.

Aelbrecht, L. (2010), *The Syntactic Licensing of Ellipsis*, Amsterdam: John Benjamins.

Arregui, A., C. Clifton Jr., L. Frazier and K. Moulton (2006), 'Processing Elided VPs with Flawed Antecedents: The Recycling Hypothesis', *Journal of Memory and Language*, 55(2): 232–46.

Baltin, M. (2006), 'The Non-Unity of VP-Preposing', *Language*, 82(4): 734–66.

Baltin, M. (2012), 'Deletion Versus Pro-Forms: An Overly Simple Dichotomy?', *Natural Language and Linguistic Theory*, 30(2): 381–423.

Biber, D., S. Johansson, G. Leech, S. Conrad and E. Finegan (1999), *Longman Grammar of Spoken and Written English*, London: Longman.

Bîlbîie, G. (2011), 'Grammaire des Constructions Elliptiques. Une étude Comparative des Phrases sans Verbe en Roumain et en Français', PhD diss., Université Paris Diderot-Paris 7, Paris.

Bîlbîie, G. (2012), 'Right-Node Raising in the Penn Treebank', Paper presented at the Topics in the Typology of Elliptical Constructions Conference, Université Paris-Diderot Paris 7, Paris.

Bîlbîie, G. (2013a), 'Une perspective quantitative du Gapping dans le Penn Treebank', Paper presented at the Séminaire ellipse, Université Paris-Diderot Paris 7, Paris.

Bîlbîie, G. (2013b), 'A Quantitative Study on Right-Node Raising in the Penn Treebank', Paper presented at the International Congress of Linguists (ICL), University of Geneva, Geneva.

Boeckx, C. (2006), *Linguistic Minimalism: Origins, Concepts, Methods, and Aims*, Oxford: Oxford University Press.

Bos, J. (1994), 'Presupposition & VP-ellipsis', in *Proceedings of the 15th International Conference on Computational Linguistics* (Coling 1994), 1184–90, Kyoto, Japan.

Bos, J. and J. Spenader (2011), 'An Annotated Corpus for the Analysis of VP Ellipsis', *Language Resources and Evaluation*, 45(4): 463–94.

Carlson, K. (2002), *Parallelism and Prosody in the Processing of Ellipsis Sentences*, New York: Routledge.

Chao, W. (1988), *On Ellipsis*, New York: Garland.

Chomsky, N. (1965), *Aspects of the Theory of Syntax*, Cambridge, MA: MIT Press.

Chomsky, N. (1982), *Noam Chomsky on the Generative Enterprise*, Dordrecht: Foris Publications.

Chung, S. (2006), 'Sluicing and the Lexicon: The Point of No Return', in R. T. Cover and Y. Kim (eds), *Proceedings of the Annual Meeting of the Berkeley Linguistics Society 31* (BLS), 73–91, Berkeley, CA: Berkeley Linguistics Society.

Chung, S. (2013), 'Syntactic Identity in Sluicing: How Much, and Why', *Linguistic Inquiry*, 44: 1–39.

Chung, S., W. Ladusaw and J. McCloskey (1995), 'Sluicing and Logical Form', *Natural Language Semantics*, 3: 239–82.

Clifton Jr., C. and L. Frazier (2010), 'Imperfect Ellipsis: Antecedents Beyond Syntax?', *Syntax*, 13(4): 279–97.

CorpusSearch Home (2005). Available online: http://corpussearch.sourceforge.net/ (accessed 29 November 2018).

Craenenbroeck, J. van (2010a), *The Syntax of Ellipsis: Evidence from Dutch Dialects*, New York: Oxford University Press.

Craenenbroeck, J. van (2010b), 'Invisible Last Resort: A Note on Clefts as the Underlying Source for Sluicing', *Lingua*, 120: 1714–26.

Craenenbroeck, J. van and J. Mechant (2013), 'Ellipsis Phenomena', in M. den Dikken (ed.), *The Cambridge Handbook of Generative Syntax*, 701–45, Cambridge: Cambridge University Press.

Craenenbroeck, J. van and T. Temmerman (2019), *The Oxford Handbook of Ellipsis*, Oxford: Oxford University Press.

Culicover, P. and R. Jackendoff (2005), *Simpler Syntax*, Oxford: Oxford University Press.

Culpeper, J. and M. Kytö (2010), *Early Modern English Dialogues. Spoken Interaction as Writing*, Cambridge: Cambridge University Press.

Dahl, Ö. (1974), 'How to Open a Sentence. Abstraction in Natural Language', in *Logical Grammar Reports 12*, Gothenburg: University of Gothenburg.

Dalrymple, M. (2005), 'Against Reconstruction in Ellipsis', in Reinaldo Elugardo and Robert J. Stainton (eds), *Ellipsis and Nonsentential Speech* (Studies in Linguistics and Philosophy), 31–55, Dordrecht: Springer.

Dalrymple, M., S. M. Shieber and F. C. N. Pereira (1991), 'Ellipsis and Higher-Order Unification', *Linguistics and Philosophy*, 14: 399–452.

Depiante, M. A. (2000), 'The Syntax of Deep and Surface Anaphora: A Study of Null Complement Anaphora and Stripping/Bare Argument Ellipsis', PhD diss., University of Connecticut, Connecticut.

Ericsson, S. (2005), *Information Enriched Constituents in Dialogue*, Göteborg: University of Göteborg.

Fiengo, R. (1980), *Surface Structure: The Interface of Autonomous Components*. Cambridge: Harvard University Press.

Fiengo, R. and R. May (1994), *Indices and Identity*, Cambridge, MA: MIT Press.

Frazier, L. and C. Clifton Jr (2005), 'The Syntax-Discourse Divide: Processing Ellipsis', *Syntax*, 8(2): 121–74.

Frazier, L. and C. Clifton Jr (2006), 'Ellipsis and Discourse Coherence', *Linguistics and Philosophy*, 29(3): 315–46.

Gallego, Á. J. (2011), *Sobre la Elipsis*, Madrid: Arco Libros (Cuadernos de Lengua Española).

Garnham, A. and J. O. K. Cain (1998), 'Selective Retention of Information about the Superficial Form of Text: Ellipses with Antecedents in Main and Subordinate Clauses', *The Quarterly Journal of Experimental Psychology. Section A: Human Experimental Psychology*, 51(1): 19–39.

Gazdar, G., E. Klein, G. K. Pullum and I. A. Sag (1985), *Generalized Phrase Structure Grammar*, Oxford: Basil Blackwell.

Gengel, K. (2007), 'Focus and Ellipsis. A Generative Analysis of Pseudogapping and Other Elliptical Structures', PhD diss., University of Stuttgart, Stuttgart.

Gengel, K. (2013), *Pseudogapping and Ellipsis*, Oxford: Oxford University Press.

Gergel, R. (2009), *Modality and Ellipsis: Diachronic and Synchronic Evidence*. Berlin: Mouton de Gruyter.

Ginzburg, J. and I. A. Sag (2000), *Interrogative Investigations*, Stanford, CA: CSLI Publications.

Grice, H. P. (1975), 'Logic and Conversation', in P. Cole and J. L. Morgan (eds), *Syntax and Semantics: Speech Acts*, vol. 3, 41–58, New York: Academic Press.

Gundel, J. K., N. Hedberg and R. Zacharski (1993), 'Cognitive Status and the Form of Referring Expressions in Discourse', *Language*, 69(2): 274–307.

Haddican, B. (2007), 'The Structural Deficiency of Verbal Pro-Forms', *Linguistic Inquiry*, 38(3): 539–47.

Haegeman, L. (2006), *Thinking Syntactically. A Guide to Argumentation and Analysis*, Malden and Oxford: Blackwell Publishing.

Halliday, M. A. K. (1994), *Introduction to Functional Grammar*, 2nd edn, London: Edward Arnold.

Halliday, M. A. K and R. Hasan (1976), *Cohesion in English* (English Language Series 9), London and New York: Longman.

Halliday, M. A. K and C. Matthiessen (2004), *An Introduction to Functional Grammar*, 3rd edn, London: Hodder Arnold.

Hankamer, J. (1978), 'On the Nontransformational Derivation of Some Null VP Anaphors', *Linguistic Inquiry*, 9: 66–74.

Hankamer, J. and I. A. Sag (1976), 'Deep and Surface Anaphora', *Linguistic Inquiry*, 7: 391–428.

Hardt, D. (1990), 'A Corpus-based Survey of VP Ellipsis', University of Pennsylvania Ms., Philadelphia, PA.

Hardt, D. (1992a), 'Some Problematic Cases of VP Ellipsis', in *Proceedings from the 30th Annual Meeting of the Association for Computational Linguistics*, 28 June – 2 July 1992, 276–8, University of Delaware.

Hardt, D. (1992b), 'An Algorithm for VP Ellipsis', in *Proceedings from the 30th Annual Meeting of the Association for Computational Linguistics*, 28 June – 2 July 1992, 9–14, University of Delaware. Available online: http://dblp.uni-trier.de/db/conf/acl/acl 92.html#Hardt92 (accessed 29 November 2018).

Hardt, D. (1993), 'Verb Phrase Ellipsis: Form, Meaning, and Processing', PhD diss., University of Pennsylvania, Philadelphia, PA.

Hardt, D. (1995), 'An Empirical Approach to VP Ellipsis', in *Proceedings, AAAI Symposium on Empirical Approaches in Discourse and Generation*, 53–7, Palo Alto, CA, March 27–29, 1995.

Hardt, D. (1997), 'An Empirical Approach to VP Ellipsis', *Computational Linguistics*, 23(4): 525–41.

Hardt, D. and O. Rambow (2001), 'Generation of VP Ellipsis: A Corpus-Based Approach', in *Proceedings of the 39th Annual Meeting on Association for Computational Linguistics*, Toulouse, France, 9–11 July 2001, 290–7.

Hardt, D. and M. Romero (2004), 'Ellipsis and Discourse Structure', *Journal of Semantics*, 21: 375–414.

Hendriks, P. and J. Spenader (2005), 'Why Be Silent? Some Functions of Ellipsis in Natural Language', in J. Spenader and P. Hendriks (eds), *Proceedings of the 17th European Summer School on Logic, Language and Information (ESSLLI 2005) Workshop on Cross-modular Approaches to Ellipsis*, 29–36, Edinburgh: Heriot-Watt University.

Hoeksema, J. (2006), 'Pseudogapping: Its Syntactic Analysis and Cumulative Effects on Acceptability', *Research on Language and Computation*, 4: 335–52.

Houser, M. J. (2010), 'The Syntax and Semantics of Do So Anaphora', PhD diss., University of California, Berkeley, CA.

Huddleston, R. and G. K. Pullum, (2002), *The Cambridge Grammar of the English Language*, Cambridge: Cambridge University Press.

Hulsey, S. M. (2008), 'Focus Sensitive Coordination', PhD diss., MIT, Cambridge, MA.

Jackendoff, R. S. (1971), 'Gapping and Related Rules', *Linguistic Inquiry*, 2(1): 21–35.

Johnson, K. (2001), 'What VP Ellipsis Can Do, and What It Can't, but Not Why', in M. Baltin and C. Collins (eds), *The Handbook of Contemporary Syntactic Theory*, 439–79, Oxford: Blackwell Publishers.

Johnson, K. (ed.) (2008), *Topics in Ellipsis*, 2nd edn, Cambridge: Cambridge University Press.

Johnson, K. (2009), 'Gapping is Not (VP) Ellipsis', *Linguistic Inquiry*, 40(2): 289–328.

Johnson, K. (2013), 'Licensing Ellipsis', *Studies in Chinese Linguistics*, 34(2): 71–98.

Johnson, K. (2014), 'Gapping', University of Massachusetts Ms., Amherst, MA.

Keenan, E. (1971), 'Names, Quantifiers, and the Sloppy Identity Problem', *Papers in Linguistics*, 4: 211–32.

Kehler, A. (2000), 'Coherence and the Resolution of Ellipsis', *Linguistics and Philosophy*, 23: 533–75.

Kehler, A. (2002), *Coherence, Reference and the Theory of Grammar*, Stanford: CSLI Publications.

Kehler, A. (2005), 'Coherence-driven Constraints on the Placement of Accent', in *Proceedings of the 15th Conference on Semantics and Linguistic Theory (SALT15)*,

Los Angeles: University of California. http://idiom.ucsd.edu/~kehler/publications.htm (accessed 17 July 2019).

Kertz, L. (2008), 'Focus Structure and Acceptability in Verb Phrase Ellipsis', in N. Abner and J. Bishop (eds), *Proceedings of the 27th West Coast Conference on Formal Linguistics (WCCFL)*, 283–91, Cascadilla Proceedings Project.

Kertz, L. (2010), 'Ellipsis Reconsidered', PhD diss., University of California, San Diego, La Jolla, CA.

Kertz, L. (2013), 'Verb Phrase Ellipsis: The View from Information Structure', *Language*, 89: 390–428.

Kim, C. and J. T. Runner (2013), 'Anaphora and Ellipsis from a Psycholinguistic Perspective', Lectures given at University of Paris Diderot-Paris 7, Paris.

Kim, C., G. M. Kobele, J. T. Runner and J. T. Hale (2011), 'The Acceptability Cline in VP Ellipsis', Syntax, 14: 318–54.

Kroch, A., B. Santorini and A. Diertani (2010), Penn Parsed Corpus of Modern British English. Available online: http://www.ling.upenn.edu/hist-corpora/PPCMBE-RELEASE-1/index.html (accessed 29 November 2018).

Kubota, Y. and R. Levine (2014), 'Pseudogapping as Pseudo-VP Ellipsis', in N. Asher and S. Soloviev (eds), *Logical Aspects of Computational Linguistics (LACL 2014)*, 122–37, Berlin: Springer-Verlag.

Lappin, S. (1992), 'The Syntactic Basis of Ellipsis Resolution', in S. Berman and A. Hestvik (eds), *Proceedings of the Stuttgart Workshop on Ellipsis*, Bericht Nr. 291992, Stuttgart: University of Stuttgart.

Lasnik, H. (1995), 'A note on Pseudogapping', *MIT Working Papers in Linguistics*, 27: 143–63.

Levin, N. S. (1978), 'Some Identity-of-Sense Deletions Puzzle Me. Do They You?', in D. Farkas, W. Jacobsen and K. Todrys (eds), *Papers from the 14th Regional Meeting of the Chicago Linguistic Society (CLS)*, 229–40, Chicago, IL: University of Chicago, Chicago Linguistic Society.

Levin, N. S. (1986), *Main Verb Ellipsis in Spoken English* (Outstanding Dissertations in Linguistics), New York: Garland.

Levin, N. and E. F. Prince (1986), 'Gapping and Causal Implicature', *Papers in Linguistics*, 19(3): 351–64.

Levine, R. D. (2012), 'Auxiliaries: *To*'s Company', *Journal of Linguistics*, 48(1): 187–203.

Lobeck, A. (1995), *Ellipsis. Functional Heads, Licensing and Identification*, New York and Oxford: Oxford University Press.

Martin, A. E. and B. McElree (2008), 'A Content-Addressable Pointer Mechanism Underlies Comprehension of Verb-Phrase Ellipsis', *Journal of Memory and Language*, 58: 879–906.

McCawley, J. D. (1993), 'Gapping with Shared Operators', *Annual Meeting of the Berkeley Linguistics Society (BLS)*, 245–53. Available online: http://journals.linguisticsociety.org/proceedings/index.php/BLS/article/view/1507/1289 (accessed 29 November 2018).

Merchant, J. (2001), *The Syntax of Silence: Sluicing, Islands, and the Theory of Ellipsis*, Oxford: Oxford University Press.

Merchant, J. (2004), 'Fragments and Ellipsis', *Linguistics and Philosophy*, 27(6): 661–738.

Merchant, J. (2006), 'Rethinking the Identity Conditions on Ellipsis', Talk given at Ealing 2006, École d'Automne de Linguistique, Paris.

Merchant, J. (2008a), 'An asymmetry in Voice Mismatches in VP-Ellipsis and Pseudogapping', *Linguistic Inquiry*, 39(1): 169–79.

Merchant, J. (2008b), 'Variable Island Repair under Ellipsis', in K. Johnson (ed.), *Topics in Ellipsis*, 132–53, Cambridge: Cambridge University Press.

Merchant, J. (2013a), 'Ellipsis: A Survey of Analytical Approaches', University of Chicago Ms., Chicago, IL.

Merchant, J. (2013b), 'Voice and Ellipsis', *Linguistic Inquiry*, 44(1): 77–108.

Merchant, J. (2013c), 'Diagnosing Ellipsis', in L. L. Cheng and N. Corver (eds), *Diagnosing Syntax*, 537–42, Oxford: Oxford University Press.

Miller, P. (2002), 'Les emplois non finis de *do* auxiliaire', in C. Delmas (ed.), *Construire et Reconstruire en Linguistique Anglaise: Syntaxe et Sémantique* (CIEREC Travaux 107), 185–98, Saint-Étienne: Publications de l'Université de Saint-Étienne.

Miller, P. (2011), 'The Choice Between Verbal Anaphors in Discourse', in I. Hendrickx, S. L. Devi, A. Branco and R. Mitkov (eds), *Anaphora Processing and Applications: 8th Discourse Anaphora and Anaphor Resolution Colloquium (DAARC 2011), Lecture Notes in Artificial Intelligence*, vol. 7099, 82–95, Berlin: Springer.

Miller, P. (2013), 'Usage Preferences: The Case of the English Verbal Anaphor *do so*', in Stefan Müller (ed.), *Proceedings of the 20th International Conference on Head-Driven Phrase Structure Grammar*, 121–39, Berlin: CSLI Publications.

Miller, P. (2014), 'A Corpus Study of Pseudogapping and its Theoretical Consequences', in C. Piñón (ed.), *Empirical Issues in Syntax and Semantics 10*, 73–90. Available online: http://www.cssp.cnrs.fr/eiss10/ (accessed 29 November 2018).

Miller, P. and B. Hemforth (2014), 'Verb Phrase Ellipsis with Nominal Antecedents', University of Paris Diderot-Paris 7 Ms., Paris.

Miller, P. and G. K. Pullum (2014), 'Exophoric VP Ellipsis', in P. Hofmeister and E. Norcliffe (eds), *The Core and the Periphery: Data-driven Perspectives on Syntax Inspired by Ivan A. Sag*, 5–32, Stanford, CA: CSLI Publications.

Murguia, E. (2004), 'Syntactic Identity and Locality Restrictions on Verbal Ellipsis', PhD diss., University of Maryland, College Park, MD.

Nielsen, L. A. (2003a), 'A Corpus-Based Study of Verb Phrase Ellipsis', in *Proceedings of the 6th Annual CLUK Research Colloquium*, 109–15, Edinburg: Edinburg University.

Nielsen, L. A. (2003b), 'Using Machine Learning Techniques for VPE Detection', in *Proceedings of Recent Advances in Natural Language Processing (RANLP)*, 339–46, Borovets, Bulgaria.

Nielsen, L. A. (2004a), 'Robust VPE Detection Using Automatically Parsed Text', in *Proceedings of the ACL (Association for Computational Linguistics) 2004 Workshop on Student Research*, 31–6, Barcelona, Spain.

Nielsen, L. A. (2004b), 'Using Automatically Parsed Text for Robust Verb Phrase Ellipsis Detection', in *Proceedings of the Fifth Discourse Anaphor and Anaphora Resolution conference (DAARC)*, 121–6, Sao Miguel, Portugal.

Nielsen, L. A. (2004c), 'Verb Phrase Ellipsis Detection Using Automatically Parsed Text', in *Proceedings of the 20th International Conference on Computational Linguistics (COLING)*, 1093–9, Geneva, Switzerland.

Nielsen, L. A. (2004d), 'Verb Phrase Ellipsis Detection Using Machine Learning Techniques', in N. Nicolov, K. Bontcheva, G. Angelova and R. Mitkov (eds), *Recent Advances in Natural Language Processing (RANLP)*, vol. 3 (CILT vol. 260), 317–26, Amsterdam and Philadelphia: John Benjamins.

Nielsen, L. A. (2005), 'A Corpus-based Study of Verb Phrase Ellipsis Identification and Resolution', PhD diss., University of London King's College London, London, UK.

Nykiel, J. (2006), 'Ellipsis in Shakespeare's Syntax', PhD diss., University of Silesia, Silesia.

Nykiel, J. (2015), 'Constraints on the Ellipsis Alternation: A View from the History of English', *Language Variation and Change*, 27: 1–8.

Pérez-Lorido, R. (2011), 'Coordinación y Ellipsis en Inglés Antiguo: Un Estudio Diacrónico de Corpus de la Interacción Modular en el Lenguaje', PhD diss., University of Oviedo, Oviedo.

Pullum, G. K. (1982), 'Syncategorematicity and English Infinitival *to*', *Glossa*, 16(2): 181–215.

Quirk, R., S. Greenbaum, G. Leech and J. Svartvik (1985), *A Comprehensive Grammar of the English language*, London: Longman.

Radford, A. (2004), *Minimalist Syntax. Exploring the Structure of English*, Cambridge: Cambridge University Press.

Rooth, M. (1992), 'Ellipsis Redundancy and Reduction Redundancy', in S. Berman and A. Hestvik (eds), *Proceedings of the Stuttgart Ellipsis Workshop*. Arbeitspapiere des Sonderforschungsbereichs 340 (Vol. 29), Heidelberg: IBM Germany.

Ross, J. R. (1969), 'Guess Who?', in R. Binnick, A. Davison, G. Green and J. Morgan (eds), *Papers from the 5th regional meeting of the Chicago Linguistic Society*, 252–86, Chicago, IL: Chicago Linguistic Society.

Sag, I. A. (1976), 'Deletion and Logical Form', PhD diss., MIT: Cambridge, MA.

Sag, I. A. and J. Hankamer (1984), 'Toward a Theory of Anaphoric Processing', *Linguistics and Philosophy*, 7: 325–45.

Schachter, P. (1977), 'Does she or doesn't she?' *Linguistic Inquiry*, 8: 763–7.

Shapiro, L. P., A. Hestvik, L. Lesan and A. R. Garcia (2003), 'Charting the Time-Course of VP-Ellipsis Sentence Comprehension: Evidence for an Initial and Independent Structural Analysis', *Journal of Memory and Language*, 49: 1–19.

Sharifzadeh, S. (2012), 'Recherches sur Do, Lexique et Grammaire', PhD diss., University of Paris-Sorbonne, Paris.

Siegel, M. E. A. (1987), 'Compositionality, Case, and the Scope of Auxiliaries', *Linguistics and Philosophy*, 10(1): 53–75.

Sundby, B., A. K. Bjørge and K. E. Haugland (eds) (1991), *A Dictionary of English Normative Grammar*, Amsterdam: John Benjamins.

Thompson, G. (2003), *Introducing Functional Grammar*, London: Arnold.

Thoms, G. (2010), 'Tolerated Lexical Mismatches in Ellipsis', Strathclyde University Ms., Glasgow.

Thoms, G. (2011a), '"Verb floating" and VP-Ellipsis: Towards a Movement Account of Ellipsis Licensing', in J. van Craenenbroeck (ed.), *Linguistic Variation Yearbook 2010*, 252–97, Amsterdam: John Benjamins.

Thoms, G. (2011b), 'From Economy to Locality: *Do*-Support as Head Movement'. Available online: http://ling.auf.net/lingbuzz/001198 (accessed 29 November 2018).

Thoms, G. (2013), 'Lexical Mismatches in Ellipsis and the Identity Condition', in S. Keine and S. Sloggett (eds), *Proceedings of the Forty-Second Annual Meeting of the North East Linguistics Society (NELS 42)*, Amherst, MA: GLSA Publications.

Warner, A. R. (1993), *English Auxiliaries: Structure and History*, Cambridge: Cambridge University Press.

Warner, A. R. (1997), 'Extending the Paradigm: An Interpretation of the Historical Development of Auxiliary Sequences in English', *English Studies*, 78(2): 162–89.

Webber, B. L. (1978), 'A Formal Approach to Discourse Anaphora', PhD diss., Harvard University, Cambridge, MA.

Williams, E. (1977), 'Discourse and Logical Form', *Linguistic Inquiry*, 8(1): 101–39.

Winkler, S. (2005), *Ellipsis and Focus in Generative Grammar*, Berlin and New York: Mouton de Gruyter.

Zagona, K. (1982), 'Government and Proper Government of Verbal Projections', PhD diss., University of Washington, Seattle, WA.

Zribi-Hertz, A. (1986), 'Relations Anaphoriques en Français', PhD diss., University Paris 8, Paris.

Index

algorithm   8–9, 52–4, 71–84, 138, 267–72
anaphora
   endophoric   98, 201
   exophoric   13, 20–1, 57–9, 98, 201
antecedent
   adjectival   40–1
   anaphoric   14–15, 20–1, 44, 59, 98–9, 201–4, 262 (*see also* retrospective ellipsis)
   cataphoric   14–15, 66, 68, 98–9, 201–4, 253, 262 (*see also* anticipatory ellipsis)
   nominal   38–41, 148
antecedent-contained deletion   89–90, 128, 134, 258
as-appositive   53, 56, 89, 128–30, 132–8, 169, 204, 258
aspect   104, 173–7, 261, 266

Backwards Anaphora Constraint   204
Bare Argument Ellipsis   45, 277 n.21, *see also* Stripping
binding Theory   34–6
boundedness   90–1, 95, 240–5, 251, 265
British English *do*   62–4, 278 n.12

complexity   42, 54–7, 71, 91–4, 141–6, 241–5, 266
Corpus of Contemporary American English (COCA)   57–60, 67, 131–2, 210–11, 226, 252–3, 278 n.9
CorpusSearch programme   71, 81
CP question   89, 95–6, 98, 128, 139, 141, 143, 146, 221, 254, 258
Cross-Conjunct Binding   4

discourse
   coherence   19, 34–7, 166–7, 169–72
      Cause-Effect coherence relation   5, 34–7, 166–7, 171
      Resemblance coherence relation   5, 34–7, 166–7, 169, 171
   cohesion   11–14, 19, 21–2

distance   41–2, 236–51, 265
   lexical   53, 94–5, 236–45, 248–51 (*see also* word distance)
   syntactic   53, 91–3, 246–51 (*see also* sentential distance)
domain   95–8, 139–46, 254, 258–9

ellipsis resolution   31, 37, 51–2, 54–6, 138

F-1 Measure   81–2
finiteness   23–5, 29
focus   46–7, 105, 108–11, 138, 166–7, 171, 205–15, 253–4, 262–3
   auxiliary choice   108–10, 171, 205–7, 213, 215, 253–4, 263, 277 n.17
   object-auxiliary choice   110, 207–9, 214, 262, 279 n.6
   object choice   109–10, 206–7, 209, 215, 254, 256, 263
   subject-auxiliary choice   108–9, 206, 213–15, 254, 263
   subject choice   108–9, 171, 205–7, 214–15, 254, 263, 277 n.17
   subject-object-auxiliary choice   110, 207–9, 215, 263
   subject-object choice   109–10, 207, 209, 215, 254, 263

Gapping   3, 13, 66, 276 n.6
genre   86, 226–35
   speech-related   86, 121–4, 132, 219, 232–5, 239–40, 256, 263
   writing-related   86, 115, 121–4, 132, 232–5, 239–40, 256, 264

identity   10, 31–3, 39, 46, 146, 148–53, 165–8, 260
   sloppy   6–7, 36–7, 39, 56, 100–1, 215–20, 254, 256, 263–4
   strict   5–7, 36–7, 39, 101, 215–18

licensing condition   1–2, 31–3, 138
licensor   32, 61, 65–6, 69, 72–4, 80, 86–8, 106, 114–27, 143, 145, 149–54, 177, 181, 188–95, 202, 253, 256–7, 259, 262, 271
linking   89–91, 95, 127–39, 141–6, 196, 213, 221, 252, 257–9

mismatch   2, 9, 17, 30, 100, 266
   aspect   173–7, 261
   category   40–1, 100, 148–9, 153, 260
   clause type   198–200, 262
   finiteness   29
   modality   105, 179–81, 184–8, 262
   polarity   158–63, 261
   tense   29–30, 189–90, 192–5, 262
   voice   25–7, 34, 39–40, 46–8, 100, 103–4, 165–72, 252–3, 261, 279 nn.4, 5

Null Complement Anaphora (NCA)   62

Penn Parsed Corpus of Modern British English (PPCMBE)   69–71
   parsing conventions   71–84
   Part of Speech labels (POS)   273–5, 278 n.18
   query language   71–84, 267–72
polarity   22–3, 53, 57, 63–4, 66, 74, 78–9, 82, 101–3, 107–8, 110, 158–64, 171, 195, 205, 217–20, 261, 263–4, 266
   polar alternative   41, 57–8, 102, 159, 163
Post-Auxiliary Ellipsis (PAE)   7–9, 61–2
precision   54, 57, 81–4, 278 n.7
presupposition   20–2, 24, 27
processing   34–48, 236–51
Pseudogapping   8–9, 61–2, 66–9
   comparative   60–1, 67, 110, 126, 131–2, 156–8, 169, 171, 195, 209, 211–12, 215, 252, 263
   non-comparative   60–1, 67, 109, 131–2, 157–8, 171, 206, 209–11, 215, 252, 263
      mirror pattern   211–12, 215, 263
      parallel pattern   211–12, 215, 263
psycholinguistics   34–48

recall   54, 57, 81, 277 n.6
recoverability condition   1, 13–17, 31–2, 58–9
situational recoverability   13–14
structural recoverability   13–14
textual recoverability   13–14
remnant   8, 59–60, 66, 109, 111, 131–2, 154–8, 168, 206, 209–15, 222, 226, 252, 257, 260–1
   AdP   111, 154–5, 158
   CP   154–5, 158
   deprepositionalized   156, 158
   double NP   154–5, 158
   infinitival VP   111, 154–5, 158
   NP   111, 131–2, 154–5, 157–8, 168, 209–15, 226, 252, 257
   PP   111, 154–5, 158
   ProNP   111, 154–5, 157–8
Rheme   19–21

situational ellipsis   14–15
Sluicing   3–4, 33–4, 276 n.7
split antecedents   56–7, 99–100, 148–9, 153–4, 255, 260, *see also* combined antecedents
Stripping   277 n.21, *see also* Bare Argument Ellipsis
substitution   12, 19, 64
Systemic Functional Grammar (SFG)   11, 18–30

tag question   81, 89, 95–7, 107, 110, 128, 139, 141, 143, 146, 161–2, 196–200, 207, 213–14, 220–1, 254, 258, 271
tense   23, 27–30, 55, 105–6, 108, 118, 120–4, 171–2
Theme   19–21, 41
Transformational Generative Grammar (TGG)   30–3

vehicle change   100–1, 215–21, *see also* sloppy identity
voice   25–7, 34, 40, 46, 47, 53, 99–100, 103–4, 146, 164–72, 195, 252–3, 261, 266, 279 nn.4, 5
VP Ellipsis (VPE)   1, 8–9, 61–2, 64–9
VP recycling hypothesis   34, 37–9

What you hear is what you get (WYHIWYG)   31
What you see is what you get (WYSIWYG)   31

www.ingramcontent.com/pod-product-compliance
Lightning Source LLC
Chambersburg PA
CBHW070018010526
44117CB00011B/1623